The Professio

Palgrave Study Skills

Business Degree Success
Career Skills
Cite Them Right (9th edn)
Critical Thinking Skills (2nd edn)
e-Learning Skills (2nd edn)
The Exam Skills Handbook (2nd edn)
The Graduate Career Guidebook
Great Ways to Learn Anatomy and
    Physiology
How to Begin Studying English Literature
    (3rd edn)
How to Manage Your Distance and Open
    Learning Course
How to Manage Your Postgraduate Course
How to Study Foreign Languages
How to Study Linguistics (2nd edn)
How to Use Your Reading in Your Essays
    (2nd edn)
How to Write Better Essays (3rd edn)
How to Write Your Undergraduate
    Dissertation
Improve Your Grammar
Information Skills
The International Student Handbook
IT Skills for Successful Study
The Mature Student's Guide to Writing
    (3rd edn)
The Mature Student's Handbook
The Palgrave Student Planner
Practical Criticism

Presentation Skills for Students (2nd edn)
The Principles of Writing in Psychology
Professional Writing (2nd edn)
Researching Online
Skills for Success (2nd edn)
The Student's Guide to Writing (3rd edn)
The Student Phrase Book
Study Skills Connected
Study Skills for International Postgraduates
Study Skills for Speakers of English as a
    Second Language
The Study Skills Handbook (4th edn)
Studying History (3rd edn)
Studying Law (3rd edn)
Studying Modern Drama (2nd edn)
Studying Psychology (2nd edn)
Teaching Study Skills and Supporting
    Learning
The Undergraduate Research Handbook
The Work-Based Learning Student
    Handbook
Work Placements – A Survival Guide for
    Students
Write it Right (2nd edn)
Writing for Engineers (3rd edn)
Writing for Law
Writing for Nursing and Midwifery Students
    (2nd edn)
You2Uni

Pocket Study Skills

14 Days to Exam Success
Blogs, Wikis, Podcasts and More
Brilliant Writing Tips for Students
Completing Your PhD
Doing Research
Getting Critical
Planning your dissertation
Planning Your Essay
Planning Your PhD

Reading and Making Notes
Referencing and Understanding Plagiarism
Reflective Writing
Report Writing
Science Study Skills
Studying with Dyslexia
Success in Groupwork
Time Management
Writing for University

Palgrave Research Skills

Authoring a PhD
The Foundations of Research (2nd edn)
Getting to Grips with Doctoral Research
The Good Supervisor (2nd edn)

The Postgraduate Research Handbook (2nd
    edn)
The Professional Doctorate
Structuring Your Research Thesis

For a complete listing of all our titles in this area please visit
www.palgrave.com/studyskills

The Professional Doctorate

A Practical Guide

John Fulton
Judith Kuit
Gail Sanders
Peter Smith

First published 2013 by
PALGRAVE MACMILLAN

Palgrave Macmillan in the UK is an imprint of Macmillan Publishers Limited, registered in England, company number 785998, of Houndmills, Basingstoke, Hampshire RG21 6XS.

Palgrave Macmillan in the US is a division of St Martin's Press LLC, 175 Fifth Avenue, New York, NY 10010.

Palgrave Macmillan is the global academic imprint of the above companies and has companies and representatives throughout the world.

Palgrave® and Macmillan® are registered trademarks in the United States, the United Kingdom, Europe and other countries

ISBN: 978-1-137-02419-0

This book is printed on paper suitable for recycling and made from fully managed and sustained forest sources. Logging, pulping and manufacturing processes are expected to conform to the environmental regulations of the country of origin.

A catalogue record for this book is available from the British Library.

A catalog record for this book is available from the Library of Congress.

Contents

Acknowledgements

We would like to thank the many students who have been kind enough to share their doctoral journeys with us. We are privileged to have experienced their highs and lows, and their ultimate triumphs as they graduated. This book would not have been possible without them. In particular, we would wish to thank the following, who allowed us to use their work in this book: Lisa Alcorn, Paul Andrew, Richard Bain, Alison Beaney, Kathy Bland, Angela Brown, Dave Camlin, Carol Candlish, Luke Feeney, Liz Herring, Simon Kerridge, Ron Lawson, Andrew Maxwell, Dawn Price, Jane Thompson, Mick Thurlbeck, Rob Warrender, and Phillippa Ryan Witheroe. Thanks to Julie Bradford and Chris Bland for help with Chapter 9, and to Helen Curtis for help with the student survey work.

1 Introduction

On completion of this chapter you will:

▶ understand the structure of this book, and be able to begin to use it to support yourself in your doctoral studies
▶ understand the standard expected of a doctoral level qualification, and start to think about how you might develop a doctoral project that works for you
▶ understand the history of the doctorate, the nature of the professional doctorate and the range of professional doctorates available
▶ feel competent to choose a programme which suits your own needs

1.1 Chapter overview

Welcome to this book. The fact that you have started to read it suggests that you are seriously considering undertaking a professional doctorate. You probably have lots of ideas and concerns – you may be quite unsure what a professional doctorate actually is, and whether studying for one can work for you. We have written this book for students like you, and we have tried to make it as interesting and useful as we can. We have based the book on our own experiences of running a professional doctorate programme and of supervising students (now graduates!) who have successfully completed our programme. We have tried to make the book as useful as we can by giving examples of student work and discussing our own experiences of the students we have personally supervised. In doing so, we hope you can use this book to support you throughout your own doctoral studies.

In this first chapter we will try to answer your initial questions about doctoral study and run through some of the reasons why you may, or may not, choose to study for a professional doctorate. We will also briefly explain the history of doctoral degrees and what is meant by 'doctoral standard'. The term 'professional doctorate' can mean many different things, and there are many different forms and structures for a professional doctorate programme. This book is based on our experiences of our own programme but we have tried to make it useful for students in a range of study situations. In this chapter we explain the sort of programme we have focused on, and define the terms which we will use throughout the book. In the next section we give an overview of what we cover in the rest of the book.

1.2 Summary of the contents of the book

The book covers all of the stages that you will go through in your professional doctorate studies, and uses examples throughout which are drawn from the work and experiences of real students. We hope that including real student work and experiences will help you with your own doctoral project; you will be able to see how other students have approached their projects and how they dealt with the issues that they had during their doctoral journey.

The first thing that you will need to do when starting your professional doctorate programme is select your project. It is, of course, vitally important that you make a good choice by selecting a project that can be developed to doctoral level and also fits within your own professional context. We cover this in the next chapter, where we help you to choose your research project and frame your research question. The chapter draws on case studies of real doctoral student projects, giving you some examples of projects that these students chose for their doctoral study.

Part of your doctoral journey is about exploring what drives you as a professional, what your professional values are, and how these relate to the professional issues which you are covering in your project. Chapter 3 considers practical techniques that you can use to analyse your own professional identity and how this contributes towards your ability to make professional judgements. It will also include practical tips on how to use techniques of reflection within your own doctoral study.

Chapter 4 considers your research methods, which underpin the core of any professional doctorate programme. There are many possible approaches available to you, and choosing the right one (and there may be more than one) for your project can be challenging and confusing. We cover the most useful research methods for exploring practice, including action research, case study approaches, mixed methods approaches and auto-ethnography. These methodological approaches are considered to be appropriate ways of developing the work of the professional doctorate, and their relative strengths and weaknesses are discussed.

You will need to place your project in the wider context. This means addressing the questions:

- How does my work compare with that of others?
- Do any previous academic studies exist?
- What professional work has already been undertaken?
- How will I measure and evaluate the impact of my work on the community of practice?

Chapter 5 helps you to answer these questions and shows you how to undertake a literature review. The importance of considering the ethical aspects of your project, and of project planning, is also outlined.

The concept of personal transformation is a key component within any professional doctorate programme. You will be an experienced professional. However, you may not be used to doctoral-level writing, and your information and research skills may require further development. Chapter 6 discusses the personal qualities that are desirable to help you become a researching professional, and will help you to understand some of the approaches that can help facilitate lasting personal transformation. We also discuss the need for you to develop a new level of criticality, including deep self-criticality.

The concept of the work-based portfolio is integral to many professional doctorate programmes. Chapter 7 discusses various ways in which you can structure your work into a portfolio format, and the tension in developing a project which includes your past, present and future work is considered in some detail. The types and relative strengths of evidence are analysed for you by presenting and discussing the contents of the portfolios of several students on a professional doctorate programme.

Your relationship with your supervisors is key to your success. Chapter 8 draws on recent research suggesting that the diversity of students' career positions is not normally taken into account in the relationship. A homogeneous approach is (usually) taken to doctoral supervision and sometimes this is not in the student's best interest. Further we will show how forging working relationships with other key stakeholders – other students within the cohort, the core programme team, your employer – can be just as important as working with a single supervisor. We consider how different models of supervision can improve your relationship with your supervisor.

Chapter 9 focuses on the importance of disseminating your work. The different avenues for dissemination are explored, along with practical tips on how to succeed. This addresses the following questions: 'Who is my community?', 'How do I demonstrate my influence?', 'When should I publish?', and 'Where do I publish?' We discuss the differences between, and roles of, academic journals, professional publications, conferences, virtual communities and peer meetings.

Chapter 10 helps you to prepare for the final assessment. Presenting your work, developing a coherent and confident defence, preparing with a mock (or practice) oral examination and selection of the examiners are discussed. The chapter will also cover the final oral examination, or viva, drawing from the experience of doctoral graduates. Clear advice on preparing for your examination is given. We also address the key questions: 'How do I know when I am ready to submit?' and 'What is my contribution?'

Chapter 11 presents a series of eight case studies of successful professional doctorate projects. These are drawn from students who have recently graduated from a professional doctorate programme. The case studies present the candidate's project, their professional and academic background, the methodological approach taken, the impact of the project on their community of practice, reflections on the examination, and the impact which studying the programme has had on the individual.

The eight case studies are:

- A pharmacy lecturer who explored different models of interprofessional education in her teaching.
- An equality and diversity professional who developed a model for corporate social responsibility.
- A local businessman who followed a doctoral project in quality and management information systems.
- A senior member of staff from a local college who undertook a project in shared services.
- A healthcare professional who developed a commissioning framework.
- A senior administrator from a university who explored research administration systems.
- A financial risk auditor who worked on methods for minimising financial risk.
- An information systems specialist who worked in healthcare.

We hope you will gain a deep understanding of the whole professional doctorate process from these case studies, and see how other students have structured their projects.

The final chapter, Chapter 12, draws together all of the main points raised throughout the text, which we hope you will find useful as a checklist of the things you need to cover throughout your doctorate. We also give some final reflections on our own experiences of working with professional doctorate candidates. The chapter addresses the question: 'What happens next?' and encourages you to view your professional doctorate study as one part of a lifelong learning journey, to recognise the personal transformation that this implies, and to continue studying, exploring, learning, pushing boundaries and disseminating throughout your professional life (and onward!).

The text is supported by a full set of current references which will cover the following topics: professional doctorates, doctoral studies, work-based learning, methodology, reflective practice, professional issues, communities of practice, professional identity, transformational learning.

Sample coursework assessments are included as an Appendix to give you an example of assessments from the taught element of a professional doctorate programme.

1.3 Why study for a doctorate?

Studying for a doctorate can be a long and lonely business. You are committing yourself to studying one topic for several years, so you must be really sure that you want to do it. Students will quote many different reasons for opting to study for a doctorate including: promotion, to develop my

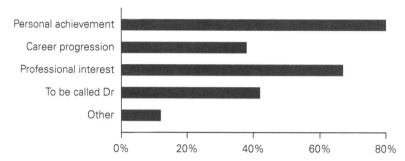

Figure 1.1   Reasons for studying on a professional doctorate programme

practice, to become an academic, to make a difference, love of my subject, to become a Doctor and personal satisfaction. Whatever your own reason for deciding to study for a doctorate, the most important thing is that you are totally committed to it. You need to feel very positive indeed about studying, so much so that you get a buzz from starting on your doctoral work. Being half-hearted just isn't good enough and won't get you through those long hard days when the project isn't going quite right for you. You must really want to do this!

We asked some of our doctoral students: 'Why did you choose to study on the professional doctorate programme?' The results were reported in Smith et al. (2011), which you may want to have a look at. Students could choose more than one answer and Figure1.1 shows that the most frequent response was 'For a sense of personal achievement'. The next most popular choice was 'For professional/subject interest'.

You will already be very busy in your professional life. So why would you dream of giving yourself more work, and potentially putting yourself under more stress by registering for a professional doctorate programme? As mentioned above, each and every doctoral candidate has their own set of reasons for embarking upon their doctoral journey. In general, however, candidates have a genuine interest in their practice which they wish to develop further, and see a professional doctorate as a vehicle for doing so. You will find that studying on a doctoral programme will have a significant impact upon you, and that you will undergo personal change and transformation.

In terms of impact upon themselves (see Figure 1.2), 68% of our students felt that they thought more critically as a direct result of studying on the programme, 71% felt that they understood relevant theory more deeply, and 50% felt that they understood professional issues more deeply. All of the students recognised that studying on the programme had changed the way in which they approached their professional practice. 93% of students stated that they had begun to use reflective practice within their work context.

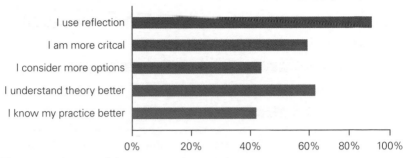

Figure 1.2   Impact of the programme on students

In response to the question: *"Why did you choose to study a professional doctorate?"*, our students replied:

"It best fits with my learning journey. I began a PhD but it didn't naturally lend itself to my portfolio career path."
"To support my desire to publish my theories and frameworks."
"To explore professional issues."
"Because of the flexibility."
"I wanted a structured programme."
"The opportunity to site my project within the workplace."

The following quotes come from professional doctorate students, and will give you some idea as to why those students decided to follow this particular route.

"The opportunity to study for a professional doctorate presented itself when I had just returned to work full time after six months' maternity leave and a year working part-time. On reflection, perhaps full time work, a demanding toddler and a part-time professional doctorate were not an ideal combination but my employer was willing to part-fund my doctoral studies and this was too good an opportunity to miss. Studying for a professional doctorate has introduced me to the power and practical application of reflective practice and I can see how my work projects have benefitted from this additional perspective.

I found studying for a professional doctorate a hugely positive and enriching experience which has without doubt made me a better healthcare professional in my field. Key experiences included: getting to grips with the evidence-based literature and better understanding my professional practice; meeting fellow students and faculty on the programme; and the support of my understanding, if long suffering, family.

Undertaking a professional doctorate is not for the faint hearted. You need to be very motivated; big doses of perseverance; dedication and commitment and the ability to be absolutely determined to see it through to the end. However, it is all worth it in the end and the personal satisfaction when you are officially awarded your doctorate will be one of the proudest days of your life."

If you are considering starting a professional doctorate, you should ask yourself the following questions:

- Do you have the opportunity to make a difference to practice?
- Are you in a position to manage a change project in your workplace?
- Are you able to demonstrate innovation and creativity in your workplace?
- Can you design a major project which is aligned with your work activities and will give you the opportunity to undertake research within the workplace?
- Do you have the time to commit to this major project? Although you will be able to base your project on things that you do as part of your day-to-day work, you will still need to devote time to additional reading, thinking and additional data collection and analysis.

If the answer to most of these questions is 'yes' you may well be in a position to undertake a professional doctorate. The academic qualifications required for entry to a professional doctorate are likely to be a good honours degree or a Master's degree, and significant experience of operating as a professional.

1.4   What is a doctorate?

The doctorate is the highest level of academic qualification and is recognised internationally as an award of academic excellence. Traditionally the title of the award has been PhD (Doctor of Philosophy). However, in recent times universities have begun to offer other forms of doctoral qualification which are of a similar standard to the PhD and are targeted at individuals working within specific professions. This book is aimed at students who intend to follow a professional, or practice-based, doctoral route, such as DProf (Professional doctorate), DBA (Doctor of Business Administration), or EdD (Doctor of Education). In all cases the award of a doctorate signifies that the holder has undertaken a major piece of research work which makes an original contribution to the subject. The doctorate is also recognised internationally as a formal training in research, and signifies that the holder has demonstrated a level of knowledge and expertise which is at the forefront of their discipline. The holder is expected to have undertaken a substantial focused programme of work which has moved their subject forward, used research methods in a competent manner and generated some new knowledge within their subject area.

The PhD has traditionally taken around three years of full-time study, and has resulted in the production of a substantial report, or thesis. The thesis summarises and evaluates the work which has been undertaken, discusses the methodological approach taken by the candidate, relates the work to the current literature in the field of study, and highlights its contribution to the subject area.

The thesis is usually assessed by a small team of examiners who have been appointed because of their expertise and knowledge of the subject area. These examiners will read the thesis and question the candidate in a viva, or oral examination. They will then make recommendations to the university as to the outcome of the examination, and whether the degree of PhD should be awarded, or whether further work needs to be done to the thesis. The doctorate first appeared in medieval Europe, and was seen as a licence to teach at a university. Its roots can be traced back to the early church when the term 'doctor' referred to scholars who taught and interpreted the Bible (Verger, 1999). Doctorates were originally awarded by the church, and involved the student passing an examination and taking an oath of allegiance.

The structure of the doctorate varies from country to country. In the USA a doctorate may consist of a taught element with examinations followed by a research project. In some European countries, the doctorate is almost always studied part-time and the candidate is required to publish a series of papers in academic journals as part of the doctoral process.

Professional doctorates have been awarded for some time in fields such as law, medicine and theology. However, since the 1990s there has been a large growth in the range and type of professional doctorate awards offered within universities around the world, including the UK (Powell and Long, 2005). In the USA Stewart (2010) has identified the issues relating to the growth of professional doctorates, with a number of new programmes emerging in recent years, some of which are called 'Clinical doctorates' or 'Practicing doctorates'. Maxwell (2011) has surveyed the growth of awards in Australia, where the number has doubled in recent years, with particular growth in specialist awards. Fell et al. (2011) identified 'confusion caused by the burgeoning number of professional doctorate titles'. Internationally there has been significant growth in the number and titles of professional doctorate programmes – and it is true that this can cause confusion – with Brown and Cooke (2010) listing 100 different titles in the UK alone. However, this also shows the growing demand from professionals who wish to register on a practice-based doctoral programme and a growing acceptance that this doctoral route is just as valid as a traditional PhD route.

The traditional PhD is said to be the training for a career in research or academia (Bourner and Bowden, 2001) whereas the professional doctorate is usually concerned with the development of professional practice. It would be easy just to assume that the PhD and the professional doctorate are very distinct, but the reality is much more complex. PhDs are not homogeneous; individual PhD studies can, and do, differ greatly. The vast majority of PhD studies are presented in the form of a thesis. However, an increasing number of practice-based PhDs use alternative approaches to the final submission of the student's work, particularly in the arts. They are usually based on the development of an artefact, such as a sculpture, painting or conceptual art, and accompanied by a thesis. Similarly, the professional doctorate does not have one single structure, and individual universities around the world take many different approaches. Perhaps the commonest model involves some taught modules at the start of the programme and a substantial thesis based on research into an area of professional practice. The thesis may also take the form of a portfolio of work, accompanied by a shorter report or dissertation. We cover the subject of portfolios in Chapter 7.

In general, the professional doctorate has grown out of recognition of the need, and demand, for doctoral programmes which enable practising professionals to study part-time alongside their job, and to base their project within their workplace. This has several attractions:

- You can obtain a doctoral qualification which draws from your professional experience.
- You can base your project upon work which you are doing as part of your practice.
- You can further develop your practice.
- You can provide evidence for the impact that your professional work is having on your employer and your broader community of practice.

Doctoral standards are set by a number of bodies; for example in the UK the QAA (Quality Assurance Agency) have published a framework for higher education qualifications in England, Wales and Northern Ireland (QAA, 2012). The following aspects are common to all doctorates:

- The requirement to produce new knowledge. In a professional doctorate programme, this may also be interpreted as contribution to, or impact upon, practice.
- Deep understanding of the relevant academic literature, or in the case of a professional doctorate, relevant professional policy and practice.
- Systematic application of appropriate research methodology.
- The undertaking of a very substantial piece of work.
- Good communication skills, both written and oral.
- Application of sound judgement and ethical principles.
- Demonstration of skills of criticality, synthesis and evaluation.

Whatever the structure of the doctorate, there are always the following elements:

- The doctorate is a research degree with a significant research element which is demonstrated by a substantial project (or series of projects).
- The candidate is required to demonstrate a contribution to knowledge, or originality.

1.4 Definitions

In this section we define some of the important aspects of terminology that we use throughout the book.

Community of practice: A set of relationships between people and activities that are bound together by the specialist knowledge required to engage in the practice that is common to the community.

Profession: We will use the word profession to describe an occupation which is usually backed up by a body of experience, the need for training, and qualifications. This does not necessarily imply that the individual is a member of a professional body (although they might be); however they will belong to a recognised community of practice.

Professional doctorate: We use the term professional doctorate to refer to a programme which is aimed at practitioners who wish to develop their practice to doctoral level. Most of these programmes will include taught components on subjects such as reflective practice and research methodology. They will also include a very significant project-based component in which the candidate will undertake a work-based project. Powell and Long (2005) describe a professional doctorate as 'one where the field of study is a professional discipline and where students are supervised within professional contexts and/or within the university but in relation to that context'.

Professional identity: This is 'the relatively stable and enduring constellation of attributes, beliefs, values, motives, and experiences in terms of which people define themselves in a professional role' (Schein and Schein, 1978).

Reflection: Reflection is an in-depth consideration of events or situations: the people involved, what they experienced and how they felt about it. This involves reviewing or reliving the experience to bring it into focus and re-playing it from diverse points of view. Seemingly innocent details might prove to be key; seemingly vital details may be irrelevant.

Reflective practice: Reflective practice means paying critical attention to the practical values and theories which inform everyday actions by examining practice reflectively and reflexively. This leads to developmental insight.

Reflexivity: To be reflexive is to find a way of standing outside of the self to examine, for example, how, seemingly unwittingly, we are involved in creating social or professional structures that are counter to our espoused values. It enables us to become aware of the limits of our knowledge, of how our own behaviour is complicit in forming organisational practices which, for example, marginalise groups or exclude individuals. Reflexivity uses such strategies as internal dialogue to treat aspects of the self as strange. It requires the ability to handle personal uncertainty, critically informed curiosity and flexibility to find ways of changing deeply-held perceptions of being: a complex, highly responsible social and political activity.

Supervisor: Students on a doctoral programme will normally study under the direction of one or more members of academic staff, usually known as supervisors. In some countries (for example, the USA) the member of academic staff will be known as an advisor instead. We use the term supervisor throughout this book. Some see the supervisor's relationship with the student differently – as more of a partner (Clarke et al., 2012), or a coach (Fillery-Travis and Robinson, 2011) or a mentor. Various definitions are provided in the literature in an attempt to clarify these differences; for example, Lester (2004) would define professional doctorate candidates as undertaking a 'practitioner doctorate' whilst others call it a 'work-based doctorate' (Boud and Tennent, 2006; Costley and Lester, 2012).

Summary

In this introductory chapter we have covered the areas which we felt were important to get you started on your doctoral journey. We have explained what is meant by a professional doctorate and the standard and expectation of a doctoral level qualification, and a little about the history and aims of the professional doctorate. We have also outlined what you can expect to find in the rest of this book. We hope this will help you to decide if a professional doctorate is for you. In the next chapter we will begin to discuss how you might choose and frame your doctoral project.

2 Choosing your Research Project and Framing your Research Question

On completion of this chapter you will:

▶ be able to differentiate between Mode 1 and Mode 2 knowledge
▶ understand the relationships between theory and practice
▶ be able to choose an area of study for your doctoral project and develop your research question
▶ understand the mechanisms of support in professional doctorate programmes, and utilise these to best effect in your own studies

2.1 Introduction

In this chapter we are considering the development of your ideas and working them up into a research proposal. Doctoral studies are concerned with producing an original contribution to knowledge and, in the case of the professional doctorate, a contribution to practice. In Chapter 4 we are going to consider the research approaches which you can take in the development of your study. Before you consider the methods you might wish to use, it is useful to think about the ways in which you can shape your ideas into a focused statement or research question. This chapter will explore the ways in which ideas can be generated from your practice and the ways in which your practice can be developed to doctoral level.

The world is an increasingly complex place and this is reflected in the workplace. This often means that professional doctorate candidates are involved in a wide range of activities including high-level technical activities and management, whilst other students may be therapists of various kinds. Many students will fulfil more than one role and this breadth (and depth) of activity has to be reflected in their study. In exploring this diverse range of work-based activities, it is therefore essential that a wide range of methodological approaches are utilised.

When you embark upon your professional doctorate studies, you will have some ideas about the sort of issues which you wish to explore. Many people undertaking the professional doctorate programme will come with a body of work which may involve completed projects. This work may be used as a building block and may be incorporated into the professional doctorate study. The first stage of the programme involves reflection on the shape and direction of your study and this chapter aims to assist with this process. Whether you are starting from scratch or have been working in a specific area for some time, the same principles apply. At first, you may have some idea of a general area that you wish to explore, without being too specific, or you may be considering more than one area. It is important to make a decision as early as you possibly can about the project that you are going to follow in your doctorate.

A number of things can shape your doctoral study. It can, and should, be shaped by the literature that you read, the needs of your employer and your broader community of practice, and your own interests and professional values. Your project should focus on a topic that is of interest to you, but it needs to be more than that. It must be of use to your community of practice and, because it is a doctoral study, it needs to be in an area where you have the potential to make a contribution and to demonstrate impact. One of the most important elements of any doctoral project is the contribution that it makes to knowledge and, in the case of a professional doctorate, the contribution that the work makes to practice.

Your doctoral research project must have a clear purpose and satisfy a clear need. It must be in an area that warrants exploration and thus has a potential to fill a current gap in knowledge. It must be timely in that it must be a current topic which is of interest and relevance to yourself and your community of practice.

Before thinking about your research question or your approach to the development of your professional doctorate study, it is useful to take a step back and examine methods of generating knowledge. The professional doctorate is concerned with the development of professional practice and you are required to demonstrate that you have developed your profession and that others can learn from your work. This chapter will examine the nature of professional practice and the type of knowledge which can be generated, and consider how this can be encapsulated in a question which can guide your study.

2.2 Knowledge production

When considering the development of your ideas, it is important to contextualise professional doctorates against knowledge frameworks. Gibbons et al. (1994) explicitly address this and contextualise the many changes taking place in society and the ways in which these changes can affect knowledge production. They argue that, traditionally, knowledge has been produced in a uni-disciplinary manner, which they call 'Mode 1 knowledge production'. Mode 1 is characterised by a single disciplinary approach which produces knowledge in a clear and focused manner, following a specific and often tightly fixed methodological approach. Within this particular intellectual climate, acceptance by the community of practice might prove difficult if one were to take an unusual and perhaps more innovative approach. In Mode 1 knowledge production the disciplinary community of practice decides and controls what is considered to be a valid contribution. Kuhn (1962) in his *Structure of Scientific Revolutions* encapsulated much of this approach, and in doing so he developed the concept of a paradigm. He argued that particular disciplines function within a particular paradigm which dictates the method and area of inquiry. In the history of a discipline there are times when this paradigm or mode is challenged or a startling discovery is made, which he called 'scientific revolutions'. Once things have been well and truly shaken up, everything becomes settled and a new status quo is established.

However, Gibbons et al. (1994) maintain that there is a second kind of knowledge production which they refer to as 'Mode 2'. Mode 2 knowledge production is a particularly modern phenomenon, characterised by a focus in the real world and a concern with real-life problems. This is not to say that Mode 1 knowledge is entirely esoteric, but the key differentiation is that Mode 1 knowledge comes from a uni-disciplinary approach, whereas Mode 2 knowledge is generated in a wider context. Mode 2 knowledge production reflects the world of working practice, with all its existing complexities and, by its very essence, is multidisciplinary in its focus. Because of these practical implications, the development and generation of Mode 2 knowledge tends to be less theoretical and the knowledge itself tends to be trans-disciplinary. Gibbons et al. (1994) outline a number of characteristics of Mode 2 knowledge. Its key features are the social nature of the knowledge, the problem-orientated focus of the research and the multidisciplinary nature. Table 2.1 summarises the key differences between Mode 1 and Mode 2 knowledge. Hessels and van Lente (2008) also provide a useful comparison.

The professional doctorate tends to generate Mode 2 knowledge whereas the traditional PhD is likely to produce Mode 1 knowledge. The use of 'tends to' is quite deliberate because, as is the case with much research, things may not be as straightforward as they first appear. It is perhaps easier to think

Mode 1 knowledge	Mode 2 knowledge
Has clear academic content	Is related to the content of the application area
Focuses on a single discipline	Crosses discipline boundaries
Is of a more theoretical nature	Is applied, takes account of the political and other contexts
Is within the control of the individual and their academic peers	Reflects practice and is affected by the complexities of the real world

Table 2.1 Comparison of Mode 1 and Mode 2 knowledge production

of research programmes as being on a continuum between Mode 1 and Mode 2 knowledge production, with some projects clearly at one end or the other. Other projects will come in the middle of the continuum, and it can be debatable as to which mode best defines them. However, most professional doctorate programmes will be of the Mode 2 type of knowledge production, and many writers have situated the professional doctorate at this end of the knowledge continuum (Maxwell, 2003). Perhaps the important aspect is the dynamic nature of the study, whereby changes in the workplace can challenge the research process and require changes to be made to an otherwise well-planned and focused study. Sensitivity to internal and external forces is very important, and this requires a degree of reflection into your situation which can be built into the study and its design.

Starkey and Maban (2001) capture this idea and argue that many developments and innovations take place through the collaboration of a variety of disciplinary approaches. The world, they maintain, is unpredictable and, in dealing with work-based problems, a degree of flexibility and creativity is required. They argue that universities need to partner with workplaces. Traditionally, universities are characterised as centres of knowledge which focus along uni-disciplinary lines. This contrasts with business and industry which draw on a range of disciplines in dealing with particular work-based developments and problems. In this context business can be interpreted in its wider sense to mean the workplace in general. The partnership between the university and the workplace is a key feature of the professional doctorate.

The aim of the professional doctorate is to take an area or an aspect of practice and develop it in such a manner that others can learn from it. The development of practice has to be done in a rigorous and systematic way, and this involves a continual reflection on the process and an evaluation of the product as well as the process. The key feature is that the study is based in practice. As such, it can represent a variety of methods and disciplines which may transcend professional boundaries. For example, Ali was a physiotherapist by profession, but he became involved in quality assurance and wished to develop this aspect of his role for his professional doctorate. His particular interest was quality assurance in healthcare and his community was health professionals who were working in quality assurance – a grouping which transcended particular professions.

Activity 1

Decide whether your ideas about your professional doctorate best fit Mode 1 or Mode 2 knowledge.

2.3 The theory/practice gap

Theory, practice and the relationship between the two are important issues. It is easy to think of Mode 1 as theory and Mode 2 as practice but the reality is more complex. Professional doctorates are about the development of practice but, by definition, underpinning theoretical ideas are also developed. So when formulating the question at the heart of your study, it is a useful exercise to consider the underpinning theory. But what exactly is theory?

A useful starting point is to consider the ways in which one can look at practice, or the ideas which underpin professional practice. An oft-quoted phrase is the 'theory practice gap', implying that there is a gap between theory and practice, and this lends itself to the Mode 1/Mode 2 knowledge production divide. Wilfred Carr (1986) takes a different approach and, although he is discussing the development of education theory and practice, many of his points can be generalised to other professional settings. He suggests that there are four types of theoretical issue which one must consider when discussing practice:

- theory as applied to practice;
- the 'common-sense' approach, which considers the moral/ethical dimension;
- theory which is derived from practice;
- the critical consideration of practice.

In developing your ideas it is worth considering these dimensions of practice. The first step is to consider your practice and how you can develop your initial ideas into a professional doctorate. Carr's typology provides a useful starting point in this process.

'Theory as applied to practice' means theoretical issues directly applied to the practice setting. Whilst the term 'knowledge production' does not mean that everything you do in your professional doctorate will involve the creation of startlingly new knowledge, many studies involve the application or adaptation of established (or fairly novel) theories which can be someone else's work. The challenge lies in the application – in many instances the insights gained from theories or previous research may generate ideas or questions about practice.

In healthcare this is encapsulated in the evidence-based movement which encourages people to base their practice on well-established evidence. A good example of this is Mohammed, a professional doctorate student working in educational settings, who designed and implemented a series of curricula innovations based on established educational theories.

Mohammed led a workplace team in this practice development and he was novel in his approach, but his originality was in the application of theory to practice. Through this he achieved recognition as a leader in his area of educational practice. Another example is Bob, a youth worker who was surprised to see that one geographical area had a much higher number of alcohol-related incidents involving young people than other areas. He investigated these incidents and found that the police were particularly vigorous in their approach in this locality. This led him to implement a series of interventions and the development of different working relationships with the police served as the basis for his study.

The example above contrasts with knowledge which is implicit within the practice setting. Carr (1986) refers to this second type as 'a common sense approach' which is concerned with knowledge that is implicit in the practice setting. This type of knowledge is often taken for granted and can lead to many actions, which may be incredibly skilled, being done in an automatic or mechanical manner.

An example of the common sense approach to the development of a professional doctorate study is Rob, who is a head teacher in an inner city school. He was tired of counting the times he heard people say, "I can tell if it's a good class the minute I walk in the door" because this expression was used so often and by a range of people. It also fits in with people's common sense ideas of teaching. Rob wondered whether there was something in it and he decided he would use this as the basis for a professional doctorate study. First, he examined whether initial impressions were fulfilled and, when he found they were, he based his study on the factors which went towards those perceptions.

Carr's third type is the practical approach in which theory is derived from the practice setting. This is practical knowledge which is based on Aristotle's *phronesis,* or practical wisdom: theory informs the practitioner but the theory is informed by a desire to do the right thing or behave in an ethical manner. Patricia Benner (1984) discusses levels of expertise in nursing and argues that expert nursing is characterised by routine and automatic actions which are highly skilled and underpinned by knowledge. The point is that much of this knowledge and skills are acquired through experience and are often never fully articulated. A professional doctorate study may be focused around the exploration of what is implicit in practice and, by making it explicit, developing practice in a very powerful way. Whilst an ethical dimension underpins all research it is perhaps more explicit in this particular approach. It is often brought out through reflection by individuals, both on themselves and on their areas of practice. It requires people to examine good practice and the moral ethical dimension to decision-making. Jean, one of our professional doctorate students, encapsulated this approach. She was interested in exploring the ways in which people determined their staffing needs in healthcare settings and used focus groups as a way of finding out exactly what happened in practice.

Carr's fourth area is that of critical theory, and this requires close examination of practice and consideration of the wider factors which may impinge on it. It means uncovering practice, questioning why things are done in a particular way at a point in time and asking what forces are shaping the initiatives. Much can be traced to government policies and the changes they bring about in healthcare and educational policy, for example. Many professional doctorate students in considering policies find it useful to explore the origins of their initiatives and the social forces which shaped and developed them.

Jean found that people were very interested in her work on staffing levels and approaches to determining staffing requirements. In the prevailing economic climate healthcare organisations were particularly concerned with finance and expenditure; any mechanism which would provide accuracy and justification for decisions was very welcome. It is important, therefore, to consider the wider contextual issues and why a particular study is relevant at a point in time.

Activity 2

When developing a proposal it is useful to consider the elements of Carr's typology, and use this approach to structure your thinking. You may want to consider these questions:

- Do you wish to apply theory to your practice or examine the theoretical underpinnings of practice?
- Do you wish to uncover the common sense ideas people have on practice and explore them in a little more detail?
- Are you concerned with the moral and ethical dimensions of practice?
- Do you wish to look critically at the forces which shaped or continue to shape your area of practice?
- Are there some elements of all of the above aspects?

Activity 2 lists some suggestions for the thinking that is required when you are shaping up your proposal. The key point is that you may draw on a wide range of disciplines and underpinning ideas on practice. The following chapters approach the reflections which will further shape your ideas and consider the research methods which will help you to explore the ways in which these ideas can be investigated.

2.4 Framing your research question

It is useful to frame your potential project as a clear aim, statement of purpose or a research question which your doctoral study is setting out to answer. Parahoo (1997, p. 396) defines a research question as 'the broad question which is set at the start of a study'. Cormack and Benton (1996) state that there are two types of research question: interrogative and declarative. An interrogative research question is written as you would expect a question to be written, while a declarative research question is a more like a statement of purpose. So an example of an interrogative research question is:

"Can Electronic Research Administration systems improve research quality and quantity?"

whilst an example of a declarative research question is:

"The purpose of this research is to evaluate the impact of an interprofessional education approach on undergraduate pharmacy students."

It is not easy to decide on your project and to specify it precisely, but it is important that you do so. The stated purpose of your project should pass the 'so what?' test. Will satisfying the aim, fulfilling the purpose or answering the question have an impact? Will it show clear benefit? It is also important that the focus of your work is quite narrow. This is a doctoral project, and you will not be able to use it to address all of the issues or solve all of the problems within your practice.

Your question should be SMART, that is:

Specific – be as specific as you possibly can about what you intend to do.

Measurable – you should be able to measure the impact of your project.

Attainable – your research should be achievable in the timescale of your doctorate.

Relevant – your research should be of use to you, your employer and your community of practice.

Timely – current, a 'hot topic' and relating to relevant issues within your practice and the profession.

The remainder of Section 2.4 presents the actual research questions addressed by six professional doctorate graduates. In only one case (David) is the purpose set out as an interrogative question. In the other examples, the purpose is given in the form of an aim or a narrative, sometimes accompanied by a set of objectives. You can find fuller treatments of these six projects in Chapter 11 where they are included in the eight case studies.

Case studies

Example 1 Claire

Claire's project, entitled *A Contribution to Pharmacy Practice Education*, explored novel approaches to Pharmacy Education at first degree and masters levels, and she defined her aims as follows:

> *"The first aim is to provide undergraduate pharmacy students with a learning experience which will prepare them for practice in a multi-professional environment and help them to improve patient care.*
>
> *The second aim is to offer a postgraduate educational provision which will help qualified students to build upon the basis of their undergraduate education and initial working experiences. These programmes will prepare them for advanced practice as clinical pharmacists, anticoagulant clinic specialists, and supplementary and independent prescribers."*

Example 2 Ian

Ian's project was entitled *Making a Difference – My Contribution in a Journey towards Corporate Social Responsibility in a Modern Civic University*. His aims were to:

- *"Reflect on a journey towards corporate social responsibility (CSR) in a modern civic university and my role in this.*
- *Evaluate the impact of CSR on stakeholders and the wider community.*
- *Propose a new framework for CSR in a modern civic university."*

He also set out the following objectives:

- *"To reflect on my early experiences in order to explore my core values and to understand how individuals can make a difference.*
- *To critically review literature relating to CSR and the civic university.*
- *To undertake action research and reflect on the development of a range of activities which I propose pave the way for a CSR culture.*
- *To reflect on the introduction of a CSR statement and the embedding of principles into corporate strategy and practice.*
- *Based on the evidence in the literature and the action research and reflections above, to propose a framework for CSR within a civic university.*
- *To evaluate the impact of CSR at the university across its stakeholders, and wider implications for the CSR community of practice.*
- *To draw conclusions and lessons for practice, and propose a final framework of CSR in a civic university."*

Example 3 Max

Max's project had the title *Core Principles for a Successful Management System: A Professional Journey*.

The aim of his work was to "*identify best practice in management systems and to propose a set of core principles which underpin a successful management system.*" He completed a thorough reflection of his experience before undertaking an examination of quality and management literature. This strengthened and supported the evidence for how he developed and implemented a system which embodied best practice. Finally, he undertook qualitative research which examined senior management views on management systems.

Example 4   Siobhan

Siobhan's title described the project, which was developing a new model: *Shared Services in Further Education.*

The aim of her research was: *"To investigate models of shared services and to develop and evaluate a new model of shared services for application in the Further Education sector."*

The specific objectives of the research were:

- *"To critically review the current state of the art of shared services, with particular reference to the Further Education Sector.*
- *To undertake a detailed case study with local Further Education partners to develop a shared services model to match their requirements.*
- *To analyse the case study and draw out lessons, and recommendations for, shared services, with particular reference to the Further Education Sector."*

Example 5 Fiona

The title of Fiona's project was: *A Commissioning Improvement Framework: The Development and Implementation of a Lean Organisational Improvement Approach for NHS Commissioning*, and she summarised it as follows:

"The purpose of this study was to develop an organisational improvement approach in NHS commissioning using the principles of Lean. This report presents the development and installation of a novel NHS Commissioning Improvement Framework (CIF) within a primary care trust context and discusses the impacts made in practice. Through a programme of action research, this study has been able to show how the principles of Lean can be introduced into the day-to-day practice of a commissioning organisation and deliver measurable benefits to both patient and the organisation through the application of the CIF."

Example 6 David

David's project was entitled: *Electronic Research Administration: Reflections on Research Management and Administration (RMA) in UK universities and in particular on Electronic Research Administration (ERA) and its perceived effect on the quality and quantity of research*

"There were two main strands of work, the development of the wider profession of research management and administration (RMA) in the UK and a specific research focus of ERA systems, in particular attempting to answer the question, 'can ERA systems improve research quality and quantity?'"

These research questions are set out as they were within the students' final submissions. Each has its own strengths and weaknesses. However they all state the purpose of the candidate's doctoral study, and they were all deemed acceptable by their examiners. (You can read how each of the candidates tackled their research questions in Chapter 11, as they are all covered in the case studies.)

The grid in Figure 2.1 can be used as a guide for establishing how SMART a question is. Try applying the statements in the grid to the six students' questions above. You can also use the grid to assess your own project.

Does the research question satisfy the following SMART criteria:	Rate on the scale Not at all Completely
The question is **Specific**, with a clearly defined focus	
The impact is **Measurable**, and you are able to clearly evaluate the contribution	
The outcome is **Attainable** within the timescale of a doctorate	
The project appears to be **Relevant** and of use, and will make a contribution to practice	
The research is **Timely**, and investigates a topic which is of current interest	

Figure 2.1   Is a research question SMART?

2.5 Learning sets

Many professional doctorate programmes have a taught component, the content of which will vary depending on the particular scheme. However the main aim is to provide an underpinning for the professional doctorate study which you will undertake. Common to most professional doctorate programmes are reflective practice and research methods, whether as specific modules or as themes running throughout the taught component. We have considered reflective practice (Chapter 3) and research methods (Chapter 4), both of which will be useful in the development of your ideas.

One thing that is common to all programmes – and something which all of our students have found helpful – is the interaction with the staff teaching on the programme and particularly with the other students. In the taught modules the interaction with other students, some from a similar background and others from very different backgrounds, is something many of our students consider invaluable.

One of the most valuable features of a professional doctorate is the chance to study within a cohort of like-minded students with whom you can share your learning journey. The opportunity to work with and learn from the interactions with their colleagues is one of the positive messages that we receive from our students on the professional doctorate programme (Smith et al., 2011):

- *Meeting up with the other students in the cohort, as we spur each other on.*
- *Interaction with a cohort of people from different disciplines and seeing how common themes emerge even from quite disparate areas.*
- *The taught sessions and cohort days help to keep you 'on target'.*

The remainder of this section will outline how you can capitalise on interactions with your fellow students, which are helpful not only in providing an opportunity to shape and develop your ideas but throughout the programme of study. This is particularly the case when the cohort contains an eclectic mix of students from a variety of professions and alternative communities of practice. Such a grouping concurs with the concept of the *practitioner doctorate* proposed by Lester (2004). Students feel that there is much to be gained from discussing their experiences with others and from hearing the views of other students who work within different disciplinary and subject contexts (Smith et al., 2011) and who may have had similar experiences and issues but with different outcomes and solutions. Conversely, having several students from the same profession in the cohort tends to stifle open discussion as one view predominates – pooling ignorance (Malfroy, 2005) – and learning tends to be single-loop (Smith et al., 2011).

The authors have found that students perceive and enjoy an element of peer pressure and competitiveness within their cohort group, and this spurs them on. They keenly anticipate the cohort study days and use them as an opportunity to share tips or ideas and compare progress. They enjoy the experience of the shared learning journey and everyone feels a shared sense of achievement as one by one they pass their viva and graduate. We intentionally arrange for the successful graduates from the programme to give a presentation on their experiences to the following cohorts, and these are always well attended and a source of useful advice. Indeed, our students have requested that there should be more of these learning opportunities in the programme.

If your particular professional doctorate programme doesn't formally provide an opportunity to work with your fellow students then there is no reason why you can't do this informally if there are other like-minded individuals on the programme. You could arrange to meet up somewhere on or off campus that suits all of you, or meet virtually using a blog, for example. It is a good idea to make these informal meetings focused so that it is worthwhile for all of you to participate. But social learning will only work effectively if you reach consensus on how the learning set should operate, with everyone agreeing to behave with mutual trust and respect. One of the most useful things that you can do is engage in peer review of your written work, particularly when you are new to academic writing and need to practise. You could for example, read aloud to each other and ask for feedback. Lee and Boud (2003, p. 187) argue that 'writing is best seen as a starting point, rather than an endpoint, of the research process' and describe the effective use of writing groups to foster academic writing. As well as encouraging formal writing skills, participation in writing groups will also encourage you to think and write critically and to engage in objective and analytical academic discussions which will help to develop your higher reasoning skills.

These are essential skills for you to acquire as you undertake your research and challenge accepted professional practice. Argyris (2002) suggests that this will take place when you engage in double-loop learning which goes beyond the single-loop learning of simple problem-solving and involves a new and deeper interpretation of the problem in the context of new theories and models. Kirkham et al. (2012) would argue that double-loop learning takes place when professional doctoral students are in learning sets and they have deliberately structured their DBA programme to reflect this.

If your learning set is maintained and developed throughout the lifetime of your professional doctorate then you will find that you have created a new community of practice. Lave and Wenger (1998) would argue that, for this to take place, you require three things:

● A shared domain of interest, such as the professional doctorate;
● A community which shares activities, such as peer review; and
● Members who are practitioners and share resources.

However, unlike your professional community of practice, this set may not survive once you graduate from the programme. This does not deny the value of this social learning experience – you may have made friends who will remain so for a lifetime.

Summary

This chapter has examined approaches you can take to the development of your ideas based on your work practice. The following areas have been explored:

● Mode 1 and Mode 2 knowledge production, their differences and similarities.
● The types of knowledge involved in practice and how these can be a starting point in your development of the professional doctorate study.
● The ways in which your ideas can be framed and shaped into specific aims, objectives and a research question.
● How your colleagues on the programme can support you and enhance your experience.

3 Developing as a Researching Professional through Reflective Practice

On completion of this chapter you will:

▶ understand what it means to be a professional, and be able to define the professional community to which you belong

▶ be able to consider the way that professionals learn within their community of practice, and understand how ways of learning within a community can be both enabling and restrictive

▶ understand the role that reflective practice plays in helping you to become a true researching professional, and understand some of the techniques that can help you to become more reflective

3.1 Introduction

This chapter explores what it means to be a researching professional, and introduces the concept of reflective practice. By embarking upon a professional doctorate programme you have signalled your intention to become a *researching professional*. This is a professional whose actions and decision-making processes are not bound by the traditional ways of doing things; who has critical curiosity about their professional world; who keeps up-to-date with developments in their field and understands how they can be applied to benefit the profession; is eager to contribute to the development of the profession and to share that development with others; and who has the ability to look at challenges through a 'fresh lens' to come up with novel and imaginative solutions to professional problems or challenges.

This way of operating does not come naturally to most of us. Once we get into our day-to-day work we often find it easier to just slip into a routine that we rarely question until problems or crises occur. Breaking out of this comfort zone requires a reflective practice approach. Applied properly, this will help you to step back from events and the emotional 'noise' associated with them, and to consider them more critically and objectively. This, in turn, leads to better professional judgements and decision-making, and can often lead to solutions that you may not otherwise have thought of. This is really important in terms of achieving doctoral-level thinking and demonstrating that you can be an effective thought-leader. This chapter has been designed to help you become a reflective practitioner. In it we will look at what reflection means, and how to build reflection into both your research and working life. It is about changing the way you think. We start, though, by setting these ideas in context and taking a look at why changing the way they think can be often difficult for established professionals.

3.2 The profession

Traditionally, the term 'profession' was used to refer to occupations such as doctor and lawyer – what we have come to know as '*the* professions'. In this book we use the term 'profession' much more inclusively to mean a paid occupation that requires an advanced degree of education or training, and the term 'professional' to mean someone who is highly-skilled and competent within their profession. In a fast-changing world, individuals' notions of their profession and the standards by which they are judged to be skilled and competent can be extremely flexible and move through many stages in the course of a career. Take, for example, someone who completes a degree in engineering, but then several years into her career starts to specialise in project management, taking a master's degree and professional qualifications in that field. She works on many projects at increasing levels of responsibility and seniority. She may then come to consider herself as a professional project manager. Others may see her as that, and some colleagues may not be aware that she used to be a practising engineer, valuing only her expertise in project management. Her engineering education has formed the foundation for this profession, but the advanced knowledge and expertise that makes her a professional is in a different field. For many of us, our career history will follow this pattern. As we move through our working lives, the specialisms and expertise that we develop and through which we define ourselves in a professional role may be only weakly linked, if at all, to our original education or training. If you are in this position, then unpicking exactly what your profession is can be very important to how you approach your doctoral studies.

This is important because your doctorate requires you to demonstrate a *unique contribution to your profession*. Within that small phrase lie a number of very fundamental questions:

1 What do you mean by your 'profession'?
2 Can you demonstrate that you understand what is already known about your profession?
3 Can you demonstrate that the contribution that you intend to offer is truly unique, and that no one else has already done it?
4 Can you demonstrate that you have made a genuine contribution that advances the state of the profession in some practical way?

You will be asked to explain and defend your answers to these questions at your *viva voce* examination, and your defence will be much more convincing if you are clear about your responses from the start. Fundamental to all of this, of course, is that first point – your definition of a profession. Given what we have discussed above, this is not always straightforward. Taking the example of our engineer again, if she were to undertake a professional doctorate she may decide that her main interest is in making a contribution within the field of project management rather than to her original discipline of engineering. Once she has made this decision about where her research effort will be focused it will determine the course that her work will take, including the literature she accesses, the methodologies she employs, the supervisory team that supports her, and ultimately the constitution of the examination panel.

Activity 1

Take ten minutes out to write down a definition of your profession.

When we ask our doctoral candidates to do this activity, one of two things normally happens: either they write down what they *do* (usually a reprise of their job description) or they write down the prescribed standards of their profession (for example, those stipulated by their professional body). Neither of these is helpful in terms of their doctoral work. The first is too narrow; working within the confines of their current job role is unlikely to produce work that makes a contribution to the wider profession. The second is too broad and non-specific to who they are as a professional. To make a real contribution, they must start to explore where they fit within that broad professional context. We have already discussed how this is rarely straightforward for experienced professionals because most of us have a professional journey that has carried us away from our original professional roots and developed into something more specialist, or indeed sometimes something quite different from where we started.

When faced with this question, one candidate, Siobhan, described how her changing job role – from a nurse on the wards to an operational manager, then to a strategic manager – has changed her perception of her chosen profession, and caused her to re-evaluate who she is as a professional. Now, some of the decisions she has to make as a manager conflict with her professional nursing values and beliefs, but the management values 'win', because she now has a different professional perspective. She described just how much this results in challenge, discomfort and conflict for her. Many of us with an established career history will tell a similar story; we develop into different roles, and of course the nature of the profession also changes over time so that often it is very different from that which we joined at the start of our career.

Why should this matter? There are several important reasons for taking the time to clearly identify and scope your profession at the start of your doctoral journey. Most significantly, it helps you to answer questions 2–4 on the list that we considered above. If you are to demonstrate that you understand what is known about your profession and that you are making a unique contribution, you first need to set the context for your work. You will be required to conduct a literature review to establish current knowledge in the field, and you will need to defend your contribution to experienced professionals who will judge whether or not your work is original and unique. These responses will be shaped by the context that you have set for your work. Take Siobhan again as an example. If she claimed her profession to be simply 'nursing', where she had started her career, she would have been left with a very broad field from which to draw both her literature review and potential experts that might examine her final work. How could she possibly conduct a review of all of the literature about nursing in its broadest sense? But, similarly, if she had defined herself as a professional 'manager', she would not have narrowed the field in any useful way. By defining her profession as 'strategic management in healthcare', she has defined a field that is very specific, and one which reflects both her original profession, and consequently much of her existing knowledge and expertise, and her developed role into management, in which she can make a current and informed contribution. She can start to explore the current strategic challenges facing the healthcare professions, and how these might be managed. By defining her current profession in this way, she has set a clear context for her research work.

3.3 Professional identity

We have used Siobhan so far to demonstrate how people can develop into particular professional roles. That process of development can itself be very important to how each of us carry out our roles – how we think, make judgements, interact with other professionals and, most importantly to the subject of this book, *how we learn*. All are shaped by our journey. There is a close relationship between professional learning and personal development (Olesen, 2001). The values, beliefs and attitudes that we gain from childhood and which develop through our personal and professional experiences over the years all shape who we are as a professional. That very unique mix that each of us has defines how we behave and distinguishes us from others in the same role; it gives us our professional identity. Professional identity can be defined as:

> The relatively stable and enduring constellation of attributes, beliefs, values, motives, and experiences in terms of which people define themselves in a professional role. (Schein and Schein, 1978)

Developing an understanding of your own professional identity and how that determines your behaviour is important if you are to make sense of the professional environment and interrelationships in the critical, analytical way demanded of you for your doctoral studies. In undertaking a professional doctorate you are inherently linking your research work to practice, so understanding the nature of that practice is fundamentally important. Wenger (1998) explains that there is a profound connection between identity and practice: developing a practice involves the formation of a community (of practice) where each of the individuals engages with and interacts with each other as participants. Thus, understanding who you are in that community and what you can contribute to it are key issues. Wenger argues that how we define our identities affects such things as:

- How we locate ourselves in a social landscape (of our community of practice).
- What we care about and what we neglect.
- What we attempt to know and understand and what we choose to ignore.
- With whom we seek connections and whom we avoid.
- How we engage and direct our energies.
- How we attempt to steer our trajectories within the community (for example, on joining or deciding to leave a community of practice, or deliberately choosing to stay on the periphery of a community rather than embracing full membership).

It is clear to see that the items on this list all have the potential to affect how you will conduct your doctoral work. Clarity of your own professional identity will help you to define the scope of the practice within which you locate your work, indicate what things you care most about and wish to study in depth, and help you to understand and appreciate the actions of others. This last point is especially important, because undoubtedly during the course of your doctorate there will be times when you are really excited about something you have discovered, only to find that those around you do not share your enthusiasm. At best they may be indifferent, at worst they may be actively antagonistic towards your ideas. At those times it can be very easy to become despondent, doubtful of your own judgement, and sometimes even to feel like giving up. If, however, you can take a step back and try to understand why they are reacting in such a way and why their perceptions are so different from yours – understanding 'where they are coming from' – you will have a much better chance of persuading others to consider your ideas. This is fundamental to reflective practice, and is one of the key skills required at doctoral level.

Consider Roy's experience.

Roy's story

Roy's story starts with a trip to visit a partner school in another country that he, as a headmaster, had planned in order to engage with what he considered to be a very exciting project. After months of planning, the trip turned out to be a disaster, the blame for which Roy placed squarely on the shoulders of the partner school's head teacher. He expressed a raft of negative emotions – he was rejected, bitter, let down, disappointed, insulted, angry, ashamed and guilty. At that point, there was no way that anything constructive was going to come from the experience. Then Roy was encouraged to reflect on the episode, and explore it from other points of view. Here's a shortened version of what he had to say:

"Have I learned to understand and forgive Anne by writing from her point of view? Well, yes; it has helped. I still feel disappointed for what might have been, but I don't feel personally affronted any more. What has been interesting though is to start to reflect on why I was nursing a grudge in the first place. Something must have touched a nerve, for, as I say, nursing grudges is most unlike me. What was it that made me so sensitive?

Unfairly and unreasonably I had been blaming Anne personally for being an inadequate part of something that was probably doomed to failure anyway and that she had never chosen to be part of.

As a head I have become increasingly outward looking. I seek opportunities to reach out to and cooperate with other schools. Though all the heads on our visit shared some of this outlook, I held it most strongly; probably this outward focus is what is most distinctive about my headship. Reaching out across to another country was a particularly exciting opportunity and I was frustrated and resentful at finding that opportunity balked.

The partner schools and their principals seemed terribly insular. It's not just that they weren't interested in us; they weren't even interested in each other. Partnership and cooperation between schools appeared to be minimal. Each principal was narrowly focused on achieving the best for their own students with little regard for the effect on other schools. This insularity was not just alien to me, it was anathema. And Anne became, for me, the embodiment of that anathema.

*As a head in a fairly successful school I failed to understand the extreme pressure the principals were under. The schools had been nationally pilloried. The mayor had been elected on an education ticket. Principals could be – and were being – summarily dismissed. Teachers were being assessed five times a year and sacked if they failed to meet the grade. I knew all this, but I failed to really **feel** it.*

Since my visit the political climate in schools in my own country has changed significantly and some of those pressures are starting to hit us. The government has raised 'floor targets' which all schools are required to meet or face threat of closure. They are threatening no-notice inspections from next year. The grade of 'satisfactory' has been changed to 'in need of improvement'. The level of grading has been significantly raised and it is much harder for a school to be good or outstanding than it was before. And they now say that if any significant group of students has inadequate

> performance in any major subject, then the whole school is considered to be inadequate.
>
> I suspect that to some extent I transferred my hostility to a cruel, unfair and insensitive system to Anne, a victim of that system who ought to really have excited my sympathy.
>
> As the political climate changes I can see the naïveté in my own approach and I am more sympathetic to Anne's relentless focus on examinations. I think at the time I saw her as someone who had capitulated to the system and I blamed her personally.
>
> I observed that the system in the partner schools was highly stratified. I saw the contrast between the private schools, and the state schools with a high degree of selection within the state schools. I saw the marked racial and social distinctions. I disliked it; I disliked it intensely, but I didn't really feel it.
>
> I think I saw the principals, and specifically Anne, as choosing a bunker mentality, as choosing to be competitive and insular. I observed, but did not sufficiently recognise, that the principals had much less power and independence than heads in my own country. I saw them as actors, when they were really victims. And now that I too am becoming a victim...
>
> I can taste the rage and bitterness as I write it.
>
> I suppose I could sum it up by saying that poor Anne, dear Anne, has been acting in my subconscious as a substitute to absorb my growing anger and frustration."

Through reflecting on this experience from the other person's point of view, Roy has started to unpick his own professional identity and has begun to develop a vision of the future where the community of practice to which he belongs is changing markedly. Will he be able to continue working in the same way – the way that matters so much to him – when that change occurs? The work that he completes for his doctorate will need to allow for the new educational environment and, by starting to understand the implications now, he is ensuring that his work remains relevant and is not situated in a professional world that no longer exists.

The ability to achieve the level of self-awareness where you can be cognisant of the professional changes around you and can appreciate the actions of others comes from a reflective practice approach to your work. However, achieving this level whilst embedded in a community of practice can be difficult because of the constraints exerted by the community itself. It is this topic that we now go on to consider.

3.4   How do we know?

This is a question that will undoubtedly be asked of you in one form or another during your viva. Your examiners will ask you to convince them that your claims to new knowledge or insights about your profession are valid.

A clear research philosophy and methodology will help you to do this – this is explored in the next chapter. But the question that we are asking here is more fundamental than that. We are alluding to how we know things in a professional sense. How do we acquire, interpret and use professional knowledge? How does it help us to become successful in our field? And what are the problems with professional knowledge? An understanding of these things forms the foundation for your subsequent development of new insights into your profession.

Think about a time when you joined a new community of practice – it could be a new job, a new department, a different role, or even the professional doctorate programme. How did you feel? How long did it take you to feel like a true member? What was it that helped you to 'become' one of the community?

We start to feel part of a new group when we start to learn its language and culture. Learning is a social process (Lave and Wenger, 2009; Wenger, 2010). Any group tends to have its own jargon, insider knowledge or 'in jokes'. Newcomers at first do not understand, and need to learn through observation and experience. Similarly, the newcomers will gradually learn through experience about the informal hierarchy in the group – who is the most powerful member, who is respected, who can and cannot be trusted and so on. None of these things are written down anywhere – they are *tacit*. We introduced this idea in Chapter 2 when we looked at Carr's typology. Tacit knowledge is common sense knowledge that cannot be easily articulated. For example, most people know how to ride a bike, but few could actually explain in detail *how* they do it. This is a very simple example, but riding a bike is nevertheless a complex skill, much of which is tacit. We learn through trial and error how to maintain balance, make different manoeuvres and so on. In the same way, learning how a profession operates is largely tacit. There may be lots of procedures written down, but finding out how the profession *really* works through things such as the underlying culture and working norms is tacit. Nevertheless, to be effective professionals in any organisation we need to learn these things. So how do we do this if the knowledge is not written down and cannot be articulated to us by those that are already 'in the know'? In practice we absorb this professional know-how in the same way that we learn to ride a bike – through observation, experimentation, reflection and trial and error. For example, medical students learn much about being a doctor by accompanying consultants on their rounds, observing how they interact with patients and other professionals. Role-modelling is an important process in developing the identity of a profession (Ibarra, 1999).

A lot has been written about the development of tacit knowledge because it is considered so important to the performance of organisations. Researchers have developed ideas about how the processes of knowledge transfer occur, and have identified *socialisation, articulation* and *internalisation* as being key (Schön, 1983; Nonaka, 1994; Baumard, 1999; Ibarra, 1999; McNett et al., 2004). So, as a newcomer to a group we absorb knowledge such as appropriate mannerisms, attitudes and social rituals through action, observation and reflection whilst we are working with the more experienced members: this is socialisation. The process of articulation happens when we work together on problems, talking around the issues and gradually teasing out the different elements of the situation to make it more explicit. Then, when we internalise this expanded knowledge, we are able to access it without conscious thought so that it simply becomes part of the toolkit with which we are able to do our job – the new tacit knowledge of our profession. This is done through reflection on our actions. Many professionals move through these processes unwittingly. A key objective of the research that is being done in this area is to identify how organisations can drive the processes more proactively to make learning more efficient and thereby improve performance.

Activity 2

As an experienced practitioner within your own specialist field, you will have acquired the tacit knowledge that has enabled you to operate successfully. Now, however, you are faced with a challenge. You are moving into a new community of practice – not simply as a professional, but as a *researching professional* – and that implies a shift in mind-set that will move you out of the normal cycle of transferring existing professional knowledge (both explicit and tacit) into an area where new knowledge can be generated. You need to develop the 'know-how' of the research community.

- How might you use the processes described above to develop that know-how?
- Do you wish to apply theory to your practice or examine the theoretical underpinnings of practice?

In the same way that we learn to integrate with any new profession, integration into the field of professional research involves the process of socialisation, articulation and internalisation through reflection. During your doctoral programme you should take the opportunity to engage with the *professional research community* as much as you can. Simply confining yourself to your normal community of practice is unlikely to stretch your thinking beyond its normal boundaries, as we discuss in more detail in the next section. You should discuss your work regularly with academics as it progresses; seek out opportunities to present your work at conferences or research seminars; and discuss your progress with your peer researchers and professional colleagues. When you start out on the research journey it is quite normal to be fearful of presenting your ideas in this way, especially when you are not yet sure where the work is taking you. Your ideas will be challenged; there will be questions that you cannot answer, there may be comments that make you doubtful about what you are doing, but that is all part of the process. Only by socialising with the research community in this way will you learn to become a true researching professional and learn the language of research. Although this can be a daunting prospect when you first start out on your research journey, the advice offered in Chapter 2 suggests a good way to start: use your peer learning group as a sounding-board, share your ideas with them and read your work aloud. Learn to give each other constructively critical feedback, and learn how to use it. You need to reflect on the exchanges that you have and use that reflection to build your knowledge base. We will consider the mechanisms of reflection in more detail in Section 3.7, but first we look at an aspect of professional knowledge that has the potential to hinder your research efforts: territorialisation.

3.5 Barriers

We have discussed how the development of tacit professional knowledge enables individuals to become part of the professional community. Despite this acknowledged value of tacit knowledge, there are limitations on its usefulness which stem largely from the fact that its development is contextual. An individual who possesses tacit knowledge of one particular organisation may become what Baumard describes as 'territorialised' (1999). That is, their knowledge, and therefore the strategic approach they take to their work, is bounded by the cognitive map that they have created within that context, and that can be a barrier to the creation of new knowledge in different situations. (See the discussion about 'pooling ignorance' in Chapter 2.) Roy's story demonstrates this really well. An experienced head teacher, he thought he knew exactly what to expect when he worked with another head teacher. What he failed to see initially was the different context within which his colleague was working, and that became a barrier to the success of the project that he had spent so long planning. The effect can be even greater when we are required to work with people from different professions who sometimes can seem to speak a completely different language.

All of us, when we have spent a significant amount of time in a particular profession, will have some degree of territorialisation. We will have a tendency to look at things in a certain, perhaps routine, way. We will have a tendency to bias, to think of things from our own perspective. We find it difficult to understand different or opposing views. It is much easier to accept what we know and devise solutions to problems that are familiar and unchallenging. This is a real barrier to creative thought and the introduction of new ideas that are the essence of doctoral study. Let Laura explain.

"There were no professional standards within autism until 1995 when the National Autistic Society developed the accredited standards scheme. The statutory framework was more concerned about closing long stay hospitals and there were no unified principles to ensure consistent and good standards of social care. At the time though, this was innovative practice and cutting edge provision.

I was still considered relatively new to the profession even with five years' experience; however I do feel that this was more to do with the people within the service who considered themselves to believe that more time served meant that you were more qualified. This would cause difficulty, particularly when practitioners would ask why they practised the way they did which would often lead to conflict and practitioners being told that this is how they had always done things. This would stifle change and result in lack of innovation and not to mention the lack of progression that service users would make. There was little evidence of best practice and value for money to service user provision.

I was eager to learn and I felt like a sponge, taking everything in, asking questions and always asking 'why'. At the time I was working a lot with one service user who had very profound and complex autism. Until I started to work with him, I wasn't sure if I would stay in the profession for long; however his complexities and uniqueness intrigued me. Many practitioners that I worked alongside considered this service user extremely difficult to work with and would often avoid opportunities to spend time with him. I found this very difficult to understand as we choose to come into this profession to care and support; however at times we have to alter our own attitudes in order to empower people with autism to develop their own values and attitudes and not impart our own to them.

This young man I feel was starting to be ostracised from his peers and the wider community because of the perceptions of others. When I identify others, I mean social care practitioners. I would often look at the duty rota to see who I was working with and feel a sense of anxiety when certain individuals were on duty. Their values and attitudes were very much to get through the shift as quickly and as calmly as possible.

The structure of a group reflected the established patterns of behaviours that were distinctive within this particular group of practitioners and this acted as an objective constraint. There were also several other factors involved with this group of practitioners.

Early on in the group's history a group leader emerged because she was perceived by other members as the most competent (or longest serving member) at the functional requirements of the leadership role.

Group members were defined as individuals who had accepted group goals as relevant and recognize interdependence with other group members in the achievement of these goals.

The decision making abilities were very poor and even the manager would discuss decisions with the longest service practitioner before agreeing to anything. As a result lots of errors were made, wasting valuable time at the cost, sometimes, to a service user's quality of life.

continued overleaf

Laura's story continued

> The group's identity therefore was affected due to all of these complex forces and caused the cohesiveness of the team to be affected, which had a significant impact on the team's functioning. This of course created a headache for management in looking to support the longer term employees but also in realising that new thinking was bringing change that was greatly needed at the time.
>
> The service user who I had taken great interest in was noticeably changing, and not for the better. Members of the group would say, 'He often goes like that' or 'that's just his autism'. I knew 'knowledge' was the key to the answers but I wasn't sure where to start or who to really go to, so I purchased some books on autism and started the lengthy process of reading them. I started by reading some autobiographies of people with the condition and this opened my eyes into the mind of a person with autism. The more that I read, the more that I questioned and when I received an answer I was able to debate the subject area and offer a valid argument which some people started to listen to."

Laura's story holds a number of interesting lessons. Firstly, it is clear that established ways of working, especially of those who held power within the group, were creating a barrier to change. Laura (and probably others) could see this, but it was much easier to conform to the group norms than to 'rock the boat'. When Laura did start to question, she quickly became an outsider. Secondly, although Laura knew that things had to be done in a different way, she wasn't sure *how*. All of her background knowledge, all of her training, had been in the established ways of working. She knew that she couldn't find the answer from within the community of practice, so she began to look outside, and in her case she chose to consider the issue from the user perspective. She had taken her first steps towards becoming a researching professional, trying to see things in a different way, seeking to understand how alternative knowledge could enhance her work practice, and developing the skill of persuading others that her arguments were valid. However, to be able to do this, it was not enough for Laura to simply find out about different aspects of the issue in hand. She had to make her new knowledge useful, and to do that she required one further, crucial, skill: critical reflection.

3.6   Making new knowledge useful: becoming a reflective practitioner

'Reflective practice' and 'reflection' are popular and frequently-used terms in modern professional life (Sanders, 2010), and the skills of reflection are an integral part of many training programmes. Many of you will be familiar with Kolb's learning cycle (Kolb, 1984) and the part that reflection plays in experiential learning. The ideas about tacit knowledge transfer that we looked at earlier showed how reflection is a key process in the internalisation of knowledge in that professional knowledge becomes tacit, allowing individuals to operate without constant recourse to written instructions or other directives. Yet despite all of this, many practitioners who claim to be reflective are merely 'going through the motions'; when asked to write reflectively they produce work that is largely descriptive. So what is it that we are really looking for, and why does the skill of reflection seem to elude so many of us?

There are a great many texts written about reflection in professional life. Schön's *The Reflective Practitioner* (1983) is perhaps one of the most influential, but others you may find useful are Kuit et al. (2001), Moon (2004), Bolton (2010) and McIntosh (2010). It is not our intention to revisit their various models and theories of reflection. Here we want to give attention to practical techniques that can help you learn how to use reflection effectively in order to develop critical research skills and for your professional development. However, it will be useful to remind ourselves of some of the definitions that we will be working with.

Reflection: Reflection entails careful and deep analysis of past events. This involves considering the situation from the viewpoint of all stakeholders; thinking about what each of them experienced and how they will have felt at the time. The event should be viewed through as many different, and relevant, lenses as possible, being careful not to make assumptions or jump to conclusions.

Reflective practice: Reflective practice involves including reflection within your everyday practice, and using the reflections to shape what you do on a day-to-day basis.

Reflexivity: Reflexivity is generally recognised as being much deeper than reflection. To be truly reflexive, one needs the ability to be very self-aware in order to find a way of stepping outside yourself and being self-analytical. This means truly understanding yourself as a professional, being aware of your values, prejudices and limits and ensuring that you act in full knowledge of why you are doing something. It also means doing this in the moment.

By now, many of the ideas involved in these definitions should seem familiar to you, relating back to our discussion about becoming a researching professional. You should recognise that reflection does not mean simply thinking about an event after it has happened and contemplating what you might have done differently (a common misinterpretation of the reflective process). It is much more than that, It involves·

- self-awareness, understanding how your own values and beliefs affect a situation;
- understanding the motives and actions of others;
- being able to step back from the emotions of a situation to judge it rationally;
- critically examining a situation, using not just your own inherent knowledge, but knowledge sought from alternative, reliable sources;
- a willingness and flexibility to see the situation differently; and
- being able to step outside of yourself so that you are not blinkered by your own prejudices and biases.

The ability to step outside of yourself is the crucial feature of reflection. It is important for any professional operating in a fast-changing environment, but more so for you when you are engaged in your doctoral study because you will be expected to demonstrate your ability to think critically and show that you are cognisant of the different perspectives on your topic. Understandably, most people find this an incredibly hard thing to do. A common technique that is used to help individuals develop as reflective practitioners is the reflective learning log, whereby individuals are asked to write a regular diary and reflect on the events. However, unless the skills of reflection are already developed, the results are often descriptive and insufficiently reflective. So, to help you along the way to becoming a critically reflective practitioner and researching professional, we next offer some practical techniques.

3.7 Practical techniques

Professional community map

We started this chapter by discussing how important it is for you to be able to clearly define your professional community. Simply describing yourself as 'a nurse' or 'a teacher' or 'an accountant' will not help you with your doctoral work. Instead, map out your community in terms of the people (described in terms of roles) that you liaise with to make your job work. Who do you influence? Who influences you? Who do you need to work with to make decisions? Who depends upon the decisions you make? How far does your influence reach? (There is always a 'ripple effect' to any of the decisions we make as professionals. Where do your ripples go?)

Professional identity metaphor

We discussed how professional identity is not just about what you do, but about who you are: your values, beliefs, motives, experiences and so on.

However, because these things are so much a part of us, they can be hidden to us. A useful way to start exploring them is by using a metaphor for your identity. The most useful that we have found is the photograph. Take a photograph or draw a picture that represents who you are as a professional. (This must NOT be a photograph or picture of you.) Then, explain it to someone, preferably someone who does not know you very well (we use the peer group for this exercise). Let them question you on the symbols that you have used in your photograph. Afterwards, reflect on the exercise. Did the image really represent who you are and how you've got to where you are? Had you missed anything out? Could you clearly explain to your partner what your symbols meant? Had you hidden anything? Do you need to change the image to make it more honest/representative? Consider how Paul uses a simple metaphor in a very powerful way to explore the conflicts between his 'research self', his 'artist self' and his 'personal self'.

Paul's reflection

"'Reflection is one of the key building blocks of human learning; it has become established at the core of management and organizational learning' (Vince and Reynolds, 2009)

To add to Vince and Reynolds' (2009) comments on reflection, I would propose that professional identity is a secondary and complementary key building block of management and organisational learning. In my current role as a leadership and management educator, teaching professionalism to practising professionals, I find professional identity and reflective practice to be the threshold concepts (Mayer and Land, 2005) fundamental to my students' understanding of their own professionalism. However, the challenges of thinking and writing reflectively have proved difficult for those professionals who have honed their mechanistic and manageresque analytical approaches over many years. In an attempt to increase their levels of personal and professional self-awareness, the use of creative writing and imagery have proven beneficial to the reflective process, which helps the students explore their current and possible new identities (Ibarra, 1999; Hargrove, 2009). Although I can now contextualise my creative approach within the contemporary discourses on the subject, my initial explorations into the use of narrative and imagery came about when I was struggling with my own personal identity as an artist and my developing professional identity as a researcher back in 2004. I reflect in both narrative and image formats.

My watch showed 11:45am as I walked out of Building 3 with my head and heart buzzing with artistic enthusiasm, generated and fuelled by the tangible positive energy of the many delegates attending the second Art of Management and Organisation conference, held in the European School of Management. It was approaching lunchtime on that sunny Parisian Thursday and for the first time during the conference, I took some time out from the proceedings to sit and reflect. Alone, apart from a few of my fellow delegates scurrying their way to the next presentation in another building I sat down on a

continued overleaf

bench in the centre of the courtyard. I greedily stretched myself out, lounging on the five-foot long wooden laths, which despite their hard angular appearance were surprisingly comfortable, having been gently warmed by the late morning sun. For the next fifteen minutes or so, I enjoyed some solitary, quiet time to reflect on my experiences. This in itself seemed quite a surreal experience in the centre of one of Europe's busiest cities at midday. The protective high walled university buildings that surrounded this oasis struck dumb the noisy traffic outside and yet on the inside provided the courtyard sparrows with the perfect acoustics to amplify their tiny cheeps as they dropped from the sunlit trees to squabble over crumbs in the shade. 'Was I truly in Paris?' I questioned. My senses sang a resounding 'yes'. My aesthetic receptors had been super charged by the conference's events so far with streams of: Art and Aesthetics; Artful Intervention; Art of Subversion and Art of Oppression; Creativity and Poetry, all tied together with threads of dramatic performance; visual arts and music.

12 o'clock now and the multicultural MBA students and conference delegates were starting to spill into the courtyard for lunchtime. I sat up allowing two students to share the bench, and watched them as they chatted and ate food. I reached for my sketchbook. My faculties were now so highly strung and in tune with my surroundings, that all five senses were absorbing every morsel of aesthetic data. My pen danced across the page in a frenzy to capture each transient moment. I observed their brightly coloured summer clothes illuminated by the sunlight and the abstract shapes formed by the shadows of their single and grouped bodied against the age-distressed walls. I could smell the food drifting from the refectory and hear the young musicians tuning their instruments and playing snippets from the jazz medley that they were about to perform to delegates over lunch. This was a truly wonderful and artistically inspiring time and after I had exhausted my short frenetic sketching, I joined my colleagues to enjoy the good food and jazz.

The following day on my return home, I was still on an artistic high and I guess the process of making my rough sketches had embedded those moments in my mind. I felt compelled to relive the experience through my painting and attempt to convey the same experience to others through the two-dimensional medium of oil paint. I share the image of my painting artefact, see Fig 3.1.

As I now reflect on this aesthetic experience, I can firstly see myself as artist absorbing through all of my faculties each aesthetic detail in the context of that time and place. I accepted some at face value; the heat of the sun; the smell of the food; and the sound of the music accompanied by the soft chatter of the students and sparrows. Other details I abstracted, seeing positive and negative shapes in the shadows and the

Fig 3.1 'Red Shoes in Paris'

colours observed. I found myself switching to artist autopilot, constructing and deconstructing images into potential framed compositions that would help guide the viewer around my paintings enabling them to share the same aesthetic values as they stand before my interpretation of that aesthetic experience. My initial sketches formed a bank of reference from which I would later draw and invest into the finished oil painting. Secondly, I can also see myself as a social science researcher gathering data ethnographically about the social actors who in that day, in that organizational setting, played out their individual and group roles on that courtyard stage. My sketches were my field notes and the finished painting was a graphical research paper, or should I say canvas, presenting my findings. Thirdly, I can see the power of creating your own artistic image of an experience where subconscious imagery presents itself for reflection. Although it was not immediately apparent during the painting process, the abstracted image of Christ on the cross with Mary on bended knee looking up at him (see Fig 3.2 detail below) caused me, in reflection to consider the spiritual aspects of my personal and professional identity. This was something very important to me and influences how I see myself, but it was not front-of-mind at the time of the Parisian experience or at the time of painting, it was only apparent when engaging in conscious reflection. Bringing together storytelling and the creation of images are powerful reflective tools to explore and enhance self-awareness in professional identity.

Fig 3.2 Detail

This dichotomous dilemma between the intuitive artist and rational researcher posed an identity challenge to me at the time. I so much wanted to be both, allowing each to influence the other. The truth is they did. I cannot detach my personal self from my professional self and the narrative storytelling and painting artefact above are auto ethnographical tools (Muncey, 2010) that enabled me, back then, to explore my personal and professional identity, as indeed the same processes enable my students to explore their own professional identity through their storytelling and images now.

In this abstract Paul has used both creative writing and artistic imagery very effectively in his efforts to explore who he really was as a professional. The story is even more powerful when one knows more of the background to this story. Paul had wanted to be an artist from childhood, but had been prevented from following that route by his father, who maintained that it was not a real career path. As a result, Paul found himself progressing through a series of jobs in heavy industry and then the police force. He was successful at all of them, but never entirely comfortable. He felt that he didn't fit. It was only when he moved into an educational role and discovered that he was able to use artistic imagery as both a teaching tool and as research data that he finally felt that he had found his true identity. The emotion evident in his writing is something that he would never have allowed himself to display in his earlier jobs, and he only found the freedom to release it when he felt he had found his authentic professional identity.

Biographical contents page

Imagine that you are planning to write your professional biography. Compose your imagined contents page, i.e. the chapter headings. Write it in a way that would interest the reader (it would be boring to simply call each chapter something like 'The period from 1994 to 2001'!). Use some imagination to give the chapters titles that really represent the meaning of what was going on in your professional life during significant periods. Then choose the chapter that interests you most, and write your story of that period. Use the story to explore not just what happened at that time, but why. Why is this chapter most significant to you? What were your feelings? What were the repercussions of what happened in that period on your subsequent career progression and decisions? Use this story to start unpicking what really matters to you in terms of your professional life. Examples from two candidates in the same cohort will demonstrate how this works (Figures 3.3 and 3.4).

Chapter	Age	Job
1	14	Shop Assistant
	15	Babysitter
2	16	Pharmacy Assistant
	17	Student Pharmacy Tech
	19	Pharmacy Technician
3	20	Student (part-time)
	21	Mature Student
4	25	Pre-Reg Pharmacist
	26	Community Pharmacist
	28	Community Pharm/Student
5	32	Prescribing Adviser
6	33	Clinical Pharmacy
	36	Hospital Pharmacist
	39	Chief Pharmacist
7	40	Exec Committee Member
8	41	Exec MBA Student
9	42	Displaced Chief Pharmacist
	44	Secondment Chief Pharmacist
	45	Returned to Previous Role
10	46	MD of Own Company
11	47	Prof Doc Student

Figure 3.3   Ashraf's list of chapters

Chapter	
1	The Roar of the Greasepaint, the Smell of the Crowd (1975–1981)
2	Sky Blue Formica (1981–1984)
3	William Millington Gives Wittgenstein a Bang On the Ear (1986–1989)
4	Running Away to Nottingham (1989–1990)
5	A Fish On Toot Hill (1990–1995)
6	Thomas Gradgrind and the Trykster (1995–1998)
7	The Fool's Leap (1998–2000)
8	Kindred Spirits (2000–2005)
9	If Not I, Then Who? (2005–2007)
10	Annie's Song (2007–2010)
11	An Opportunity Too Good To Miss (2010–present)

Figure 3.4   Cameron's list of chapters

You can see from Figure 3.3 that Ashraf has simply listed his jobs chronologically. This sort of factual representation of his professional career was not what we were looking for. There is no evidence of thought or reflection behind it. Compare it now with Cameron's chapter headings (Figure 3.4).

You might comment that Cameron's chapter list means nothing to you – you cannot even tell what his profession might be. But, of course, the point of the exercise is not to write a CV, it is to encourage the writer to identify significant periods in their professional life and explore what these periods meant to them – why they occurred, key influences, what they felt at the time, how they developed through that period. By inventing creative chapter headings to represent each of these periods, Cameron has had to reflect in depth on these issues in order to find words that succinctly describe them (for him). He then went on to describe one of those chapters in a very thoughtful and poignant way, describing why it was formative to his professional development.

Critical incident technique

This technique helps you explore and make explicit the norms, values and standards of the profession as a whole and compare them with your own. It can help you to see where you fit within the profession and explain any areas of discomfort you may have. Select an incident from your working life that is significant to you. It could be where something unexpected, surprising or shocking happened. Write down what your assumptions were before the incident. Then write down what happened, who was involved, and what the consequences were. Then analyse what effect your assumptions had on your actions during and after the incident. What did you learn from this? The case study overleaf presents one example.

The incident

"The central aim of the following report is to explore and analyse an incident that occurred while attending a clinical meeting about a nine year old child with autism. A number of clinical issues had been brought to my attention as the Head of Children's Services. I had received various emails and had discussions with key staff within the organisation who all shared the same concerns. As a result of this information, I convened a multidisciplinary meeting by emailing all key professionals.

On the day of the meeting both residential, school and therapy professionals attended. Residential and therapy staff appeared very relaxed and interacted positively before the start of the meeting. School staff were noticeably tense and were unusually quiet. The room management arrangements were also interesting as school staff sat at one end of the table and residential and therapy sat at the other.

I noticed these issues when I entered the meeting room so I encouraged everyone to get themselves a drink and to make the environment less formal. This also provided me with some time to get a picture of the child concerned. I had seen another senior manager use a picture of the child before in a difficult meeting. What the picture represented was to remind people why we were here, their value base of the child being at the centre of everything that we do, and directing all staffs' powerful emotions to the benefit of the child in order to ensure the child receives the best possible care and support.

I returned with the picture and placed this in the middle of the table. All staff looked at the picture and smiled. I started the meeting by saying that I could sense the emotions in the room and encouraged staff to use these emotions constructively so that the child gets the right support. What took place throughout the meeting was very interesting; when certain critical issues were raised and could have resulted in conflict, the staff would sit back and look at the child's picture.

There were a number of clinical areas that needed addressing and these were successfully achieved at the meeting. An area that was identified for improvement was communication between school and the residential home. This has historically been a long standing problem over many years. A number of actions were agreed and the result of the meeting was extremely positive.

At the end of the meeting I requested to speak with the Head Teacher to discuss the concerns about how we could work together more closely and bridge the gap between the two services. The Head Teacher expressed that the meeting was not what she had expected and she assumed that school were going to "get the blame" for some of the issues raised. When I asked the Head Teacher to explain what she meant by this, she discussed that it had always been a blame culture within the organisation and that she wished that I had spoken with her before the meeting.

As I am relatively new to the organisation, I had not identified this and did not understand why she thought that I would apportion blame to the school. We discussed this at some length and the areas of importance were:

● Lack of relationship between each other;
● Suspicion and tension due to expecting the blame;
● Lack of regular communication between each other;

- *Head Teacher accepted that communication needed to improve within the school and with her own staff;*
- *Head Teacher was able to recognise that her own anxieties had transferred to her staff and she had actually created the blame culture into their mind sets.*

We discussed these key issues at great length and this also proved to be a very positive meeting as we were able to agree a number of actions to take forward. These were:

- *Monthly Head of service meeting*
- *Monthly meetings between teachers, therapists and residential managers which would be facilitated by the Head Teacher and Head of Children's Services. Being united when working with staff in services was considered a powerful message to the workforce and to embed a unified culture and practice.*

Following on from this discussion I returned to my office and picked up my emails. What was pleasing to see were numerous emails going backwards and forwards from all staff who had attended the meeting. They had arranged meetings between themselves, communicated the necessary strategies to support the child, agreed these and confirmed dates to evaluate performance – all within the time that the Head Teacher and I had been talking. A number of staff had identified how motivating the meeting had been and expressed their enthusiasm for working jointly for the sake of the child.

I spent some time afterwards on my own thinking through the incident. The meeting had been more successful because I was able to reflect 'in' action which avoided potential conflict during the meeting. I was able to keep control over my emotions and channel them for the needs of the child which others were able to do due to this role modelling. I agreed with the points that the Head Teacher had raised and our relationship can only become stronger as a result of regular meetings and this can also support a greater partnership working through the organisation.

Assumptions

My assumptions before the meeting were that this was going to provide a multidisciplinary perspective over a complex issue that would provide a deep critical review of the strategies that had been put in place for the child. My view was one of positivity that by everyone sitting around a table, we would be able to resolve these concerns to ensure that the child had a better quality of life and achieve all of the principles set out in social care. I had also received a number of emails from my own staff that suggested that they were keen for this meeting to take place. I did not receive any email from the school staff however they all accepted the invitation and did not question the purpose of the meeting. I assumed that all practitioners were willing to work in partnership with each other which was certainly a learning point as I cannot expect all professionals to share my professional ethics and values.

My assumptions changed when I visibly saw the demeanour of the school staff and the atmosphere that could be felt within the room. By taking myself back out of the environment for a short time assisted me in reflecting about

continued overleaf

The incident continued

what actions I needed to take to ensure that this was going to result in a successful meeting. I also needed to keep my own emotions controlled as I was feeling anxious about why they were behaving like this.

I questioned my professional role and those of other practitioners who were attending the meeting. I understood that possibly our expectations of the meeting were in conflict and I knew that I would have to address this at the start of the meeting.

Using the photo of the child was a good move as staff visibly changed their body language and identifying people's interpersonal relationships and emotions assisted everyone to channel these to the benefit of the child. I was also knowingly internalising my professional role and seeking confirmation from others in the form of feedback, e.g. nodding, positive eye contact, etc. My responses or possibly my emotions meant that I needed an endorsement by others of my claims to be a professional (Olesen and Whittaker, 1968). I was evidently using a 'reflection in action' model as described by Schon."

Storytelling

There is a significant body of literature on the value of storytelling to professional development, but of course we don't need the academic literature to convince us how important storytelling is to learning. Knowledge in all cultures and societies is passed on through stories. As children we learn about the rules of our society from the fairy stories that our parents tell us; our history is passed down through stories of myth and legend. Stories can help us to detach ourselves from 'the self' that can be limiting to creative thought, and can free us to include the feelings and emotions that are important to true reflection; stories tend to be more memorable than the simple recounting of the facts. And, storytelling can help you to unlock some of your tacit knowledge and to appreciate alternative views. Roy's story (p. 30) is a successful example of this. Asked to recount a critical incident in his career, he struggled to be truly reflective when he wrote about his trip to Washington. Then he decided to write the story of the trip from his American colleague's point of view. This unlocked his understanding and appreciation, not only of the event itself but also of his own identity, as it forced him to revisit his previous assumptions and question why he had acted the way he did. Try this technique when you are struggling to understand something that is happening in the workplace – you will be surprised at the result.

Summary

In this chapter we have considered what it means to be a professional, and the importance of defining the professional community to which you belong. Because many professional doctorate candidates have a complex career history and have moved across role, and perhaps even discipline, boundaries, this task is not straightforward. It is, nevertheless, crucial to the doctoral process in order to clearly articulate your unique contribution to the profession.

We have considered how our professional identity – defined as the attributes, beliefs, values, motives and experiences in terms of which we define ourselves in a professional role – can affect:

- How we locate ourselves in a social landscape (of our community of practice).
- What we care about and what we neglect.
- What we attempt to know and understand and what we choose to ignore.
- With whom we seek connections and who we avoid.
- How we engage and direct our energies.
- How we attempt to steer our trajectories within the community (for example, on joining or deciding to leave a community of practice, or deliberately choosing to stay on the periphery of a community rather than embracing full membership).

We have considered learning as a social process by which people learn within their community of practice, adopting not only the expert knowledge that allows them to function as competent professionals, but also the norms, rituals and the tacit knowledge that are equally important to that functioning. However, we have also learned that sometimes this can restrict an individual's ability to see things from a different perspective, hindering their ability to solve unexpected problems or to work with others from outside of their profession. This we have called 'territorialisation'. Such territorialisation can act as a barrier to becoming a true researching professional.

Reflective practice has been considered as a way to break down territorialisation, help us to become more self-aware, understand the things that might affect our decisions and behaviours, and develop as more critical professionals.

Reflective practice is not an easy process and requires some practice. Techniques that can help you to master the processes are:

- Professional community mapping
- Professional identity metaphor
- Biographical contents page
- Critical incident technique
- Storytelling

4 Methods of Enquiry

On completion of this chapter you will:

▶ be able to examine the philosophical basis of research studies
▶ be able to explore mixed methods approaches to research
▶ be able to identify means of structuring the professional doctorate study
▶ be able to outline the importance of reflexivity in research

4.1 Introduction

This chapter aims to explore the research methods appropriate to the development of a professional doctorate study. As was outlined in Chapter 2, by its very nature, the professional doctorate is generic and students can choose from a vast and often bewildering array of research approaches. It is important that the approaches selected are in keeping with the aims of the study. An additional, and perhaps complicating, factor is that a professional doctorate can be trans-disciplinary, drawing from disciplines which may take very different approaches in their methods of enquiry. However, there is one element which is common to most professional doctorates: the use of more than one research approach. An additional feature is the importance of reflection as an integral part of the research process. Because of this eclecticism it is easy to think that 'anything goes' when it comes to methodologies and the methods used, but it is important that the research design does not come across as disorganised. The final product of the professional doctorate should be a logically sequenced account and, whilst a range of approaches may have been used, there has to be an internal logic and consistency.

When a diverse approach is taken to the research design it can be a particular challenge to try and reconcile many of these differences. This chapter will explore this issue in some detail and investigate some of the strategies which can be utilised in the design and implementation of your study. The methodologies outlined in this chapter are not inclusive of all possible approaches but represent those commonly taken by professional doctorate students.

4.2 Study design

Professional doctorates are, by definition, generic; they cover a number of different disciplines. It is important to spend some time thinking about the design of your study. You should also bear in mind that, due to the dynamic nature of the process, the approach that you take may need to be altered, sometimes several times, in the course of the study.

Maxwell (1996, p. 25) states that the *'system of concepts, assumptions, expectations and beliefs and theories that support and inform your research is a key part of its design'*. Before you begin to think about the design of your study, it is useful to spend some time asking yourself exactly what your position is, what are your basic values and beliefs. This will help you to determine approaches and methods you are comfortable with.

Activity 1

Answer these questions, relating your responses to your proposed study.

- What is your professional background?
- How does this link with your ideas on your proposed research?
- How do you expect your study to impact on your professional practice?

The answers to the questions in Activity 1 will be diverse; groups of professional doctorate candidates have supplied a wide range of answers. Once you have established in broad terms the area of interest and your particular skills, it is useful to consider the theoretical basis for the development of your study. This can present a challenge for many professional doctorate students because people working in practice very often do things on a needs-must basis rather than a planned and focused manner. One of the particular challenges, when formalising work-based practice, lies in identifying and establishing a framework on which to build the research. Research methodologies are based on certain philosophical assumptions and it is useful to consider these underlying tenets before thinking about the methodologies.

4.3 Philosophical underpinnings

As discussed in Chapter 2, professional doctorates often use a range of methods and one of the key criticisms of taking a variety of approaches is that they can have very different, and often incompatible, philosophical underpinnings. The multidisciplinary nature of the professional doctorate will involve a wide range of methodological approaches and, before mixing the research methods, it is appropriate to consider their basic assumptions and underpinnings. It is important to ask: How can the underpinning philosophical bases of the different methods, which can be *very* different, be reconciled? The orthodox view is that, when designing your research study, there should be congruence between the methods employed. The techniques you use, such as a questionnaire or observational schedule, and the methodology that create the overall structure of your study should reflect the theoretical perspectives and the underlying assumptions. This section will consider the philosophical underpinnings of research and the thinking in this area.

Reading about the philosophy of research is not made easy by either the language often used or the range and variety of configurations. There is no clear agreement on the different paradigms which are available for you to apply to your study. For example, Blaikie (2007) offers eleven different paradigm approaches to research, whilst other authors suggest different numbers and different arrangements of paradigms. Most of this work is drawn from the social sciences which has developed much of the thinking and has gone on to influence other fields, such as education and health. Hammersley and Atkinson (1996) offer a fairly succinct approach and, whilst they are discussing a particular research approach, their discussion can be generalised and applied to the context of a professional doctoral research study.

When examining philosophical underpinnings, Hammersley and Atkinson (1996) maintain that there are two contrasting poles: realism and naturalism. Realism takes the position that there is an external reality and the goal of the researcher is to discover and unpick this particular reality. This is linked to positivism, which is the methodology of choice in the natural sciences. Positivism maintains that all the focus of science is on that which is directly observable and measurable, and by definition this reflects a realist position. One of the difficulties with positivism is that people use the term in different ways. However, its concern is always with directly observable phenomena and facts which exist independently of the research study. The task of the researcher is to identify this independent underlying reality.

Blaikie (2007) also emphasises the ways in which realism – the underlying philosophy of both positivism and naturalism – is primarily interested in observable data. This contrasts with interpretivist approaches in which the researcher has to interpret, or give meaning to, the emergent data. To put this in a different way, the researcher has to find meaning which is inherent in the data. However, both approaches are based upon the fundamental assumption that there is an underlying truth or reality. The role of the researcher is to uncover this truth or reality.

In direct contrast to this is the constructionist approach where knowledge is seen as constructed or formulated by people at a particular point in time and the concerns and nuances of the time are reflected in the construction of that knowledge (Blaikie, 2007). Constructionism is a fairly recent development and came into prominence in the latter part of the twentieth century. For the constructionists, reality does not exist but is something which must be uncovered by the researcher. 'Reality' is created by individuals at a particular point in time, and it is the task of the researcher to uncover and explore that particular reality. It would, therefore, follow that the researcher can never be an independent observer, but is always an active participant in the process. Their very presence can shape the environment under investigation so the impact of the researcher is a central concern. This is of relevance to the professional doctorate student who is concerned with, and immersed in, the world of work and is very much part of the process. In a professional doctorate study the student is aiming to bring about very real changes in their practice, and their presence is central to the research study.

Hammersley and Atkinson (1996) also make the point that positivism and naturalism strive for objectivity and often ignore the political dimension. In professional doctorate studies, the researcher, rather than being neutral, is a very powerful vehicle for change. The research may uncover inequalities which can be articulated and become a motivation for bringing about change. Hammersley and Atkinson refer to this stance as 'critical theory', which includes critical feminism and critical race theory.

To summarise, there are four broad philosophical underpinnings which can serve as the basis for a research study:

- positivism,
- naturalism,
- constructionism,
- critical theory.

In professional doctorate studies one often finds a mix of these philosophical approaches. A good example of this is Peter, a scientist working in the pharmaceutical industry who was involved in the formulation and clinical trials of a drug (in the positivist paradigm). He then became involved in the marketing of the drug and did some research into patient experience (moving to a constructionist approach). This then begs the question of how the professional doctorate, which by definition is multidisciplinary in its focus, reconciles an eclectic approach to contrasting, and possibly conflicting, paradigms?

The remainder of this chapter addresses this question by considering some of the research approaches which are available to you.

Activity 2

Before reading the next section, consider the approaches you might take when collecting data.

4.4 Qualitative versus quantitative approaches to research

As implied in the previous section, the professional doctorate study may not be a single overarching study but may be a series of small-scale studies.

A complex reality is being investigated and different methods may be used to investigate this reality, methods which may involve both qualitative and quantitative research.

Qualitative and quantitative approaches usually address different focuses or research aims, and therefore require different kinds of data. The most obvious difference between the two approaches is the concern of qualitative research with textual information and the concern of quantitative methods with numerical data. The primary purpose of quantitative research is to test or verify a theory, whereas the primary purpose of qualitative research is theory generation. Because of these differences, different data collection methods are used in qualitative and quantitative research.

Blaikie (2007, p. 205) lists the various data collection approaches to research design. He is talking about methods of social enquiry, as a laboratory-based scientist would take different approaches to their data collection.

Quantitative approaches are:

- questionnaire, both self-administered and by a structured interview,
- structured observation,
- content analysis of documents.

Qualitative methods of data collection are:

- participant observation,
- non-participant observation which can be semi-structured and unstructured,
- focused and in-depth interview,
- oral life history,
- thematic analysis of documents.

Plowright (2011) devised a typology which organises research methods into structured and unstructured approaches rather than qualitative and quantitative. He also considers the analysis of artefacts, which can be of particular application in the professional doctorate where many candidates explore documentation and records as a unit of analysis. It is important that there is logic and consistency to the methods used; each should be selected for a particular reason, to address specific aims and objectives of the study.

An important issue is that quantitative research strives for generalisability; that is, the results are applicable to the population being studied and not just the sample taken. Qualitative approaches do not attempt to generalise, but rather study and explore people or situations in depth. By definition, they use a small sample of people. Any generalisation in qualitative research will originate from considering how the findings stand against the relevant theoretical issues and how these findings will add to the theory.

These issues should be identified at the outset of the study and are important considerations in the design of the research.

The question of description as opposed to explanation is another consideration. The findings from research can both describe and explain, and indeed many studies do both. It is important that the purpose of the findings is articulated clearly and that the data collected will address the issues identified at the beginning of the study. In quantitative research explanation can come through the establishment of a co-relationship or a causal relationship, whereas in qualitative research explanation can come through investigation of the relationship between categories established in the qualitative analysis.

Having demonstrated a clear division between qualitative and quantitative approaches, the remainder of this chapter will discuss ways in which differences can be reconciled and how a variety of methodological approaches can be combined within the design of a professional doctorate study. The thrust of the argument is that the development of Mode 2 knowledge requires a flexible approach which draws on a range of research methods.

The professional doctorate is seldom a single study with a highly-focused approach. More often than not, it is an eclectic mix of small- to medium-scale studies, all linked to an overarching situation and it is important to ensure there is a logical and consistent framework. Three approaches to the development of the study will be considered: mixed methods, action research and case study.

One approach to multidimensional study is that of 'bricolage', an eclectic style using whatever materials are to hand. In research studies bricolage represents a mixture of research approaches used within a study. Denzin and Lincoln (2000) emphasise how multiple perspectives can be viewed when a particular phenomenon is being investigated. The idea of bricolage acknowledges that in exploring a particular phenomenon the multi-perspectives are unpicked and examined, and this requires a range of methodological approaches to ensure that all viewpoints are expressed.

The professional doctorate is about examining a practical situation with all of its complexities, and the principle of bricolage can capture this multidimensional perspective. It is similar to Mode 2 knowledge production by emphasising the variety of perspectives which can be explored and the ways in which the impact of these perspectives can be determined and articulated.

The term 'bricoleur' traditionally refers to a handyman or woman who makes use of the available tools to do a particular task (Kincheloe and Berry, 2002). In research terms, the researcher draws on a range of methodologies, methods and theoretical approaches which may give multiple interpretations. Denzin and Lincoln (2000) discuss the multiple viewpoints from which a situation can be explored and the richness which follows when these perspectives are developed. The basic premise is that you should use the tools most appropriate to doing the task in hand which, in the context of study, is exploring the particular dimension of an issue. This means an emphasis on the wider social factors and many of the critical issues involved in the particular scenario (Denzin and Lincoln, 2000). Denzin and Lincoln draw an analogy with the quilt-maker who makes a patchwork quilt from a series of sections. Although each section is different, the quilt is presented as a whole.

4.5 Mixed methods approaches

The professional doctorate is tied into the workplace and it is almost inevitable that a mixed methods approach, involving qualitative and quantitative methodologies, will be taken during the the study. For example, an engineer who develops a technical innovation will in this development take a structured positivist research approach. However, in developing the innovation he may need to employ a wider range of methods based on quite different philosophical ideas.

Creswell (2007) defines mixed methods as:

> an approach to enquiry which combines and associates both qualitative and quantitative approaches. It involves philosophical assumptions and the use of quantitative and qualitative approaches in a study. It is more than just collecting and analysing both types of data but consists of using both approaches in tandem so as the overall strength of a study is greater than either qualitative or quantitative approaches.

When following a particular paradigm, the researcher is tied to the collection of a particular type of data. For example, positivism requires quantification and the collection of numerical data, whereas a constructionist approach is concerned with eliciting narrative accounts of people's perceptions and experience. Paradigms are translated into different methodologies, which serve as guides to the development of the research. The particular methodologies which are chosen can then provide a broad overarching framework for the development of the study.

People using mixed methods approaches are not following a particular paradigm and, therefore, have to reconcile diverse approaches in their study design. One suggestion is to take a pragmatic approach which is based on the work of John Dewey (de Waal, 2005). He argued that, rather than agonise over reconciling different approaches, you should just look for what works in practice – what method will get the information to answer a particular problem – and go with that. For pragmatists, the important issue is the practical outcome because that is the meaning of truth (Plowright, 2011). Another slant on this debate is taken by the philosopher of science Paul Feyerabend. Although addressing issues in the physical sciences, he also suggested that the researcher should not be tied to methodological approaches because the important issue is the discovery and development of knowledge (Feyerabend, 1975).

Bryman (2008) traces the history of mixed methods approaches and maintains that the debate can be centred on two positions. The first is the paradigm argument that the research design must be cognisant of the philosophical tradition in which the research is situated, and the methods used must be true to this position. The second position is a technical one in which the deficiencies of one approach are rectified by the other: 'use one method to correct the deficiencies of another which you have used' (Wacquant, 2012).

It would seem that, whilst paradigms have been debated and are prominent in the literature, many research designs have been pragmatic. Although debates on mixed methods are a fairly recent addition to the literature, it can be argued that they have been around for longer than is usually supposed, as Jennifer Platt suggests when discussing the Chicago School of Sociology:

> Research methods may on the level of theory, when theory is consciously involved at all, reflect intellectual *bricolage* or *post hoc* justifications rather than the consistent working through of carefully chosen fundamental assumptions. Frequently methodological choices are steered by quite other considerations, some of a highly practical nature, and there are independent methodological traditions each with their own channels of transmission ... In many cases general theoretical/methodological stances are just stances: slogans, hopes, aspirations, not guidelines with clear implications that are followed in practice. (cited by Bryman, 2008, p. 593, italics in original)

Bryman (2008) also considers that qualitative and quantitative approaches to research are not such a dichotomy as they may first appear and have many similarities. For example, many qualitative researchers implicitly quantify by use of terms such as 'normally', 'often' and 'occasionally'. Conversely, whilst quantitative researchers may be focused on numerical information, they can and do interpret their findings, and thereby give them meaning. The elucidation of subjective meaning is said to be the province of qualitative research, yet in quantitative research the use of questionnaires to elicit opinions is also concerned with the identification of subjective meaning.

When utilising a diverse range of methods it is important that the researcher develops the skills necessary to undertake the particular activity with which they wish to engage. For example, the researcher undertaking in-depth interviews should have the skills to carry out this activity. It is also important that mixed methods research is not done in a piecemeal manner, but rather the design should demonstrate logic and consistency throughout the process. This point is illustrated by Hammersley and Atkinson (1995) who give three approaches to the use of mixed methods in a research study:

● *Triangulation* – the use of qualitative findings to corroborate quantitative findings. This process can also be reversed. For example, one of our students was involved in an activity for young people from which some of them appeared to benefit. Although he only examined a few of the young people, he thought that it was a good and purposeful activity and he went on to test out his ideas by distributing a questionnaire to a much larger sample of people. The analysis of the questionnaire confirmed his original findings.

● *Facilitative* – one research strategy aids the other. An example of this is the researcher who develops indicators through qualitative research which are tried out through a questionnaire. To continue with the previous example, when exploring activities for young people, the researcher identified some ideas through qualitative research, which he then developed through a questionnaire.

● *Complementary* – one research approach complements the other and explores a different aspect of the issue. In effect, this means collecting different types of data to explore quite different aspects of the same phenomenon. In the activities example, it would mean using a questionnaire to determine the policy-makers' rationale for the choice of activities on offer, and exploring the views of the young people through qualitative approaches such as in-depth interviews and observation.

4.6 Reflectivity in the research context

In the generation of Mode 2 knowledge, the role of the researcher is very much part of the process. Bringing about change and exploring areas of work-based practice usually means dealing with people who are in complex situations. The researcher must be conscious of how their research fits into the situation, and in particular on their influence, as there is no real blueprint. This can be one of the major challenges of the professional doctorate. The researcher is not a neutral observer but his or her very presence is part of what is being researched. Their reflections on the process become one of the research methods, as important as, say, a questionnaire; they are not just an adjunct to the research process. Reflection can, in fact, be said to be a research method in its own right.

Traditionally, reflection has been integral to research and, in particular, qualitative research has emphasised the importance of the researcher reflecting on their part in the process. More recent work has emphasised the need for the researcher to formally document the ways in which their presence, background and discipline can affect the process, context and interpretation of the research.

Woolgar and Ashmore (Woolgar and Ashmore, 1988) outline three phases of reflexivity in research:

- *Phase One* is the 'pre-Kuhnian phase' in which the researcher is seen as a neutral observer and thereby stands outside the process, neutrally recoding his or her findings.
- *Phase Two* is the phase of knowledge deconstruction when the debate becomes polarised between realist and constructionist domains: the realist as a neutral observer and the constructionist recognising the part played by the researcher in the collection of data and the interpretation of the findings.
- *Phase Three* is the reflective phase. This comes from the social sciences where a good deal of emphasis is placed on reflective processes.

Reflection on the research process is an integral part of most qualitative research traditions (such as grounded theory and ethnography). It is also of central concern to a professional doctorate study. It is important to be clear and focused about the design of the study at the outset. It will take place in the real world, and changes and contingencies will almost inevitably be required. It is therefore important, at the outset, to establish a clear reflective strategy which should be built into the study. The structure and design of the study should be reflected upon so that any changes can be made quickly should they be required in response to the researcher's findings or because of changes in structure, personnel and function of the workplace.

An important consideration is that the reflections should be structured. Woolgar (Woolgar and Ashmore, 1988) make the point that there are two levels of reflection: description and critical analysis (or radical constructive reflexivity). This distinction is fairly consistent across models of reflection. For example, Capobianco and Feldman (2010) suggest that reflective levels are:

- descriptive or technical dialogue, whereby insights come from discussions with other people,
- critical, where the basis of the knowledge and its underlying assumptions are considered.

Any framework used should ensure that the user will move beyond the descriptive and explore the wider contextual issues.

Reflective accounts tend to be presented as such and may be structured according to the models of research as outlined in Sections 4.7 to 4.9. This is acceptable and is an often-used approach. Duncan (2004) provides an interesting account of her auto-ethnographic study in which she treats her reflections as data in a similar way to her consideration of data from a qualitative interview.

It is important that your professional doctorate study is appropriately structured, and the remaining sections of this chapter consider methodologies which will give an overarching framework to your work.

4.7 Action research

Action research, by its very nature, is grounded in practice and is therefore a very attractive approach for professional doctorate students. It is also popular in educational research and is becoming increasingly widespread in health and social care. Hart and Bond (1995) emphasise the emancipatory dimension of action research.

There are a variety of names for action research, such as participatory action research, critical action, research developmental action research. Similarly there are a number of definitions of action research but all have the following features:

● Action research should result in changes in social practice.
● Action research should involve collaboration.
● Action research is cyclical in nature.
● Reflection is integral to the process of action research.

Action research is concerned with social practice and bringing about change in practice or the practical situation. It is not an armchair activity but involves bringing about change within an area of practice which can range from the work-based situation to community development on a large scale. Collaboration is integral to the whole process. Unlike many other types of research, where the researcher is an impartial, often outside, observer, the researcher works with the participants in the research setting, interacting with them to identify problem areas, bring about change in practice and monitor and evaluate that change. This is why action research is attractive to the professional doctorate candidate whose aim is to improve practice in their area. Some writers emphasise the dialogic aspect of action research as a distinct entity (Winter, 1989; Heikkinen et al., 2007). This means, in effect, that ideas and knowledge are created through discussion with others.

Woolgar (1988) captures this point when he states that, in the early days of ethnography, the researcher was very much a neutral observer who impartially recorded and objectively interpreted. Although attention was paid to reflection, and it was recognised that the researcher's views must have an impact on the process and the product of the research study, yet the goal was to objectively record and analyse. Woolgar (1988) makes the same point regarding research design: it is often a co-interpretation between the researcher and the respondents which creates the view of the situation, and this is acknowledged as part of the study. The co-interpretation and creation of an image is what is meant by the dialogic aspect.

Action research is cyclical and involves identifying problems, planning a strategy, acting on it, and reflection and evaluation, as illustrated in Figure 4.1. This cyclical process may be repeated several times. It can take place either in a short timespan or over a much longer timeframe, but the important issue is that each cycle develops and advances from the previous

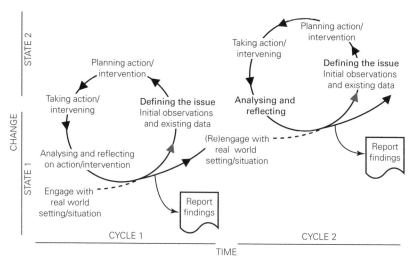

Figure 4.1 Action research
Source: Muir (2007).

one. The domain of the critical is also very important because it is through this aspect that the researcher can take a wider view of the social domain and the political and contextual issues which affect the workplace.

Two important areas which are built into the process are mixed methods and reflection at each stage of the research. The various typologies or models of reflection are covered in Chapter 2. As well as describing the situation, a degree of criticality in the reflection is also important. This criticality will allow the wider contextual features to be identified, which is particularly important if the research is focused on bringing about change in a practical context.

One professional doctorate student, Fiona, examined issues in workforce planning and structured her work around the action research cycle. She had accumulated a great deal of experience in workforce planning, and this formed the first phase of her action research cycle. She then became involved in another project, which formed the second phase of the action research cycle. The insights gained formed the next stage, which was a logical development of the previous two phases. Fiona did not work with a regular group of people, but she was central to the process and her reflections and insights informed each stage.

4.8 Case studies

Case studies are another methodological approach to the structuring of the professional doctorate, and can provide a useful framework for the development of the study. Case studies fit in well with workplace learning and allow an in-depth exploration of a real-world situation. They also facilitate the use of a wide range of research methodologies and methodological approaches. A case study can refer to a specific situation or organisation or to a theme which can be applied across a range of organisations and situations. Yin defines the case study as:

> an empirical inquiry that investigates a contemporary phenomenon within its real-life context; when the boundaries between phenomenon and context are not clearly evident; and in which multiple sources of evidence are used. (Yin, 1984, p. 24)

Yin draws on the range of cases which can be used in case study research: individual case studies, phenomena which consist of a social group and cases relating to more formal structures such as institutions and organisations. Alternatively, rather than an organisation or a particular group of people, cases can comprise situations such as a series of events, relationships or roles across a variety of organisations.

Within this approach, evidence is collected from the particular case then analysed in some detail. The evidence may be wide–ranging, extending from formal reports and statistical information to the perceptions and feelings of individual participants.

Stake (1995) discusses three types of case studies:

- *Intrinsic case studies* in which the researcher attempts to understand a particular case with a view to addressing theoretical issues and concerns.
- *Instrumental case studies* in which the researcher attempts to use a case as an exemplar and to draw inferences which can be applied to a wider range of cases.
- *Collective case studies* in which more than one case is studied.

Yin (1984) makes a slightly different classification in which he refers to three types:

- *Descriptive case studies*, where the case is described usually in some detail.
- *Interpretative case studies* in which the case is analysed and inferences drawn.
- *Evaluative case studies* in which detailed evaluations are made.

The Commonwealth Association (2010) presents yet another typology of case studies. They outline four main approaches:

- The *traditional approach* which comprises Yin's three categories of 'descriptive, exploratory and explanatory case studies'.
- *Business school approaches* include field case studies of the real world and particular cases, literature case studies and hypothetical case studies in which particular scenarios are considered.

- *Learning history* in which a reflective account of past cases is considered and lessons and future plans are drawn from these accounts.
- *Best practice accounts* in which best practice is considered or a case which works really well. This category could also include failure case studies – the main theme is to draw out issues and learn lessons from the particular cases.

The types of case study given above illustrate approaches which can be taken. They are not mutually exclusive and you can use more than one type to pull out and explain points from a particular case. It is worth emphasising that a key feature of the professional doctorate study is its impact on professional practice and, to ensure this emerges, there should always be a focus on real-world cases.

For example, Rafiah explicitly structured her work around case studies. Rather than considering a case to be an organisation or an institution, she studied different educational innovations: one case looked at the ways in which assessment was approached in different organisations and another examined projects in teaching information retrieval to students.

4.9 Auto-ethnography

Auto-ethnography is a fairly recent development in research and has become increasingly popular as a mode of investigative enquiry since the 1990s (Duncan, 2004). It stems from the narrative research tradition which allows the respondent to tell their story. An understanding of the situation is gained through these stories, and they are thus considered to be valid data. To an extent, the professional doctorate is about narrative and the telling of a particular story against a professional background so it is important that the story comes through in the research account, whether through reflection or auto-ethnography.

Auto-ethnography can be considered as a research approach in its own right. It has a strong focus on self-reflection and is therefore attractive to the professional doctorate candidate. Auto-ethnography comes from *auto* meaning 'self' and *ethnography* meaning 'a study of cultures', so it can be seen as combining an autobiographical account with an exploration of a culture or sub-culture. The professional doctorate explores the world of work, and the individual experience is articulated against the particular situation or sub-culture in which the researcher operates.

This leads to the question of when something is autobiography and when it is auto-ethnography. David Mathews, a journalist with no previous boxing experience, wrote an interesting account of training to become a professional boxer (Mathews, 2001). There are no claims that this is an auto-ethnographical account but nonetheless it describes both his personal experience and the sub-culture of boxing. So how does it differ from auto-ethnography?

Carolyn Ellis defines auto-ethnography as:

research writing and method that connect the autobiographical and personal to the cultural and social. This form usually features concrete actions, emotions and embodiment, self-consciousness and introspection and claims the conventions of literary writing. (Ellis, 2004, p. ix)

All of Ellis' elements are evident in Mathews' work. He presents readers with a fairly clear account, which is largely descriptive in nature, but leaves them with a good understanding of the world of professional boxing. There is a tension between the different definitions of auto-ethnography: some, like Ellis, emphasise the autobiographical aspect but other definitions are broader than hers. They include an acknowledgement of the role of ethnography in explaining and exploring other cultures and understanding their customs and practices. The personal experiences must be emphasised, but, in auto-ethnographical accounts, they must also be set against the wider environment . There should be a linkage to theory, and this is what is missing from Mathew's account of boxing.

It is Ellis' statement that the auto-ethnographic form 'claims the conventions of literary writing' which is perhaps the most contentious. Auto-ethnographers present their findings in what are (in research terms) rather unconventional approaches. For example, Ellis' account of her experiences in teaching auto-ethnography is subtitled "an auto-ethnographic novel", and ethnographic work can be presented in poetry or painting which, it is argued, captures the essence of the experience.

How then does this help the professional doctorate student? In the previous two approaches – action research and case studies – we considered ways of framing the research and presenting the study in a logical and coherent manner. It is possible to represent the entire process of the professional doctorate as auto-ethnography. However, it is more likely to be used as part of the data, and it will provide a narrative account which will be read in conjunction with other data. It is important that any accounts are presented in a logical manner which is in keeping with the main thrust of the research. The more ambitious or unconventional approaches to the presentation of research accounts should be considered with caution.

Summary

It is important to consider the stance you are taking and the basic philosophical assumptions which lie behind your research design. This chapter has outlined some of these approaches and the research methodologies which may be useful in structuring your work. They are not exclusive but representative of the approaches you may wish to take and the ways in which a professional doctorate may be structured.

5 Contextualising and Planning your Doctoral Project

On completion of this chapter you will:

▶ understand how to undertake a literature review, why it is important to do so, and be able to critically review the literature relating to your project
▶ be able to produce a detailed plan for your doctoral project
▶ be able to demonstrate an understanding of the importance of making a contribution to practice, and identify the impact which you have made through your doctoral work
▶ be able to identify and interact with your community of practice

5.1 Introduction

As a candidate on a professional doctorate programme you must place your project in a wider context. This requires addressing the following questions:

● How does your work compare with that of others?
● Which methodological approach best fits with your work?
● Which theoretical model(s) can be used to situate your work?
● Do any previous academic studies exist?
● What professional work has already been undertaken within your field of practice?
● How will you measure and evaluate the impact of your work on the broader community of practice?

This chapter will take you through the process of doing a literature review so that you are able to address the above questions for your own doctoral project. The importance of project planning will also be discussed, and we will take you through the major issues which you need to consider when drawing up your plan. We will draw examples from successful professional doctorate projects, and give detailed examples of project plans which have been produced by graduates (see Figures 5.4, 5.5 and 5.6).

5.2 How to conduct your literature review

One of the first things that you need to do is undertake a review of the relevant literature. You may think that you know everything there is to know on your subject. However, be assured that there will be lots of literature out there that you aren't aware of, and lots of other practitioners and researchers working in the same, or similar, areas. As you are studying on a professional doctorate your literature review will need to cover practice, professional issues, relevant policy, and academic and research literature.

When complete, your literature review will form a critique of the area which you are going to explore within your doctoral study. It should set the baseline for what is already known about the subject and help you to pull out the main issues, problems and gaps in knowledge and practice. Your literature review will, in itself, help to define your area of research. You will no doubt have started your doctoral journey with some idea of the area that you wish to research. It is likely, however, that your ideas will only be partially formed, and perhaps quite broad. Reviewing the literature will help to confirm, or otherwise, your thoughts, and help you to further refine your area of study.

A good literature review serves several purposes. First, it informs you what other practitioners and researchers are doing. It will also show your examiners that you have a deep understanding of the relevant literature. This is important as one of the key criteria for the award of a doctorate is demonstrating command of your subject. A thorough literature review will show you the current gaps in knowledge and practice, and give you ideas as to the direction and purpose of your own project. Towards the end of your project, you will be able to return to your literature review and use parts of it to demonstrate how your work has taken the field forward and developed practice. You will be able to select articles from your literature review as benchmarks against which you can evaluate your work. You will be able to point to academic theory which underpins your work, and references which justify your choice of research methods.

Remember, one of the most important things about any doctorate is making a contribution to knowledge. This is the prime thing that the examiners will be looking for in your final submission. It is by reviewing the work on your subject that has already been published that you begin to understand the context of your studies. The literature will tell you what other practitioners and researchers have already done in terms of the professional issues which you intend to explore. This will show you the work that you need to build upon so that you can demonstrate impact and contribution at the end of your doctoral project. This also implies that you must continue to keep on top of the current professional and academic literature within your subject area as your project progresses. Your literature review must be a living, dynamic document.

So what is the 'literature'? And how, and where, do you find it? For a professional doctorate, literature can take many forms, including:

- articles in professional magazines and journals,
- articles (or 'papers', as they are more commonly known) in academic journals,

- papers in the proceedings of conferences,
- books,
- theses of other doctoral studies by PhD and professional doctorate graduates,
- material that you find on the internet,
- government and other policy documents,
- reports written by other practitioners and peers.

Covering all of the above areas will, no doubt, seem a daunting task. You will be asking yourself "How on earth can I ever read and understand everything that is published on and around my area of study?" Indeed, it is true that a professional doctorate provides an additional challenge in that you are required to review both the academic *and* the professional litera-ture relating to your subject area. However, with careful definition of your problem area and a well-designed search strategy, the task can, and does, become more manageable.

The trick is to define your problem area as tightly as possible, and to then design a search strategy to match that problem area. Once you have clearly defined your subject area, set out a series of keywords on which you can search online databases. At this stage you should ask for the advice of your supervisor and, probably more importantly, of an information special-ist from your university library. Don't be frightened of asking someone from the library to help you. They are trained information specialists and will know exactly which electronic databases your university subscribes to and how to access them. They will have helped many other students at bach-elors, masters and doctoral level with their literature searches, and they will be pleased to help you too. You may already have been introduced to them during an induction session as part of your initial doctoral training. Liam described his literature review search strategy as follows.

Literature search strategy

"To better underpin both the aim of my doctorate project as well as comply with the rigour of the mixed methods research design I had selected, my literature review needed to be a continuously informing activity throughout the lifecycle of my project. This would ensure that I would solidly underpin the iterative development of my integrated risk, incident and audit (IRIA) frame-work with the published evidence-base in an on-going manner. My literature review was divided into three streams, with each stream designed to support the requirements of my project, and provide insight for the development of my IRIA framework and my practical case study work. I identified an addi-tional fourth stream later on in my project to support the development of the final iteration of my framework.

continued overleaf

Stream one of my review focused on literature with regard to healthcare risk, incident and audit management as these are the fundamental building blocks for the delivery of high quality and safe healthcare. Stream two of my review explored key quality and safety healthcare requirements and how an integrated risk, incident and audit management core system framework could be developed to meet such requirements. This second stream of my literature review was not intended to be an exhaustive review of the use and benefits of risk, incident and audit management in healthcare; rather it sought to explore key literature to support a rationale for the design and development of my proposed IRIA framework. Stream three of my review focused on quality improvement frameworks and models which are used in healthcare and what I needed to understand from such frameworks.

Information supporting Stream one was attained from the following sources:

- *Databases (Emerald Insight, BMJ Journals, Science Direct, Google Scholar)*
- *Books on the subject area*
- *Medical and nursing journals*

The key words used for my search within Stream one were:

- *healthcare risk management*
- *incident management*
- *healthcare audit*
- *clinical audit.*

A total of 5,000 plus results were obtained through these searches. Of these results approximately 100 were reviewed initially. The remainder of the results were deemed not to be relevant. Eventually 24 texts were selected for full review and for inclusion within my literature review. I approached Streams two and three in a similar manner."

It is important to set up a system for collecting and recording your references at the outset. This will save you a lot of time when you come to producing your final submission at the end of your project. You should check which system of referencing your university regulations require you to use. The most common is the Harvard system. There are several software packages which you can use to help you organise your references. Some of these are free, and others cost a small price. Your university will be able to advise you as to which system to use, and may provide a training course on using the software package. You would be well advised to attend such a course, or ask someone to demonstrate the software to you. It is well worth making the investment in time to learn how to use a software package, as they have several features which make it much easier to collect and manage your reference list throughout your project. This will come in handy, not just for your final submission, but also for any reports or articles which you write during your doctoral project.

Many doctoral students worry about the originality of their work. Students often express the following concerns: "How can I possibly know what everyone else is doing in my field?" and "What if someone else beats me to it?"

It is important to stay up to date with the literature by continually revisiting your literature review. However, this is not the only way to keep up to speed with what is going on in your field. You should also be consulting professional magazines and taking part in discussions with your peers. The internet is now, of course, a very rich source of information about what is happening. As a practitioner you will already be keeping yourself up to date with recent developments in your field as part of your continual professional development. The internet, email lists, discussion groups and message boards are all ways in which you can interact with other professionals. It is becoming much easier to search for information these days. However, this also means that there is much more information available.

There will be people in other parts of your country, or even in other countries, who are doing similar work to you and trying to address similar issues. You need, as much as you are able, to understand what approaches they are taking so that you can learn from them, build on their work, and compare it to yours. This is very important to demonstrate your grasp of current practice. In most cases, their approach will be quite different from your own, or will deal with different issues, different clients or different problems. It is unlikely, but not impossible, that they will be taking exactly the same approach as you.

If you do discover that someone else is doing similar work, it is usually not a problem. One of the authors can speak from personal experience:

"When I was coming close to the end of my own PhD many years ago, I was in the university library reading some journal articles. To my horror I came across an article by another researcher which described a model which at first sight appeared to be almost identical to the model which I had just finished developing and testing. At first I was shocked and didn't know what to do. I considered trying to forget that I had seen the article. But I knew that wasn't the right thing to do. I also knew that realistically I would just worry, and wouldn't be able to forget that I had seen it.

Various thoughts flashed through my mind. 'What if my external examiner knew of the work?', 'Did this work invalidate my own?', 'Was my claim to a contribution to knowledge now worthless?'

I decided that the right thing to do, as a researcher, was to read the work in detail and evaluate it, to see how it related to my own work. So that is what I did. I calmed myself down, and sat down in the library there and then and started to read the article in detail. I made a photocopy of it, for my personal use, and made notes as I read. And as I read through I began to see some differences between the work in the article and my own work. Although it appeared at first sight to be identical, the approach taken was a little different. I decided to treat the work in this way. I added a short critique of the work to my literature review, and in my evaluation chapter, I added a section which compared my results to those that the authors had presented in the paper. I showed where my results were better, and where theirs were better than mine. This gave me a few extra days work, but having completed it, I felt that my own thesis was strengthened, as was my own contribution to knowledge."

Your literature review should also cover methodological aspects of your project. You need to justify your methodological approach and the methods used by referring to the literature. You should look at the methods which other researchers and practitioners have used in their work, and consider which approaches are suitable for your own study.

It is important that your literature review is critical. Being critical does not mean being negative. Rather, it means taking a balanced view of the work you read, looking for strengths and weaknesses within the work and relating to your own studies and other work that you have read. When reading a paper you should make your own notes, asking yourself the following questions:

- What are the important points?
- How does this work relate to my own project?
- How does this work relate to the work of others?
- How can I build on this work?

You might like to consider producing formal notes for each paper you cover, as Liam did for his project (see Figure 5.1).

Your literature review should not simply be a summary of each paper you read. It should also draw out themes across the articles you read. At the end, you should summarise by drawing together the important points and how they relate to your project.

It is important that your literature review is not purely academic. You are studying on a professional doctorate programme, and this means that you must have a firm grasp of current policy and practice within your field. So, as well as reviewing academic journals, you will also need to consult policy documents, professional body reports, audit reports and other documents and items of information which present current practice.

5.3 Defining your community of practice

The concept of community of practice is important. You need to show that you interact with your community of practice, and that ultimately your work influences and impacts upon the community. Your community of practice

Author(s)	Okuyama, A., Sasaki, M. & Kanda, K.
Date	2010
Title	The relationship between incident reporting by nurses and safety management in hospitals.
Publication	Quality Management in Health Care, 19(2), 164-172
Purpose	An examination of the relationship between nurses' perceptions of incident reporting, the frequency of incident reporting on wards and safety management in hospitals.
Method	A self-administered survey was conducted on 528 nurses in 8 hospitals that provide core medical care in rural areas of Japan. Each hospital is equipped with more than 90 beds. The relationship among perceptions of incident reporting, the frequency of incident reporting on wards, and safety management was examined using Pearson correlation coefficients calculated using ward scores.
Outcome	On wards where staff and safety managers discuss incidents and their root causes, staff are less fearful of incident reporting, understand the significance of incident reporting and report incidents more willingly. There is a need for ward managers not only to demonstrate leadership in terms of safety management but also to discuss incidents with staff.

Author(s)	Fukuda, H., Imanaka, Y., Hirose, M. & Hayashida, K.
Date	2010
Title	Impact of system-level activities and reporting design on the number of incident reports for patient safety.
Publication	Quality & Safety in Health Care, 19(2), 122-127
Purpose	Incident reporting is a promising tool to enhance patient safety, but few empirical studies have been conducted to identify factors that increase the number of incident reports. This study evaluates how the number of incident reports are related to system-level activities and reporting design.
Method	A questionnaire-based survey was administered to all 1039 teaching hospitals in Japan. Items included number of reported incidents; reporting design of incidents; status for system-level activities, including assignment of safety managers, conferences, and ward rounds by peers and staff education. Poisson regression models were used to determine whether these activities and design of reporting method increase incident reports filed by physicians and nurses.
Outcome	In accordance with the suggestions by previous studies that examined staff perceptions and attitudes, this study empirically demonstrated that to decrease burden to reporting and to implement staff education may improve incident reporting.

Figure 5.1   Example of a paper summary

NB The purpose, method and outcome have been quoted directly from the papers by Okuyama et al. and Fukuda et al.

are your peers, those in equivalent roles in other organisations, and those with whom you share a common interest or purpose.

> Communities of practice are groups of people who share a concern or a passion for something they do and learn how to do it better as they interact regularly. (Wenger, 2010)

According to Wenger, communities of practice have three vital characteristics:

- *Domain*. The members of the community all have a shared identity with a particular domain. They are committed to that domain, and have shared skills, abilities and experiences which bind them to that domain and enable them to practise within it. Those within the community recognise the expertise which they each possess. However, others outside that community may not recognise or value the domain in the same way.
- *Community*. The group of people must interact, and work together, as a community. They must engage in joint activities, share discussions and form relationships.
- *Practice*. The third vital element of a community of practice is the practice itself. Those within a community of practice are not simply interested in their community, they are practitioners. They work together to develop and share resources, experiences, case studies, stories, solutions, etc. They interact, and do so over a period of time.

Dianne, a doctoral student, describes her community of practice in the following terms.

Defining your community of practice

"Prior to this research, I was a specialist mental health pharmacist qualified to prescribe medication as an independent practitioner. My particular community of practice was hospital mental health pharmacy. As such my formal networks are in the specialty of mental health, with peers belonging to the College of Mental Health Pharmacy, a registered charity emerging from a former group UKPPG – United Kingdom Psychiatric Pharmacy group. I was elected and held office on the UKPPG executive committee, who were considered the national leading informative group on mental health issues, consulted on a regular basis to represent the specialty in relation to Department of Health (DOH) and NICE (National Institute for Clinical Excellence) guidance. During my time as UKPPG Secretary and Vice Chair, I was lucky to have been personally involved in the DOH secondary care guideline for the Safer Management of Controlled Drugs, and the NICE guidance for Drugs in Pregnancy review.

At a regional level and having performed as a mental health trust Chief Pharmacist in two regions across the UK, my extended external peers have included acute trust hospital chief pharmacists and informal networks have

> *included other clinical specialist and independent pharmacist practitioners around the UK.*
>
> *However, during this course with particular reference to the reflective practice assignment my community of practice described above was challenged in relation to pharmacy as a profession. In light of investigating a critical incident, the paper described the discourse in the profession of pharmacy and as a result of the paper; it reframes my community of practice to the wider practice of "clinical pharmacy". As such then this research will therefore endeavour to inform clinical pharmacy and so findings will be extrapolated to this wider community within other specialist areas. The research will be required to influence the wider network information services that include the UK Medicines Information Service (UKMI), NHS Direct and hopefully EAMC (European Association of Medicines Committee)."*

5.4 What is the potential for contribution to the profession?

One of the most important elements of any doctoral project is the contribution that it makes to knowledge. In the case of a professional doctorate, this means the contribution that the work makes to practice. In planning your project you need to consider its potential for contributing to practice. This means asking yourself the following questions:

- Who else will use my work?
- What impact on practice can I demonstrate?
- How can I impact upon the practice of others?
- What will other practitioners learn by reading my work?

You need to create a project which ultimately addresses these questions. The more you can interact with other practitioners from your community of practice during the project, the greater the chance that you will be able to influence practice. Ideally, you should plan interactions with peers into your project. Show your work to peers at key stages within your project, collect their feedback and use it to improve your work. Take notes so that you can demonstrate that you have done so. Leave plenty of time in your plan for dissemination of your work, and for a final evaluation stage when you take your outcomes to your peer group and collect feedback on how your work might influence their future practice.

5.5 Ethical issues

It is very important that you consider all of the ethical issues which come into play within your project. It is sometimes easy to dismiss the area of ethics, and to think that there are no ethical issues within your project. However, experience suggests that this is very unlikely to be the case. Any project within the context of a professional doctorate is, by its very nature, exploring professional issues, and that implies that there will be ethical issues within that context. There are also ethical issues and tensions associated with your roles as a practitioner and as a researcher, which you will need to fully recognise and manage within your project.

We will start by defining exactly what we mean by ethics. According to the *Oxford English Dictionary* (2012), ethics are 'moral principles that govern a person's behaviours or the conducting of an activity'. This is quite a broad definition. Within the context of a professional doctorate it is more appropriate to consider definitions of professional ethics and definitions relating specifically to research. Let's take professional ethics first. Your own professional body may have its own Code of Conduct, or Code of Ethics which will embody a set of ethical principles to which you are expected to adhere. For example, CIMA (Chartered Institute of Management Accountants) sets out a Code of Ethics, which states:

> As chartered management accountants, CIMA members throughout the world have a duty to observe the highest standards of conduct and integrity, and to uphold the good standing and reputation of the profession. They must also refrain from any conduct which might discredit the profession. Members must have regard to these guidelines irrespective of their field of activity, of their contract of employment or of any other professional memberships they may hold.

Check out your own professional body or, if you are not a member of one, the professional body most closely aligned to your area of practice to see if they have such a code, and consider how this might apply within your own doctoral project.

In terms of research ethics, the university where you are studying will almost certainly have a research ethics committee to which you will need to submit your project proposal in order to obtain ethical clearance before you start your study. A typical set of guiding principles for a university research ethics committee might be:

- Research should be designed, reviewed and undertaken according to the highest possible standards. It should comply with University Governance, Professional Codes of Practice and the law.
- Research with human participants must protect their dignity, rights, safety and well-being.
- Participants must be completely informed about the purposes, methods and intended uses of the research. They must be informed about what participation will involve and the risks and benefits fully explained. Any research proposing deviation from this principle may be approved; but only in very specific contexts in which the lack of complete information is justified by the benefits of the research.

- Participants must consent to participate in the research having been fully informed about what participation will involve. Participation must be voluntary. The use of incentives to encourage participation is acceptable but these must be appropriate.
- Participants must be allowed to withdraw themselves from participation at any time and for any reason without disadvantage.
- Information and data obtained about participants must be confidential.
- Anonymity should be maintained wherever possible. All information held about the participants must be processed, retained, stored, and disposed of in accordance with the law.
- The research must protect the dignity, rights, safety and well-being of the research workers who should completely understand the risks and benefits of the research.
- The research must protect the reputation, safety and well-being of the University. The University should completely understand the risks and benefits of the research. (Research Ethics Committee, University of Sunderland)

An important feature of all research ethics is that research participants must be fully informed about what participation in the research project will involve before they participate, and that they fully consent to their participation. This is known as the principle of informed consent.

The normal and accepted way to give information about your study to the potential participants is to design an information sheet. There is no absolutely correct way to construct an information sheet, but the template in Figure 5.2 indicates the sort of information that should be included. It is important that the sheet clearly explains what the participant will actually have to do in the study, and it is crucial that it is written in language that the participant will be able to understand. The wording should be simple and clear, and the sheet should explain the purpose of the research and the participants' role within it.

Each participant should keep a copy of the information sheet and you must also keep a copy. Your contact details, such as your address, email or phone number, should be your professional ones and not your personal ones.

Particular attention must be paid to providing information to participants who are children/young people and hospital patients or people under the care of a doctor. There are particular processes and laws to which you must adhere when working with young people or those under the care of doctors. You must take advice from the chair of your university ethics committee if any of your participants fall under these categories.

INFORMATION SHEET

Study Title: The title should clearly explain the purpose of the study and should be short.

Inclusion Criteria: The person is being asked to participate in your research project because they fall into certain 'Inclusion Criteria'. You should explain what these criteria are.

Study Aims: The main research aims of your study should be stated.

What the participant will have to do: You must include a description of what participation will actually involve e.g. taking a drug, operating a device or viewing a computer screen.

Risks: Every study has some risks – you should explain what these are.

Benefits: Explain the benefits of participation. There may be none apart from the potential benefit to others from the results of the study.

Expenses and payment: Explain what payment or incentives, if any, are available for participation.

Confidentiality: You should explain who will have access to their personal data. Describe how personal data will be stored and how long it will be kept for. Explain whether their personal data will be anonymised. You should also inform participants what will happen to the study data and the results. If a report or publication is planned this should be explained here.

Consent: You should explain that taking part in the study is entirely voluntary and they will be free to withdraw from the whole study at any time and without giving any reason and without any penalty.

Approval: You should inform participants that your study has been approved by your University Research Ethics Committee.

Contact details for Further Information: You should inform the participants who they can contact if they have any questions about the study, or if they have any concerns about the research.

Figure 5.2   Sample template for an information sheet

The information sheet should be accompanied by a consent form, which each participant must sign to show that they consent to taking part in the project. You should keep the original copies of the signed consent form in case they are needed for any subsequent audit purposes. It is likely that the research ethics committee will wish to see your information sheet and a sample consent form when approving your project.

The remainder of the section comprises two examples of how students handled ethical issues in their doctoral studies. Barbara discusses the ethical considerations within her own projects and George summarises the ethical issues he foresees in his project.

Ethical issues

Barbara

"Ethical consideration was especially important in this case study as participants had known me as the head of the training company which conferred their vocational competence, and as the head of the organisation which allocated working hours to them. The responsibility to conduct the research rigorously was important both for the future of the companies and the well-being of participants. The Social Research Association's Ethical Guidelines (2003) indicates four levels of obligations: to society; funders and employers; to colleagues; and to participants. I observed these guidelines throughout the study.

Obtaining informed consent of participants is key and depends upon the cooperation of subjects and significant others to take place. Informed consent also implies that the participants understand the nature of the research project.

The purpose of the research was discussed with social enterprise participants in a group meeting followed by a letter to everyone, outlining the purpose of the research. We held a further meeting to discuss the present model of training and work and gathered permission from 15 participants who agreed to supply narrative accounts of what they perceived as benefits of this model. A letter was also posted to all current members stating the purpose of the questionnaire, the ability to choose to remain anonymous, the confidential use of any findings and the right to withdraw from taking part.

I informed all participants that they would have access to the findings which I had timetabled to give in a formal meeting and also in a more informal lunch to thank them for their participation. The intention of this whole process is to benefit participants in both the social enterprise and also my own training company and morally I have a motivation to succeed in this intention. However adhering to a specific ethical code gave me a checklist which served as a reminder of good practice and ensured that I respected the needs and wishes of the participants."

George

"All the participants in my study will be healthy adults. They will be participating in interviews or discussions on non-sensitive subjects. The most important ethical consideration will be to obtain informed consent from all participants. I think that this will be fairly straightforward for each of the participants that I interview, and I will do this using a consent form. It will be less straightforward however for any situations where I am a participant-observer:

- *As a member of the education board I will need to write to all of the other board members to apprise them of my research and to ask their consent that I make notes of and may write about board meetings.*
- *There will be a number of other occasions when I may be making observations, e.g. at secondary heads' meetings or at head teachers' briefings where the issues of partnership are raised. These may be quite large meetings with 60 or more head teachers involved and it will not usually be practical to raise the issue at such meetings. My strategy will be to prepare a statement setting out the aims of my research and the way I intend to*

continued overleaf

Ethical issues continued

> use the information and to ensure that the chair of any meeting is aware of my research role. If they feel the need to ask the consent of the meeting they will do. Otherwise I will undertake to present any information that I use in a manner that is anonymous for any individual.
>
> - I will need to be particularly careful with any observations within my own school to ensure that consent is genuinely informed. However I do not at present anticipate any observations in my own school.
> - I am aware that I will be entering this research with considerable bias. I have strong views about the value of partnership and collaboration and I am likely to have a tendency to interpret my findings from this perspective. It will be very important for me to be alert to possible bias in the way that I ask questions and it the ways that I interpret the answers. I will need to use other people – colleague head teachers and my supervisor – to challenge me to justify any conclusions from an objective standpoint."

5.6 Project planning

Studying for a doctorate is a major undertaking. It is probably the largest, and most significant, project which you will ever undertake. So it deserves proper and detailed planning, starting at the very outset of your studies.

Be realistic in completing your project plan. Give yourself plenty of time in which to complete your professional doctorate. Remember that a doctorate is normally awarded for the equivalent of three years' full-time work. So if you are studying part-time for your doctorate, allow sufficient time to complete the work to the required standard. Many doctoral candidates want, for the very best of reasons, to complete their doctorate as quickly as possible, and that is fine. However, you shouldn't rush the work. You need time to consider the implications of your project.

A professional doctoral study is likely to have the structure shown in Figure 5.3. This is an outline project plan which breaks the doctoral project into four years. Let's consider each of the years in detail and think through the elements within it.

Phase 1 Preparation and reflection

You will spend the first period of your project defining the project area, your aims and research questions. You will also need to reflect on your previous experience, and on the results of any work that you have previously undertaken in the area. You will need to define the methodological approach that you will take. Plan the time it will take to do each of these tasks, the outputs they will produce and build these into your project plan, assigning specific time elements. You will also need to take account of any taught elements that are required for your programme.

Phase 1   Preparation and reflection
Determination of initial aim and purpose Reflection on critical issues, previous experience and any contribution already made Analysis of existing data to frame study Initial literature review Definition of methodological approach Project planning Formulation of aim and potential for contribution Complete taught elements of programme
Phase 2   Development
Interaction with community of practice Development of model or framework/collection of data Data analysis Report on results Continual updating of literature review
Phase 3   Dissemination and evaluation
Interaction with community of practice Dissemination of results in journal/conference/professional arena Evaluation of impact upon the community of practice, and with respect to literature Continual updating of literature review
Phase 4   Synthesis and presentation
Compiling and writing final submission Synthesis of evidence of impact and contribution to practice Conceptualise the contribution to knowledge of the doctoral study Prepare for examination Final examination

Figure 5.3   Project plan structure

Phase 2   Development

During the development stage of your work you will be collecting data and/or developing the framework, model, processes or strategies which form the core of your final submission. These are the elements that will demonstrate how you have contributed to practice. It is important to allow plenty of time for this work and for interaction with your community of practice. Build some outcomes from these activities into your plan, perhaps in the form of reports to your employer or discussion documents which you can share with your peers. Remember to leave time to continue to update your literature review.

Phase 3   Dissemination and evaluation

Once you have completed the development stage and produced some outcomes, you should disseminate this work to your peers. Build time into your plan for writing an article for a journal, magazine or a conference. It is also important that you evaluate the impact of your work upon your community of practice and its place with respect to the literature, and time must be allowed within your plan for these tasks.

Phase 4   Synthesis and presentation

The final stage involves compiling your final submission. You will have been writing reports on your work throughout the previous phases, and you will be able to use some of these in your final submission. However, don't underestimate the time it can take to put together the final product. Build time into your plan for several iterations of your submission with your supervisors. They will want to read and comment on your work before you finally submit it to the university, and you need to allow plenty of time for this. Reading a large and complex document is a big task, and may take your supervisors several weeks. Also, plan time for preparing for your examination, including a practice or mock examination.

Throughout the planning process, and indeed throughout your studies, you will need to discuss your project and your plans with your supervisors. It is important to be honest with them and to listen to their advice, as they will have experience of working with other doctoral students. Activities will often take longer than you anticipate, or not turn out as you expected, and you need to build plenty of time into your plan to take account of this.

The way in which your project interacts with your day-to-day work activities will also impact upon the time it takes to complete your doctorate. The whole idea of a professional doctorate programme is that it should allow you to build upon and develop your own work-based practice. The more that you can do this the better. Look for opportunities to build data collection, interaction with stakeholders and dissemination into your day-to-day activities. If you are attending a meeting consider how it might be used as a data collection activity. Or, instead of simply attending a meeting, could you ask to make a presentation to collect feedback on your work? If you are continually on the lookout for opportunities to build your doctoral project into your day-to-day activities, you will not only save time, you will also ensure the relevance and practice-based nature of your work – which is exactly what is required for a professional doctorate.

Figures 5.4, 5.5 and 5.6 show actual student project plans. These are included to give you examples of different ways of structuring your own project plan. The detail in these plans will not have much meaning for you; they have been included just to give you a feel for how a plan might be

Stage #	Project stage description	Activity details	Status	Completion date
1.	Initiating the project ("getting started") + Reflection record	Contextualisation of the project and project management initiation.	Complete	January 2011
2.	Selecting the appropriate case study site + Reflection record	Investigate and select a hospital study site.	Complete	February 2011
3.	Design and develop investigative tools, instruments, protocols, etc. + Reflection record	Identification and development of multiple evidence-based valid and reliable data collection methods (qualitative and quantitative) plus the identification and training of multiple investigators.	Complete	May 2011
4.	Onsite work ("entering the field") + Reflection record	Management of case study data collection and analysis with flexible/opportunistic data collection where possible.	In progress	June to November 2011
5.	Data analysis + Reflection record	In-case analysis supported by continuing literature review to cross-match findings using differing techniques.	In progress	December 2011 to February 2012
6.	Hypothesis review and testing + Reflection record	Iterative tabulation of the evidence of the case study attempting to replicate the logic across the case and searching for evidence for "why" or "why not".	Not started	March 2012
7.	Return to the literature + Reflection record	Return to the literature to identify comparisons with supporting and conflicting research.	Not started	April 2012
8.	Project closure + Reflection record	Fine-tune the learning, theory and identify post-project actions (dissemination, etc.). Write final report and supporting portfolio.	Not started	May 2012

Figure 5.4   Example of a tabular project plan

structured. The students whose plans are shown in Figures 5.4 and 5.5 chose to structure their project plan as a table, while Figure 5.6 shows a project plan which has been produced using Microsoft Project. The important things are that you have a plan that it is shared with your supervisors, and that you continue to review your progress against it and update it accordingly throughout your doctoral studies.

Preparatory work

1. Consolidate reading on
   a. collaborations and partnerships
   b. methodology
	autumn 2012/spring 2013

2. Obtain informed consent from all participants	autumn 2012
3. Obtain ethical approval	autumn 2012

Part one

4. Plan interviews and document analysis for case studies 1
   and 2
   ● share plans with supervisors
   ● share plans with key participants for criticism
	spring 2013

5. Conduct and transcribe interviews	summer 2013
6. Analyse interviews against the three frameworks	summer 2013
7. Compare and contrast the two case studies	summer 2013

Part two

8. Prepare outline description of the current situation ● share outline with key participants for verification	spring/summer 2013

9. Plan interviews and document analysis for case study 3
   ● share plans with supervisors
   ● share plans with key participants for criticism
	summer 2013

10. Conduct and transcribe interviews	autumn 2013
11. Analyse interviews against the three frameworks	autumn 2013
12. Compare and contrast case study 3 with case studies 1 and 2	autumn 2013
13. Maintain diary for participant observations	autumn 2012 and on-going

Consolidation work

14. Review reading	spring 2014
15. Write thesis	spring/summer 2014

Figure 5.5   Example of a tabular project plan

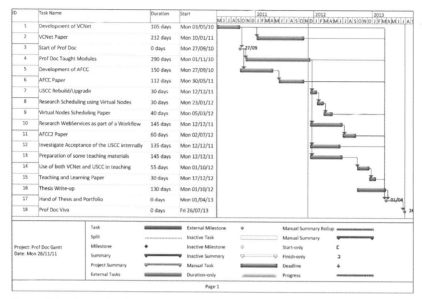

ID	Task Name	Duration	Start	
1	Development of VCNet	105 days	Mon 03/05/10	
2	VCNet Paper	212 days	Mon 10/01/11	
3	Start of Prof Doc	0 days	Mon 27/09/10	27/09
4	Prof Doc Taught Modules	290 days	Mon 01/11/10	
5	Development of AFCC	150 days	Mon 27/09/10	
6	AFCC Paper	112 days	Mon 30/05/11	
7	USCC Rebuild/Upgrade	30 days	Mon 12/12/11	
8	Research Scheduling using Virtual Nodes	30 days	Mon 23/01/12	
9	Virtual Nodes Scheduling Paper	40 days	Mon 05/03/12	
10	Research WebServices as part of a Workflow	145 days	Mon 12/12/11	
11	AFCC2 Paper	60 days	Mon 02/07/12	
12	Investigate Acceptance of the USCC internally	135 days	Mon 12/12/11	
13	Preparation of some teaching materials	145 days	Mon 12/12/11	
14	Use of both VCNet and USCC in teaching	55 days	Mon 01/10/12	
15	Teaching and Learning Paper	30 days	Mon 17/12/12	
16	Thesis Write-up	130 days	Mon 01/10/12	
17	Hand of Thesis and Portfolio	0 days	Mon 01/04/13	01/04
18	Prof Doc Viva	0 days	Fri 26/07/13	26

Project: Prof Doc Gantt Date: Mon 28/11/11	Task	▬▬▬	External Milestone	◆	Manual Summary Rollup	▬▬▬
	Split	···············	Inactive Task		Manual Summary	▬▬▬
	Milestone	◆	Inactive Milestone	◇	Start-only	⊏
	Summary	▬▬▬	Inactive Summary	▽─────▽	Finish-only	⊐
	Project Summary	▬▬▬	Manual Task	▬▬▬	Deadline	↓
	External Tasks	▬▬▬	Duration-only		Progress	▬▬▬

Page 1

Figure 5.6   Example of a project plan using Microsoft Project

Summary

This chapter has explained the importance of setting your work in the context of the literature and the practice of others. Only by doing so can you develop your own practice, make an impact and demonstrate a contribution. The importance of project planning has also been discussed. The next chapter will consider personal development and transformation and how these might be approached within your own doctorate.

6 Personal Development and Transformation

On completion of this chapter you will:

▶ appreciate the personal qualities that are desirable to help you become a researching professional with the capacity to have an on-going and enduring impact upon your profession
▶ understand some of the approaches that can help to facilitate lasting personal transformation

6.1 Introduction

In Chapter 3 we took a look at how professional identity can influence an individual's thinking, and we discussed how important it is to become a critically reflective practitioner. We also considered how profession-specific ways of thinking, despite being crucial to acceptance as a member of a professional community, can hinder critical reflection, for example by fostering a type of territorialisation of knowledge that can blind us to new and novel ways of thinking and create a barrier to inter-professional working – the very things that you are required to demonstrate if you are to be successful in your pursuit of a professional doctorate. It is this issue that we explore further in this chapter.

6.2 The problem with critical reflection

Every doctoral training programme places significant emphasis on criticality and reflection. Some have specific modules or taught elements that seek to develop these skills in their candidates. Many professions also emphasise the development of these skills, and offer training and continuous professional development programmes accordingly. The problem is that it is possible to 'go through the motions' of critical reflection without *really* changing the way one thinks about things. For example, we have seen doctoral candidates who have written a very competent critical literature review, but then resorted back to exactly the same view of their topic that they held before starting the review. There is no evidence that they have learned anything – they have gone through the motions of producing the required piece of written work, but their thinking has not developed as a result. Note that we are not suggesting that it is absolutely necessary for you to *change* your views as the result of a critical literature review; rather that whatever views you hold should be developed in an intellectually sophisticated way. You must be aware of the different arguments about a topic and how they interlink; you must be able to support your own argument (you will be required to do this at your *viva voce*). What you must *not* do is unquestioningly adopt a particular stance simply because that is the currently accepted wisdom in your profession or because it fits with what you are trying to achieve (that would be putting the cart before the horse).

In the workplace too, some individuals may be very diligent in terms of keeping, for example, reflective learning logs without ever showing any evidence of behavioural or attitude change as a result of their reflections. This is what, Fiona, a professional doctorate candidates had to say on this issue.

Case study

"At the start of my doctoral process I thought I knew why I was doing what I was doing, comfortable in my skin and prepared to take on the world. However, my real journey of discovery started when I wrote the personal reflection of my life and career, identifying some of the significant events that form my personal jigsaw. Accustomed to the practice of reflection as a nurse, I understood its value to practice, but not its value to me as a person.

When I look back at the role of reflection as a clinical practitioner and as a process of understanding me, the two processes are poles apart in terms of depth and wider meaning. In reality, the reflection I undertook as a nurse offered a 'here and now' picture of what had happened, what the consequences were, and what I should do next. I did not examine the personal impact, look at relationships, or the impact that events had on me. It has only been through the doctorate process I have taken the time to examine the situations, events, and developments I have led in more detail, adding strength to my outlook on life. In practice, I feel it is important to know who you are and what drives you, and yet it has only been over the last three years that I have achieved such clarity.

…Blinded by my passion at times, access to critical friends (both inside and outside of work and the university) has been vital in 'extracting' me from my world of improvement, in order to bring objectivity and meaning."

Fiona makes a couple of very interesting and astute observations here. First, note that at the start of her doctorate she was very focused and clear on what she wanted to achieve; she knew what her end-point was. She makes the point that she was 'blinded' by her passion for her topic. This is very common with professional doctorate students early in the programme. They feel that they already know the 'answer' to the research topic that they are undertaking, and that the doctorate is a way of giving their views greater strength and credibility within their profession. Consider what another candidate, Marie, had to say on this.

Case study

> "At the beginning my supervisor was being very challenging, questioning my views and telling me to consult the literature. I thought 'hang on, what do you mean, I have to go away and read something? I've got all of this experience, I _know_ what this is'. I started off with a huge claim: 'this is my model; it's going to change the world'. That was my starting point. And then it changed to be 'hang on, that's far too big, I don't have those claims after all'.
>
> I started to see the impact of standing back and having to look at other people's models and the things that other people did, and trying to synthesise that, because then I started to see the impact on my business. When you start to do the research and look at the problem from inside the messy world of business you realise that you have a whole new thing to capture. By doing that I identified lots of opportunities that we hadn't even thought about – it changed the business completely."

The starting points expressed by Fiona and Marie are not at all uncommon for professional doctorate candidates who have a great deal of experience in their field. We will look at an explanation for this a little later.

Our second observation on Fiona and Marie's comments is that they both experienced a change in their perspective as soon as they began to research their topic systematically. This change was, of course, partly due to the fact that they were learning research skills – how to retrieve information from the literature; how to process and formulate that information in the context of their research objective; understanding different research paradigms and how to select the most appropriate methods through which to explore their topic. But it was much more than that. You will see from Fiona's comments that she places a great deal of emphasis on the personal change that she experienced. She talks about a 'voyage of discovery' that has strengthened her outlook on life and given her greater clarity. As a nurse, Fiona was already familiar with reflective practice, but she acknowledged that up until then she had used it in a rather systematic way, applying it to individual work situations rather than in a way that would have a lasting effect on her personal professional behaviours. Marie also talks about the significance of this personal change when asked about the impact of the doctoral process:

> "From starting from the point of just wanting to tick the boxes and get the title, it has changed to being much more enabling and empowering than I thought it would be. The main thing is the impact it has had upon me as a person, and how that has changed the impact that I have on the business."

Perhaps, like Marie and Fiona, as you start out on your doctoral journey you have not anticipated that personal transformation is a feature of this experience. However, if you are to have an impact on your profession that endures beyond the specific outcome of your doctoral project, then that personal transformation is just as important as formal research skills. Throughout this book we refer to this process as 'becoming a researching professional', so now we need to look more closely at what that really means.

6.3 Beyond critical reflection: mindfulness, curiosity and imagination

It is not surprising that as we establish ourselves as professionals in our field we may start to become blinkered to other perspectives and different ideas. The educational processes through which we qualify to practise in our chosen professions are, to a large extent, focused on the specific knowledge and skills of that discipline. Although at higher levels of education we are encouraged towards criticality, it tends to be applied only within the confines of the individual discipline's knowledge structures. When we begin work, these structures are further reinforced. We learn to adopt the accepted practices of the profession, absorb the tacit as well as the explicit knowledge, and through this process we gradually become an accepted member of our community of practice. Our working lives can be driven by rules, processes and written procedures that may cover the most undemanding of operations, often in the name of 'quality'. Of course, much of this is necessary to enable us to work together efficiently and effectively, but there are negative effects too. We can sometimes act almost as if we are on autopilot, following standard practices in an unquestioning way without really considering whether or not they are still appropriate. We concur with the 'accepted wisdom' of our profession, building new knowledge on top of what we already know without challenge. This has inherent dangers. What if the situation changes so that standard practices are no longer valid? What if the accepted wisdom is flawed? Every profession needs individuals with the intellectual agility to ask these questions and to offer solutions if it is to be able to cope with change. Your professional doctorate studies will help you to develop your own intellectual agility so that you are able to be a thought leader who can pioneer development within your profession. In addition to formal research skills that will help you to achieve this goal, there are three key interrelated attributes that are more personal in nature. These are *mindfulness, curiosity* and *imagination.*

Mindfulness

Most of us work in organisations which are defined by recurring behaviours within institutionalised roles (Tsoukas, 2005). Automatic processes free us from tasks that do not require our vigilance and intervention (Bargh and Chartrand, 1999). Mental habituation to standard practices and sequences of activity makes it unnecessary for us to apply new effort and painstaking scrutiny to everything we do, greatly simplifying our working life (Weick and Sutcliffe, 2006). However, despite the benefits of adopting routine behaviours and processes, there is the danger that we can fall into what Thera calls 'mental grooves' when we follow routines thoughtlessly and without due control (Thera, cited in Weick and Sutcliffe, 2006). At best, the thoughtless following of routine operations can hinder the development of new and improved ways of doing things in the organisation. At worst, it can be disastrous. Take, for example, an incident described by Levinthal and Rerup:

> An Air Florida pilot, accustomed to uniformly warm weather, automatically responded in the affirmative to his team member's routine question 'Anti-ice off?', despite the heavy snowfall at Washington DC's National Airport. This response led to a crash into the Potomac River shortly after take-off, and the death of crew and passengers. (2006, p. 503)

This incident is an example of a *mindless* response to routine procedures. The alternative to this is a *mindful* approach. The concept of mindfulness in organisational life has been the subject of a growing body of research in recent years. Langer (1989) defines mindfulness as a state of active awareness characterised by the continual creation and refinement of categories, openness to new information, and a willingness to view contexts from multiple perspectives. For Langer, mindfulness is also about learning to switch modes of thinking and noticing new things (Langer, 2005). Levinthal and Rerup (2006) describe mindfulness as the conversion of experience into reconfigurations of assumptions, frameworks and actions.

All of this should sound familiar to you by now. If you refer back to the learning outcomes for your doctoral programme, you will see that mindfulness is just the sort of ability that you are expected to demonstrate. As a researching professional, you should strive to adopt a mindful attitude to your work, for it is through this approach that you will be able to challenge some of the organisational blindness that can be a barrier to the creation of new knowledge and alternative ways of working. When you start to do this, you will begin to realise how readily we put our experiences into conceptual boxes, how reluctant we normally are to examine those conceptual boxes, and how much we discover when we become less dependent on them (Weick and Sutcliffe, 2006).

Curiosity

Hand in hand with mindfulness goes the emotion of curiosity, that is, the innate urge to investigate, learn and find out about things. Several theories of professional education hold that the development of capacities for mindfulness and reflection represents an essential bridge between the trait of curiosity and higher cognitive skills such as problem-solving, critical thinking and self-assessment (Dyche and Epstein, 2011). Curiosity tends to be ignited by facts that contradict our cognitive mapping of the world, it stirs us to explore and expand our understanding. Take, for example, the story of Jenny Clack (now Professor and Curator of Vertebrate Palaeontology at the University of Cambridge). When she was working as a researcher early in her career the conventional wisdom was that land animals had evolved from fish that crawled out of the water using their fins, and that over time fins developed into legs. However, a newly-discovered fossil made Jenny curious – it seemed to contradict the theory by suggesting that some species had developed legs to help propel themselves along the seabed *before* they ever emerged onto land. Jenny's theory was rejected by the eminent scientists of the day, who were unwilling to have their own research and theories contradicted. Finally, however, her curiosity prevailed and, after the discovery of further fossils that supported her theory, she was able to rewrite part of the story of evolution and, in doing so, make a significant contribution to scientific understanding – a very good example of how one person's innovative thinking can revolutionise an entire discipline's body of knowledge, as we discussed in Chapter 2 (BBC, 2012).

Unfortunately, indulging in our curiosity can often feel like a luxury in our professional lives. It is often suppressed by time pressures, the drive for efficiency and the requirement to conform to standard practices. It can be suppressed by others with more power in the organisation who do not wish to see the status quo, or indeed their own position, challenged, as we have seen with the story of Professor Clack. Curiosity needs an opportunity to challenge convention and assumptions (Langer, 1989). In studying for your professional doctorate you have that opportunity – you are in the special position of being positively encouraged to engage your curiosity about your profession. However, you should beware of one of the other main killers of curiosity, over-confidence. Like the scientists that suppressed Jenny Clack's ideas because they were so confident that their own ideas were right, individuals who are over-confident can be less likely to learn and accept new knowledge. It was a trap that nearly claimed Fiona and Marie at the outset of their studies when they *knew* that they already had the answer to their research topics. Over-confidence can discourage the pursuit of feedback and lifelong learning (Duffy and Holmboe, 2006).

Imagination

So far we have looked at how mindfulness and curiosity are essential traits for your development as a researching professional, helping you to seek new knowledge and understanding. But what happens next? Raising questions is only half of the story – your programme of study requires that you can also develop meaningful solutions that make a significant contribution to your professional community of practice. Doing that often requires a leap in imagination, sometimes looking outside the boundaries of the profession to alternative approaches, and perhaps proposing ideas that seem unlikely or impossible to some. As children we all have great capacity for imagination, but as we grow older that capacity diminishes because our thinking becomes restricted by the conventions and paradigms of our formal education and working lives. But it is through imagination that some of the greatest advances have been made. For example, we all now take air travel for granted, yet it is little over 100 years ago that the Wright brothers dared to imagine that they could use their skills as bicycle manufacturers to build a machine that would allow a man to fly. It was less than 70 years after their first successful manned flight in 1901 that the imagination of others put men on the moon. Jenny Clack emphasises the importance that imagination has played in the success of her scientific research. Without her ability to imagine that things could be radically different from the established scientific wisdom of the day, she would never have formulated her alternative theories.

We are not suggesting that as part of your doctoral studies you have to make world-changing discoveries. However, with the ever-increasing rate of change in our modern world ideas often become obsolete very quickly and new solutions need to be found. People who work in the creative and technology industries will already be used to this idea, but rapid change now permeates almost every profession. Consider, for example, the retail industry. Until only a few years ago consumers would visit a shop when they wanted to buy something, just as shoppers had been doing for centuries. Now, internet shopping is becoming ever-more prominent, and retailers who have not adapted quickly to this trend by adopting new marketing approaches are going out of business.

The problem with dealing with fundamental change in our professional lives is that often we are propelled into situations for which we have no mental model. In many situations our past experience no longer helps us to make decisions and plan for the future. This is where imagination is so important. Imagination involves both the ability to form mental images without having been exposed to 'model images' and the capacity to combine and rearrange images to create scenarios which differ from real-life occurrences (Bronckart, 1991). The implication of these imagination skills is important – it means that you do not have to have concrete experience of something to develop an idea. Imaginative people can think outside of the box and contribute something different from the offerings of less imaginative people (Rozuel, 2012). Fostering your imagination can lead to originality and creativity, facilitating accessibility to more obscure informational links than those that might first occur to you and helping you to find new connections between categories and concepts (Baas et al., 2011). Thinking imaginatively makes it more likely that you will develop a significant and original contribution to your profession during the course of your doctoral studies.

6.4 Feedback, criticism and resilience

So far in this chapter we have looked at how you can improve your intellectual agility by adopting a mindful approach to your professional life and by nurturing your curiosity and imagination. We will look at some approaches to help you do this in the next section. Before that, we sound some notes of caution.

Testing your ideas

We have encountered several candidates on our professional doctorate programme who have been very excited about new ideas that they proposed as part of their research work, only to find out later that the ideas were not new at all, and that others were already using them. This is one of the initial potential pitfalls of a professional doctoral project. For anyone who has spent a number of years working in a profession, perhaps with the same organisation, the world outside can be something of a mystery. Once that person starts to look beyond their existing professional and organisational boundaries as part of their research, many things can seem novel and original. It is almost as if blinkers have been taken off, and the individual is presented with a new vision of professional life. However, in many cases, the ideas that they are excited about are not new or novel at all – they simply haven't been used before *in their organisation*. If these ideas then formed the basis of the final submission, it is unlikely that it would be judged to be of the level required for doctoral work. It is therefore very important to make sure that you are familiar with existing knowledge and theoretical approaches in your area so that when you present your final work you can be confident that your research *adds* to that knowledge. Initially you must conduct a thorough literature review for your topic, and make sure that you keep abreast of any relevant literature that appears during the course of your programme. Once you start to formulate your own ideas and theories, it is advisable that, wherever possible, you test them in the community of practice and in the academic community in order to get feedback that you can use to strengthen those ideas. The more that you can expose your work as you develop it, the less likely you are to have the undesirable experience of being told at your viva that your ideas are not viable or that your work is insufficiently original.

You can test your work in a number of ways. Your university will undoubtedly offer an in-house research seminar programme where you can present your ideas to other research students and academics. This is often the safest way to start because you will be presenting to an audience that is on your side and eager to support you with constructive feedback. Once you gain a little more confidence you may wish to submit a paper to present at a national or international academic and/or professional conference. Your academic supervisor will be able to advise you on how to prepare these submissions. Remember, though, that to present at a conference you will be required to register as a delegate and pay a registration fee.

Attendance at conferences is not only useful in terms of exposing your work to a peer community. It also gives you the opportunity to network with others working in your field. You will most likely already be familiar with how important networking can be in professional life, and it holds no less importance in academic life. It helps you to identify the key thinkers in your field, their different perspectives and how their ideas fit with your own. It can also be extremely useful to have made personal contact with these people when it comes to identifying possible examiners for your viva, as it helps in selecting someone who can give your work a fair and thorough examination.

Another way to present your developing ideas to your peer and academic communities is by writing research papers for publication in professional and academic journals. This has a couple of added advantages over presenting at conferences. First, it gives you practice at writing in an academic style, something with which many professional doctorate candidates struggle initially, and, second, it provides evidence that your work has been accepted through peer review. Your published papers can be included as part of your portfolio of evidence, adding strength to your claims of originality and contribution to knowledge in your field. We will cover these issues in more detail in Chapter 9.

Dealing with criticism

As we have seen, testing your work within the peer and academic community is an invaluable way of validating and strengthening your ideas. However, for that to happen you must receive and act on the feedback you are given. Receiving feedback can be quite a painful process, especially when it is critical of your work. If you are in a position of seniority at work you may not be accustomed to having your ideas questioned, let alone criticised, but it is important to understand that this is part of the academic process. The people offering feedback are questioning neither your authority nor your intellect; they are offering their comments and advice as critical friends in order to help you develop your ideas. If you refer back to Fiona's comments (p. 83) you will see how much she valued this process. However, it was not always thus. Like many professional doctorate candidates, Fiona had some initial problems dealing with what she saw as criticism of her work from her academic supervisor, and this caused tensions in the relationship. Then, as she learned to depersonalise the criticism and accept it in the spirit in which it was offered, she was able to progress.

You may feel the same way as Fiona when you first receive feedback on your work. It is important to remember that it is not *personal* criticism. Step back from it and give yourself time to reflect on what it means. Most of the time, you will then realise that it does help you to improve your work. On occasions when you still disagree with what has been said, even after a period of reflection, you need to think how you might answer the criticism in an objective way. You need to construct a *defence* of your argument that is not emotional and is supported by valid evidence. It is important to be able to articulate this defence without being *defensive*, which implies an emotional response that ignores objective reasoning.

Dealing with resistance: developing resilience

Throughout this chapter we have emphasised the need for you to develop a different way of thinking and to look at your profession through a 'different lens'. Whilst it is natural to become excited and enthusiastic about the different things you see through this lens, you should remain aware that your colleagues may not share those emotions. Not everyone will be able to see what you see, and even if they can they may not be enthusiastic about it. Many people dislike change, either through fear of the unknown, feelings that they will not be able to cope, worries that the change will create more work for them or because the changes challenge their own accepted wisdom or authority. You need to be sensitive to these issues. It is very common for candidates undertaking a professional doctorate to meet with resistance in the workplace. As an example, take Diane, whose professional doctorate research focused on the care of people with autism. Here she describes her experiences in her working group when she tried to propose alternative approaches to improve the care of the users of the service:

> *"I would often look at the duty rota to see who I was working with and feel a sense of anxiety when certain individuals were on duty. Their values and attitudes were very much to get through the shift as quickly and as calmly as possible.*
>
> *I soon became isolated from this group. I was not willing to change my values and attitudes and I wanted more for my service users and I wanted to ensure that they were treated fairly, as a unique individual, to be respected and empowered in their lives as much as they possibly could. Isn't this what we would all want if we needed the care and support from others?"*

Faced with almost universal resistance, and as a result suffering almost continuous anxiety, it would have been easy for Diane to give up on her ideas. Instead, she managed to remain resilient to the opposition and eventually brought about lasting change in her organisation.

You can avoid or minimise resistance to a large extent by having empathy with those who seek to resist you. Try to understand things from their perspective. It is unlikely that their resistance is personal. Do they feel threatened in any way? Why? Being open and transparent about the research you are doing, its purpose and the likely outcomes will help to allay any fears. Keep people 'in the loop' by asking for their advice, input and feedback. Most of all, make sure that you have a solid argument for the work that you are doing, just as we discussed in the previous section.

If colleagues are convinced that your ideas are clearly thought through and have a solid basis in evidence they are more likely to go along with them. If possible, it is useful to develop some resilience to any resistance by demonstrations of success. Can you run a pilot to showcase the benefits of the work you are doing? Perhaps you can persuade a few colleagues to become champions for the work, and they can help persuade others of the benefits. Customers or clients may also be valuable supporters. This is really important with professional doctorates because, unlike a traditional PhD which is often a solitary research project that can be carried out relatively independently, the success of your doctorate is likely to require the collaboration of your work colleagues and professional peers. Without their buy-in you will be unable to test and evaluate any solutions or models that you develop. Diane used just such an approach to encourage her colleagues to accept her ideas.

Case study

"Of course there was scepticism by some of the practitioners; however I believed in what I was doing. I also didn't think that some of these practitioners were just 'nasty' people but I believed that there had been a lack of leadership, continual professional development and no structured approach to knowledge management. I started to hold person-centred case meetings where we would discuss individual service users in a holistic way and I created a philosophy of 'the service being at the centre of everything that we do'. This philosophy played a significant role in changing practice, e.g. staff started to think, behave and practise differently and trying to be objective and consider it from the view point of the service user.

The organisation started to evolve with a group of practitioners with a commitment and interest to providing innovative services for people with autism. The structure of the organization was changed to promote shared activities. This created a learning environment and built relationships to learn from each other which supported practitioners to improve their work performance and strengthened the value and attitudes within social care."

It is important to remember that it is natural to feel a little fear or anxiety in a learning situation – real learning often hurts. It should not be a cue for giving up. Throughout your doctorate you will undoubtedly experience times when you feel that it is all too difficult or that no one understands your ideas. Everyone goes through this, and it is usually a sign that the process is working. Speak to your academic supervisor or perhaps a trusted work-place colleague who will be able to offer support. Your resilience to these feelings will grow as you progress.

6.5 Learning space

The emphasis in this chapter has been on intellectual agility, personal trans-formation through the development of an enquiring mind unfettered by the traditional boundaries of your profession. We have proposed that mindful-ness, curiosity and imagination are attributes that you should seek to de-velop as you progress through your doctorate. There are many resources available that can help you with this development. (Some would argue that things like curiosity and imagination are traits that we either have or don't have, but we would argue that they *can* and *should* be actively developed and nurtured.) I always start by directing my students to *Who Moved My Cheese?* (Johnson, 2001), a self-help guide to coping with change. Although this is a very simple and seemingly silly story, it provides an excellent meta-phor to explain what we are trying to achieve in terms of our candidates' mindset. Langer (1997) and McIntosh (2010) offer useful introductions to mindfulness and imagination.

None of this will work, however, if your mind is not open to new learn-ing. In this chapter we have already considered the barriers that can inhibit transformational learning in professional life and, although your doctoral studies may help to overcome these barriers, you will still need to make a conscious effort to embrace a new way of thinking. It is very important that you create for yourself a *learning space*. This does not mean an uncluttered desk, a quiet office or a comprehensively stocked bookshelf (although these things are undoubtedly valuable). We use 'learning space' here in a much broader sense to mean creating opportunities for learning where you are free from the 'noise' of your professional community, somewhere where you can 'hear things differently' (Savin-Baden, 2008). Learning spaces are different for each person and you need to discover what works best for you, but Savin-Baden insists it is vital that they have a different kind of temporal-ity and allow different ways of thinking. She suggests that:

[c]ommon types of learning space occur through:

- Physical and/or psychological removal from the normal learning environment. For example, conferences, writing retreats, or work-ing overseas. New environments often prompt new ways of seeing issues, providing opportunities for reflection and presenting chal-lenges to current ways of thinking

- The creation of specific time for writing or reflection
- Using social learning spaces for dialogue and debate
- Accessing digital spaces for discussion and reflection with and through others. (Savin-Baden, 2008, p. 8)

You are already fortunate in that your professional doctorate programme provides one kind of learning space. If your programme cohort is multi-professional this offers yet another, giving you a further opportunity to broaden your networks. We have already looked briefly at the value of networking, but we can also consider the network in terms of your personal development as an alternative learning space. Dobrow and Higgins (2005) define networks in terms of range and density, arguing that high-range, low-density networks are more conducive to development than low-range, high-density networks. The latter network is one that might be formed within a single context, where all members of the network know each other (for example, within a single organisation). In high-range, low-density networks, individuals are drawn from a range of contexts such as employers, educational institutions and professional associations, and would not necessarily know each other. Thus, a multidisciplinary cohort in a professional doctorate programme is an example of this type of low-density network. The low-density, high-range network gives you access to a much greater variety of information and resources as well as greater cognitive flexibility (Higgins, 2001), and thus offers an effective learning space. To make best use of it, you need to actively engage with the cohort in discussions and debates about your topic. Some of the best learning experiences can arise from discussions between people with completely different backgrounds – for example, a scientist with a musician, or a nurse with an engineer. If you do not have an opportunity to engage with multidisciplinary networks on a face-to-face basis, technology offers an alternative. For example, one professional doctorate student has used LinkedIn to test his ideas across the professional community worldwide.

A common problem with professional doctorate candidates is that they often do not recognise the learning that happens outside the confines of the classroom or the formal boundaries of their research objectives, and fail to record useful conversations or experiences that could turn out to be significant. This is a mistake. You will benefit by recognising all the learning spaces that are available to you, and value them regardless of whether or not they are directly attached to your research project.

Summary

In this chapter we aimed to help you to appreciate the personal qualities that will assist you to become a researching professional with the capacity to have an on-going and enduring impact upon your profession, and to understand some of the approaches that can help facilitate lasting personal transformation.

We have discussed how the development of greater intellectual agility will advance your progress towards becoming a researching professional. You need to be able to think beyond the traditional boundaries of your profession and to see your working world through a fresh lens. The qualities that will help you do this are *mindfulness*, *curiosity* and *imagination*.

We have also considered how, in order to nurture these qualities, you can create *learning spaces* for yourself. These are spaces in your life where you are encouraged to think differently, for example by sharing and debating your ideas at conferences or through written papers, and with professionals from other disciplines who might be able to offer you different perspectives.

Your ability to receive and act on feedback and constructive criticism is important to your continued development. Similarly, your ability to apply your ideas in a sensitive and empathetic manner, mindful of the effect they may have on others, and your capacity to defend your ideas in an objective manner will influence your potential to contribute to your profession.

7 Putting Together a Portfolio

On completion of this chapter you will:

▶ be able to establish a definition of the term 'portfolio' in the context of the professional doctorate
▶ be able to identify the types of evidence which are appropriate for the professional doctorate portfolio
▶ be able to establish the role of reflection in the professional doctorate portfolio

7.1 Introduction

Portfolios are becoming increasingly common as a means of assessment in professional doctorates, but it is recognised that not all professional doctorate candidates are required to compile a portfolio. This chapter will be particularly relevant if your programme uses portfolios but it will also be of general interest even if it doesn't. The development of a portfolio can be a useful exercise – it is one way for you to monitor your skills development – so the material should be of general as well as specific interest.

Portfolios came into vogue in the UK education system in the early 1990s as a result of the National Vocational Qualification (NVQ) movement which required candidates to build a portfolio of evidence against the NVQ standards or competencies of practice. Of course, the term had been in use for a much longer period of time: artists maintain and develop portfolios of their work, managers have a portfolio of responsibilities, as do most ministers of state. However, it was the NVQ movement which brought the portfolio to the fore in educational formal assessment across a wide range of programmes. Since then, the portfolio has been used increasingly as a means of assessment and, indeed, has become dominant in a number of higher education courses, mainly educational and health-related programmes of study.

Activity 1

Write down what you understand by the term 'portfolio' in three or four bullet points.

7.2 Definitions of portfolios

The free online dictionary defines a portfolio as:

> A portable case for holding material, such as loose papers, photographs, or drawings.
>
> The materials collected in such a case, especially when representative of a person's work: a photographer's portfolio; an artist's portfolio of drawings.

This definition outlines the important principle that a portfolio is a collection of work in an accessible format that is held in some sort of case or holder. In recent times, the electronic or digital portfolio has become increasingly common. Despite the fact that the concept of the portfolio has being taken up by many educational courses, there is no common understanding of the term in that context. However, the definition of a portfolio as a collection of material which has a discernible structure is fairly consistent across educational organisations.

Arter and Spandel define portfolios in the educational context as:

> A purposeful collection of student work that tells the story of a student's progress or achievement in (a) given area(s). This collection must include student participation in the selection of content; the guidelines for selection; the criteria for judging merit; the evidence of student self-selection. (1992, p. 36)

This definition contains many important ideas, but the central point that the portfolio tells the story of a student's progression is particularly relevant. The portfolio demonstrates achievement in a given area and shows development around a particular theme. Portfolios can be used as part of a programme, in the context of a module or one aspect of a programme of study (for example, work-based modules), or for the establishment of achievement against the programme of study as a whole. The portfolio can be used in a variety of ways, but it is not simply a loose collection of issues or ideas. It is a structured record of achievement and as such subscribes to certain principles or guidelines.

Activity 2

Look back at the responses you gave in Activity 1 and compare them with the definitions given above. This will help you to establish a working definition for your portfolio.

With this in mind, the major characteristic of the portfolio is demonstration of achievement against pre-set standards. In the case of the professional doctorate portfolio, this may involve showing achievement against programme learning outcomes or against national standards such as the UK QAA standards for doctoral study (QAA, 2012). In portfolio compilation, the aim is to map the material against these standards. Some evidence will map directly onto these standards, but at other times one piece of evidence may fit more than one standard and should therefore be cross-referenced. The important principle is to ensure that the reader can follow the portfolio's logic and relate the evidence to the standards. One popular approach is to compile a grid which makes explicit the relationship of the evidence to the main report. This is very helpful to the reader who must be able to navigate their way around the portfolio.

All of the above begs the question: what is evidence? Evidence can be anything which demonstrates achievement of a standard, but this does not mean that anything goes! Rather, you should collect highly-focused and relevant evidence which demonstrates the points which you are trying to address. The validity of the evidence should be ascertained in the sense that it should clearly be evidence which has been generated by the candidate or, if part of a team effort, the contribution of the person presenting the evidence should be clearly identified. Secondary material, such as reports and protocols, should be linked to the evidence and should have a purpose.

Paulson et al. (1991) outline concepts which are integral to portfolios and highlight the following areas which should be addressed:

- Rationale
- Intent
- Content
- Standards
- Judgement.

It is important that the rationale for the evidence is very clearly outlined. It must be set against the aims and objectives of the study, with clear explanations of why the evidence was collected in a particular way and how it is related to the overall aims of the study.

The intent, or the purpose, for which the portfolio was compiled must be clear. The obvious answer – 'to get the doctorate!' – will not suffice. However, the relationship of the items to the aims of the study and the programme criteria for doctoral study should be fully described.

The content, too, should show a clear rationale – it should be included for a specific reason and purpose – and it is useful to consider this in the development of the portfolio. You should ask yourself questions such as:

- Is this material original?
- How does it relate to the objectives of my study?

- Does it name people or organisations, and is its confidentiality compromised?
- If this item is excluded, would it detract from the portfolio?
- Does it require a commentary or explanation?
- Is the order and sequence of the portfolio logical?

Paulson et al. (1991) define standards for the quality of the content as well as what makes a good, or a not so good, portfolio item. This is not to say that only those items with successful outcomes should be included. Pieces of work that have not turned out as well as expected can also be included because much can be learned from these situations, and that often leads to a successful project. Judgement is very important. In a sense, the whole process is one of judgement, and decisions are being made about the appropriateness of the material as the portfolio is being complied. An overall or summative judgement is useful in considering how the totality of the portfolio meets the overall aims of the study.

Whilst high-quality evidence is important, it is also imperative to demonstrate the development of thinking over a period of time and to provide evidence that this thinking has a tangible focus in the practical situation. The portfolio should therefore, as well as demonstrating achievement, also stimulate a degree of critical thinking, which is an important part of the learning process itself. This means that, as well as reflection on each aspect which may be an integral part of professional practice, there should be an overview of the process of development of the portfolio. This section has presented a general consideration of portfolio development. The remainder of this chapter will consider portfolios within the context of the professional doctorate.

7.3 Portfolios in the context of the professional doctorate

There are many professional doctorates on offer around the world, all having different structures, but an increasing number of schemes are using portfolios of evidence accompanied by a report or dissertation. The traditional PhD thesis tends to be highly structured and is presented as a coherent body of work. In contrast, a professional doctorate submission may be a more eclectic body of work and less formally structured, but it must still be presented in a focused and coherent manner. The use of portfolios in the context of the professional doctorate draws on all of the principles outlined in the previous section. The chief aim is to demonstrate the impact of the work on professional practice and the individual student's contribution. The portfolio provides a record of this.

Professional doctorate programmes will have their own guidance and regulations which will detail the specific structure of the portfolio. However, as a generic definition, Walker defines the portfolio in the context of the professional doctorate as 'a selection of products of research which best establish(es) the candidate's claim to have carried out research of a doctoral standard' (1998, p. 94).

It is worth reiterating an important point made in the previous section: a portfolio is more than merely a collection of work put together in a file to represent engagement in the process of learning. It is also a collection of material which will be assessed against a set of outcomes. Maxwell and Kupczyk-Romanczuk (2009), in discussing Walker's definition, indicate that the portfolio is also about the clear development of an idea, and they liken the professional doctorate portfolio to the artist developing a concept and trying out ideas using different mediums. This process is often messy, but a degree of order and structure in the final product is required to make the portfolio and its content meaningful. Webb et al. (2002) discuss several models of portfolios. In the *shopping trolley* approach everything of possible relevance is included. This should be avoided, and a degree of selectivity should always be employed. Whilst it is difficult to legislate about the length of the portfolio, as a general rule the smaller and more focused the better the portfolio is. Webb et al. (2002) also outline a portfolio model that is perhaps more appropriate to the professional doctorate: the *cake mix approach* in which the different parts are integrated to make a coherent and focused document.

At an individual level, the nature of the professional doctorate and the candidate's approach to it vary, largely because candidates enter the programme at different stages in different career trajectories. However there are three broad scenarios:

1   An individual who is near the end of their career whose portfolio will consist of a body of work detailing their career pathway and achievements. It will usually comprise a fairly eclectic body of material.
2   An individual who is working on a large (research) project and their portfolio encompasses this project.
3   An individual who comes with a body of work comprising a number of research projects and details of innovation in practice. These will be pieces of work around a particular theme which will require some further development, usually through the generation of further projects. An important component is often the evaluation of achieved and on-going projects. The majority of candidates fall into this category.

Candidates often ask how recent the information contained within the portfolio should be. In practice, individual circumstances will largely determine the portfolio structure and the nature of the evidence contained within the portfolio. The portfolio can demonstrate achievement over a long time frame and in many instances can represent a lifetime's work. In this scenario it is particularly important for candidates to be highly selective and to focus the information contained within the portfolio. More commonly, the portfolio contains a mixture of past work and studies generated within the context of the professional doctorate. Here the time frame will depend on the relevance of the evidence to the overall aims of the professional doctorate. There is no hard and fast rule for the types of evidence which should be included in a portfolio, only that the evidence must be appropriate and address the particular aims and objectives set at the beginning of the portfolio compilation.

The submission of the portfolio is usually accompanied by a report, known as a thesis or a dissertation. This report must discuss the evidence and thereby demonstrate that the candidate's work is of doctoral standard and has made a professional impact. The portfolio and this report make up the thesis. It is useful to think of the professional doctorate as being no different from any other research study, and as such it should contain the following elements:

- A review of the relevant literature in which the area of investigation is fully and rigorously explored.
- The methodological approach which has shaped and focused the study.
- The aims of the work and the research questions to be addressed.
- The results, including a contextualisation and discussion of the results in which the literature is further explored.
- A demonstration of the contribution to knowledge and to professional practice.

These elements will be contained in the report which accompanies the portfolio. However, the 'results' will generally be in the portfolio itself and it is important to cross-reference from the report to the portfolio. It is also important to recognise that the results need not be results in the sense of a research study or tables; rather, they are evidence which supports the claim that the work is of doctoral standard. As such they could comprise a number of items ranging from academic publications and work-related reports to artefacts or details of particular projects.

Portfolio compilation goes well beyond the gathering of evidence and putting it in a file. The very act of compiling a portfolio is creative, and should be allocated sufficient time and intellectual resources. Moon (cited by Zubizaretta, 2009) outlines some principles of portfolio compilation:

- Portfolios demand time and intellectual space.
- The independent and self-directing nature of the process develops a sense of ownership of the learning in the learner.
- Portfolios focus attention on particular areas of, and demand the independent ordering of, thought.

● Portfolios often draw affective function into learning, and this can bring about greater effectiveness in learning.

● The ill-structured nature of the tasks ... challenges the learner and increases the sophistication of the learning process. (Zubizaretta, 2009)

The first, and perhaps the most important, issue in portfolio compilation is the need for time and space. Moon's second principle emphasises the importance of seeing the process of portfolio building as an integral part of the professional doctorate, and not just as a tedious task. It will take time to gather the evidence and that is not a mindless task but one that requires thought and consideration or, in other words, intellectual space. Physical space is also important because portfolios contain a great deal of material which needs to be spread out, so the sheer physical space required should not be underestimated. Candidates have been known to state that they could not use their dining room table for months!

The third issue emphasises the creative aspect of portfolio compilation. Compiling a portfolio is not a mechanical mindless action but is something which enhances learning. It forces the compiler to consider why certain pieces of evidence are being selected and others are rejected, and it adds to a deeper understanding of the area of practice.

The aim of portfolio compilation is to supplement the final report, and all attention should be focused on that, but the very act of portfolio compilation is of itself highly creative. Klenowski (2002) highlights the inherent tension between the focus on evidence as an indication of achievement in order to gain acceptance and the formative facilitative process of portfolio compilation. The process of selecting items, modifying them, adding to them and synthesising material is important and actually shapes thought, assisting with the development of the requisite skills. Ownership is essential and it is through these creative processes that the candidate will gain a real sense of possession.

Zubizaretta (2009) suggests there are three vital components in the compilation of the portfolio: reflection, evidence and collaboration/mentorship. He makes the point that the portfolio should be more than a series of reflective accounts and should also contain real and focused evidence. With this in mind, it is worth emphasising the reflective activity which must take place throughout the process of portfolio compilation. These reflections take place at different levels. Each project contains a reflective element or dimension and, indeed, each part of the portfolio requires some evidence of reflection. It is important to know why something is included and the reasoning behind its inclusion. It is also important to take an overview, sometimes referred to as 'meta-analysis', and in doing so reflect on the process of portfolio compilation as well as the finished product.

Discussion is important. In terms of the claims around development of practice which are made against the current literature, the focus is both on doing and on development. The impact on practice rarely comes from a 'light bulb moment' in which the innovation suddenly illuminates and changes professional practice. Rather, this process takes place over a lengthy time frame, some projects succeeding and others not, but valuable lessons being learned from both – which brings us back to the importance of reflection.

Zubizaretta (2009) also emphasises the need for collaboration and mentorship. This is collaboration in the sense of working with a mentor or, in the case of the professional doctorate, a supervisor or advisor. Through the process of discussion, questioning and challenging, the evidence can be focused and development of the reflective ability can be refined. Zubizaretta was discussing portfolios in general, and was not considering the professional doctorate specifically, but we can add a fourth component to portfolio compilation in that context – interaction with the report. Whilst they are often presented as two separate documents, the portfolio and the report are part of the same submission and together form an integrated whole. Clear cross-referencing from the report to the portfolio is essential.

7.4 Collection of evidence

The key to portfolio development is the collection of evidence which addresses the overall aims of the programme. This evidence must demonstrate achievement, usually in terms of completed projects, either done by the candidate alone or by a group in which the candidate has played a substantive part. Examples of the material included in the portfolio are reports and publications evaluating the project(s) and demonstrating the dissemination of the findings from all of the individual projects. 'Publications' is often interpreted in a wider sense than academic papers alone, and can include reports, conference presentations and articles in professional, as opposed to academic, journals.

The evidence should also include an evaluation of the degree of impact each particular project has had on an area of professional practice. It can include witness statements, usually by someone influential in the profession. Table 7.1 contains suggestions for the types of material which can be included in a portfolio. This list is not exhaustive. The important issue is that the material is presented in such a way that it has logic and consistency, and should address a particular theme or outcome.

The process of portfolio compilation is neither a paper exercise nor a technical exercise of putting evidence in a logical order in a folder. It is an active process which requires thought and development. Often writing something down can spark off renewed thinking and further development.

Strategic organisational reports
Reports of projects that have been carried out as part of the work programme
Published conference or journal papers
Work of clearly publishable quality
Strategic policy documents
Evaluation reports
CD Rom, DVD and web work
Reflections on professional practice
Reflective diary extracts
Letters of validation
Objective evidence of impact of work, such as newspaper articles, trade press articles, journal articles, minutes of meetings, letters of support, exhibition details etc.
Personal development plan
Monitoring reports

Table 7.1 Suggestions for material which could be included in the portfolio

Nor is it totally an armchair activity. It involves action, and the impact and development of practice is a very important element of the activity.

The initial decisions relate to content and identifying a framework for compiling the portfolio, that is, establishing a structure and gathering the initial evidence. Completion of this process establishes the thrust and direction of the portfolio, which in practice may often mean a change of focus. Indeed, the structure may change several times before you are happy with your portfolio. The first draft of the portfolio structure will identify the gaps and the type of evidence needed to fill these gaps. Having compiled your portfolio, the final process involves taking a *meta* view, examining the totality of the experience and focusing on how the process has impacted on individual practice and on the profession as a whole.

The professional doctorate portfolio cannot be defined against a particular blueprint. Each individual must make a logical decision about the structure of their portfolio. Clarity is the overriding principle. It is important to remember that the examiners will have to read the portfolio and it is not their job to try and find their way around it. The structure must be clear and transparent. The formative process will be messy, but the final product should be streamlined, logical and tidy!

Portfolios are not just a means of storing information in an organised way, they also demonstrate achievement. The NVQ portfolio demonstrates achievement against pre-set standards or competencies. The artist's portfolio is a little more fluid and flexible in its demonstration of artistic achievement. The professional doctorate portfolio falls somewhere between the two. It must demonstrate clearly that standards have been met, and this must be tied in with a unique and creative approach to an area of professional practice.

In the majority of portfolios, evidence is presented in some sort of written format, which can range from reports to curricular documentation and previously published material. As well as written documentation, it can also be in the form of artefacts or in electronic format, such as web-based material (which could also be printed off), or videos. These are works which are part of the individual career trajectory of the candidate's journey. Intrinsic to the achievement of outcomes is the demonstration that the candidate has contributed to the particular area of practice in a unique and individual way and that they have clearly and fully disseminated those developments to the community of practice.

The evidence, therefore, must demonstrate achievement both in terms of pre-set competencies and of creativity and originality. It can, depending on the area of practice, be a mix of materials ranging from artefacts to published formal material in an academic sense. A small amount of strong material which demonstrates a unique contribution in a highly focused manner is much better than lots of material which is fairly mundane and repetitive.

In gathering evidence it is important to remember that any material should be personally generated by the candidate. This means that the portfolio will contain work, or evidence of work, which has been done directly by you. If it is a group exercise your contribution to that group exercise must be clearly demonstrated. In professional life much of what we do is as a part of a team of people, and sometimes individual contributions are easy to identify whilst others are considerably less obvious. It is important that group material in the portfolio is presented in such a way that your personal contribution is clearly identifiable.

There may be occasions when work not directly generated by you, either individually or as part of a team, may be included. For example, your portfolio may contain research carried out by others under your direction if the idea and innovation was yours, and protocols or work done by your department as long as there is a very good reason why this material is included. This is why your reflections on the process of generating a piece of work – demonstrating the thinking behind it – are particularly important. The reader will not be able to determine this for themselves and reflections can be a powerful way of demonstrating the influence something has had on your practice and that of others.

7.5 Reflective element

Reflection is an integral part of portfolio-related activities, and it is an area which requires some discussion. Reflection takes place at a number of levels, and reflective accounts may be included as evidence. Reflections will take place as the portfolio is compiled, as well as in an overview or meta-reflective account. There are a number of models which facilitate reflection, but it is important that the reflection covers both the overview and each individual piece of work. The overview is sometimes called a 'meta-analysis' and is an important component of the portfolio. The way in which the portfolio is structured is worth consideration because it might be useful to include reflections, where appropriate, in each section, although some candidates prefer to present their reflections in the form of an overview and create a summary account. Others will use a combination of approaches. The important principle is that the portfolio must contain a demonstration of the reflections accompanying each piece of evidence as well as a reflection on the project as a whole.

An increasingly popular concept in education is a teaching portfolio, which is a compilation of candidates' teaching activities and their subsequent development. This captures the essence of portfolio compilation. It is particularly relevant to the professional doctorate portfolio because it emphasises the formative and developmental processes, as well as the summative aspect. Kreber and Cranton (2000) outline the levels at which reflection takes place in a teaching portfolio. They discuss the need to reflect on the premise, process and content of the portfolio, and this is a very useful model to transfer to the professional doctorate portfolio. They make the points that there are different levels of portfolio compilation and that candidates should establish the fundamental principles of why the portfolio is being compiled – what is it trying to achieve? They need to think about the contents of the portfolio and their reflections on the process of compilation, and how this has changed and developed the actual project.

The *premise* of the portfolio refers to its underlying idea and the overall thrust that the evidence is supporting. It is worth looking at the aims and objectives of the study and ensuring that the portfolio is congruent with these and that the evidence is focused on them. In the professional doctorate, the focus is on the development of professional practice in your discipline, and that is the case which is being put forward. Throughout the process you need to be aware of this and ensure the material is congruent with this aim, even though, in the process, the aim may be changed or modified in the light of the emerging content.

The content needs to be reflected on continually. It is very much a two-way process: ensuring that the broad aim is being met and that the evidence is congruent with that aim. The content must be focused and demonstrate that the candidate has achieved the programme's aims and objectives. It is also important to take an overview of the process, and this is sometimes called the 'metacognitive perspective'. This means reflecting on how the process facilitated learning and development and sharpened and focused your thinking. This is an activity which should really be done throughout the process of portfolio compilation and not just at the end.

Collin (2011) discusses students' presentation of their portfolios and how the process of presentation actually conveys much of the student's disposition. He draws on the theories of the French sociologist, Bourdieu, and it is worth bringing in some of Bourdieu's thinking. In the case of the professional doctorate, the portfolio is presented or examined at the viva, and we are concerned with what it conveys. Bourdieu wrote explicitly on the need for reflectivity and discussed the different ways in which one can reflect. He was writing about reflection on research projects, but his ideas can be transferred across to portfolio compilation. He maintained that it is important not just to consider the ways in which personal characteristics, such as age and gender and social class, can influence the approach, but to also think about professional background and how your profession looks at the world (Bourdieu and Wacquant, 1992). This can lead to many insights and create a more innovative approach to portfolio compilation.

Reflection is an on-going and dynamic activity and is integral to the compilation of the portfolio. There is mileage in writing down all your reflections because this can shape and focus your thinking, but it is important that the reflections included in the actual portfolio are relevant and focused to the task in hand and that they form an integral part of the portfolio.

7.6 The structure of the portfolio

It is worth spending time considering aspects of the overall structure of the portfolio and issues around its presentation. The final product must be a coherent body of work, yet at the same time the professional doctorate portfolio is often an eclectic mix of material and does not fall into a neat pattern. The evidence can come in a combination of mediums ranging from formalised reports to pictures, newspaper articles and so on. Organisation of the material is essential and it needs thought as to the best approach and the most logical sequence for the contents. It is by this engagement in the process that the individual student can gain a real sense of ownership of the material, and this sense of ownership is essential for the viva.

The presentation of the portfolio can be a particular challenge and the format requires a great deal of thought. The material presented is both evidence of development on a central theme and a demonstration of creative ability.

Clarity is essential. It is not the task of readers to work out where things are and, when cross-referencing from the report, they should be able to identify easily where the material is stored. This may seem obvious but it is often overlooked. A table of contents allows the reader to navigate their way through the portfolio. It is worth spending time on this. Sometimes a simple list of the contents is enough, in other cases a more innovative strategy is required. At the end of this chapter, examples of real portfolios are presented, showing how candidates have addressed these issues. It is important that each item in the portfolio is mentioned in the report. Issues should be grouped together in a particular order which is logical to the reader.

In the presentation of the portfolio, a degree of creativity is important. The reader should warm to the portfolio and wish to look at it rather than finding it offputting. Eisenman has highlighted different approaches to portfolio presentation:

> By definition a design portfolio is a grouping of loose sheets collected in a portable case. But today, portfolios assume a range of new forms: web sites, motion portfolios, files on a disk, portable documents (pdf). (Eisenman, 2008)

Whilst Eisenman's book is mainly concerned with an artist's portfolio there are many useful tips and hints for professional doctorate candidates.

Much of the information on portfolios is about e- or electronic portfolios and in recent years this approach has become increasing common. An e-portfolio is often web-based and open access. Professional doctorate portfolios can be presented in this manner and the same principles apply to e-portfolios as to paper-based ones. It is good practice to have both a paper-based and a digital copy of the portfolio, so that the reader can choose which format to access.

Activity 3

Spend some time outlining a possible structure for your portfolio.
When you have done this, compare your thoughts with the examples in Section 7.7.

7.7 Case studies

There is no definite blueprint on which the portfolio can be based and individual students need to determine the logic and structure of their own portfolio.

To illustrate this point, the portfolios of three successful students have been selected as case studies.

- Susan is a senior pharmacist who influenced national policy through her work. She presented a series of successful projects within her portfolio.

- Peter also had a well-established career and was involved in a number of projects. His work consisted of evaluating his existing projects and, on the basis of that work, engaging in further development.
- Jean, also a well-established professional, developed and implemented a large-scale study which addressed practice issues.

Case studies

Susan's portfolio

Susan had a body of work which she had accumulated over several years at a senior level. One of her challenges was to develop a structure which would show the innovative way in which she had approached her work at a strategic level. She was involved with the development of national standards for the preparation of medicines and she had a great deal of information. At first, the task of presenting it with some sort of structure and order seemed extremely daunting, but she persevered. Eventually she decided to use a grid with the place of preparation on the top row, forming column headings for the three sections:

1. Evidence to support the development of the standards
2. Evidence to support the implementation of the standards
3. Evidence to support the dissemination of the standards.

Peter's portfolio

Peter's doctorate contained a blend of achievement, theory, reflection and practice. This broad approach suited a mixed methods research methodology. He wrote in the first person and sought to match his chapters to his identified objectives. His structure can be summarised as follows:

Report
Chapter 1 – Introduction, methodology and structure;
Chapter 2 – Reflection on early experiences in shaping values and work – used reflective writing, including auto-ethnography, to understand experiences from personal and practitioner perspectives;
Chapter 3 – Literature review, to research and contextualise the subject area;
Chapters 4, 5 and 6 – Outline the main body of on-going work, leading to a proposed model – used action research and reflective practice to capture contribution, assess impact and improve practice;
Chapter 7 – Evaluate impact and implications for community of practice – used quantitative and qualitative research to gauge stakeholder views, cover any gaps, and provide insights to complement other work;
Chapter 8 — Conclusions, including a final model which was refined following evaluation.

Portfolio
The report should be read in conjunction with the portfolio. In Peter's case the portfolio sat alongside Chapters 2, 4 and 5. For ease of reference, the numbering systems directly mapped across. For example, portfolio

continued overleaf

Case studies continued

section 4.2 provided detail and evidence to complement report section 4.2. One additional section was inserted at the beginning of the portfolio – an explanation of the portfolio structure, followed by a table which outlined how the learning outcomes of the doctoral programme were delivered.

Jean's portfolio

Maxwell and Kupczyk-Romanczuk (2009) use the metaphor of the Greek temple to describe the concept of the professional doctorate portfolio. The floor is the portfolio, the pillars represent the themes within the portfolio and the roof represents the overarching report. This is a useful metaphor which illustrates how the portfolio is integrated into the whole. Jean used this approach quite explicitly to structure her portfolio. She had three research questions and used each question as a means of linking her portfolio to her report, representing them diagramatically. She gave this explanation:

"The guiding structure or temple embodies 6 distinct key elements. Maxwell and Kupczyk-Romanczuk (2009) describe the pediment or roof as the overarching linking paper which connects the individual segments within the portfolio. In this instance the doctoral report represents the pediment as the overarching component integrating, outlining and referencing each section of the portfolio of evidence. Within the pediment/doctoral report the reader will locate the introduction, background, research context, methodology, discussion, recommendations and reflections. Reflections are below the pediment identified as the fascia supported by the peristyle and recorded in the doctoral report. The purpose of the peristyle is to support the pediment translated as the individual pieces of research supporting the overarching doctoral report. The pediment is extended beyond the peristyle to display a developed introduction and developed final conclusions (Maxwell and Kupczyk-Romanczuk, 2009).

Each of the above three key research questions is represented on the temple as the columns. Providing the sound base on the temple is the foundation recognised as the professional experience the researcher brings to the topic. It encapsulates the researcher as an experienced professional which provides the source of its strength in the same sense that the foundation of the temple is a vital feature (Maxwell and Kupczyk-Romanczuk, 2009). The final element of the temple structure is the human figure."

7.8 Tips for portfolio compilation

You may find the following tips useful when preparing your portfolio:

- Organise yourself and develop a system for filing and storing material. As you progress you will develop increasingly sophisticated systems but from the start you need to organise your material in a systematic manner.
- Remember that someone will have to find their way around the portfolio so keep this in mind as you develop classification systems

- It can either be electronic or 'hard copies', although usually it is a mixture of the two approaches. Be clear about what is a duplicate and what is your only copy.
- It is better to collect as much as you can initially; but become more selective as you continue with your studies.
- Remember the report and portfolio comprise an integrated document so make links between the two.
- If it is unclear why some material is included put in a commentary or reflective account.
- Check against these three aspects:
  1. Match against criteria or standard for the professional doctorate,
  2. Provide evidence for any claims that are made,
  3. Make sure that everything is clear and easily identified.

Summary

A portfolio of evidence is an integral part of the professional doctorate scheme. It is important that thought is given to the overall portfolio content and structure and to its presentation in such a way as to maximise its impact. It is also very important to consider the porfolio in a formative sense as well as summative. It is a final product, but the act of compiling a portfolio is in itself creative, and leads to a much deeper appreciation and understanding of the innovations and changes which are the basis of the professional doctorate. The following example portfolio contains the opening section of a real student's work, which you may find useful in structuring your own portfolio.

Portfolio example

Section 1 – Introduction

1.1 Structure

This portfolio contains evidence of my professional practice and reflections on the impact of this practice on the broader community. It should be read in conjunction with the report which, using a blend of achievement, theory, reflection and practice, outlines my role in a journey towards CSR in a modern civic university.

The portfolio contains five sections:

- This section (Section 1) sets out the portfolio structure and outlines how the learning outcomes of the doctoral programme were achieved.
- Section 2 corresponds directly to Chapter 2 of the report and provides complementary evidence of *Early Years* achievements that influenced my thinking prior to joining the university.

continued overleaf

Portfolio example continued

- Section 3 is left intentionally blank.
- Section 4 corresponds directly to Chapter 4 of the report and provides complementary evidence of achievements at the university that constituted *Beginning the Journey* towards CSR.
- Section 5 corresponds directly to Chapter 5 of the report and provides complementary evidence of achievements at the university that constituted *Launching and Embedding Corporate Social Responsibility*.

Section 3 is left intentionally blank in order to ensure ease of navigation between the report and portfolio, in which Chapters 2, 4 and 5 map directly across to portfolio sections 2, 4 and 5. For example, references from Chapter 4.2 are supported by evidence in Portfolio 4.2.

The chapters present and discuss my personal contributions and reflect on this; the portfolio sections provide appropriate evidence and more detailed reflections of the contributions and the impact upon my community of practice.

1.2 Learning outcomes

In connection with the learning outcomes under the professional doctorate programme, students are required to demonstrate the following knowledge (see Figure 1):

| K1 | Deep understanding of the recent developments in their profession nationally and internationally. |
| K2 | Deep understanding of current theoretical frameworks and approaches which have direct relevance to their own professional context. |

Figure 1: Knowledge learning outcomes of professional doctorate programme

Students are also required to demonstrate the following skills and abilities (see Figure 2):

S1	Make a significant contribution to practice within their chosen field.
S2	Apply theory and research methodology within the workplace, and feel comfortable in integrating different approaches to address "messy" multidisciplinary problems in a rigorous yet practical manner.
S3	Recognise budgetary, political, strategic, ethical and social issues when addressing issues within the workplace.
S4	Reflect on their own work, and on themselves, and thus operate as a truly reflective independent practitioner.
S5	Present and defend an original and coherent body of work which demonstrates, reflects upon, and evaluates the impact upon practice which they have personally made.

Figure 2: Skills and abilities learning outcomes of professional doctorate programme

Figure 3 shows how these learning outcomes have been met.

NB *In the column headings in Figure 3, Sec. refers to the portfolio section and Ch. to the report chapter.*

	Learning Outcomes	How Achieved	Sec./ Ch.
K1	Deep understanding of the recent developments in their profession nationally and internationally.	Member of TUC Democracy in South Africa Committee.	2.4.1
		Invited to join Higher Education UK Dignity at Work Group due to knowledge of mediation and dignity and respect issues.	4.9.1
		Co-authoring independently refereed paper for International Journal of Diversity.	4.7.2
		Invited to join HE Equality Working Group.	5.2.4
		Invited to speak at national conferences on:	
		Equal pay	4.3.4
		Embedding gender and race equality	5.3.2
		Best practice in sexual orientation	4.5.3
		Embedding mediation into equality and diversity practice	5.2.2
K2	Deep understanding of current theoretical frameworks and approaches which have direct relevance to their own professional context.	Authoring equal pay and CSR documentation that is available online, has been embedded into corporate practice, and is cited by national organisations as best practice.	4.2.2
			5.6.3
		Featured in national professional publications and respected local, regional and national media in order to outline approaches on:	
		Equal pay	4.2.4
		Dignity and respect	4.9.1
		Community engagement	5.10.2
		CSR	5.6.1
		Review of relevant literature on CSR. Review of CSR models and frameworks	Ch. 3
S1	Make a significant contribution to practice within their chosen field.	Equal pay audits were first of their kind and cited as best practice in the sector and by the Equality and Human Rights Commission.	4.2.1
		Second UK University CSR Statement, the first to be international in dimension.	5.5.1
		Equality and diversity practices recognised at series of national and regional awards.	4.10.1
			4.3.3
		Top UK university for good LGB practice.	4.5.3
		Making meaningful engagements with the local and international community in:	2.4.1
		Monitoring free and fair elections	4.8.1
		Refugees	5.4.2
		Migrant workers	5.10.2
		Age	4.7.4
		Race	5.4.3
		Sexuality	4.7.3
		Civic integration	5.7.1
		Empowerment through Fairtrade	5.8.1
		Co-authoring independently refereed paper for International Journal of Diversity.	4.7.2
			Ch. 6
		Proposing a new CSR model	Ch. 8

Figure 3: Achievement of learning objectives (part)

8 The Student/Supervisor Relationship: Expectations and Challenges

On completion of this chapter you will:
- ▶ be able to articulate your expectations of a good supervisor
- ▶ be able to identify what should be included in your learning contract
- ▶ be able to establish an effective working relationship with your supervisor

8.1 Traditional relationships between students and doctoral supervisors

The relationship between you and your supervisor(s) is the key to the successful and timely completion of your professional doctorate. It is very likely that you will have more than one supervisor, but we will use the singular rather than hedging our bets with the clumsy 'supervisor(s)'. This chapter starts by discussing the traditional model of PhD supervisory practice and continues with the differences in being supervised for a professional doctorate. In many ways the relationship that you have with your supervisor will be similar to that of a conventional PhD student/supervisor relationship; which is based on the traditional trade model of the master and apprentice. This well-established model focuses on the generation of Mode 1 knowledge (as discussed in Chapter 2) and not on Mode 2 knowledge generated by professional practice (Gibbons et al., 1994) as is the case with a professional doctorate. In the traditional PhD model the student is usually relatively inexperienced and unknowledgeable in the subject area and learns by emulating the behaviour of the subject expert, their supervisor (Sanders et al., 2011). As a professional doctorate student, you are more likely to be mature and, although you may have been out of academic study for some time, you are also likely to be very experienced and knowledgeable about your own profession. You are an expert in the application to practice of a possibly narrow subject area (Mode 2 knowledge production) whilst your supervisor is more likely to have a broad theoretical knowledge of the subject but not of how it is applied in current practice (Taylor, 2007). Carr et al. (2010) argue that the supervisory approach required for a professional doctorate student is different from that required for a PhD student because the explicit contribution to knowledge needs to be theoretically sound, original and relevant to their practice area. As such, students and their supervisors face unique challenges of balancing academic requirements with *praxis*. Because of the parity of knowledge – and thus of power – between you, your relationship will be subtly different from a typical PhD student and supervisor, whose role can be more akin to that of an advisor.

This has been an issue within our own professional doctorate programme where we initially replaced the title 'supervisor' with that of 'advisor' to reflect the parity of the relationship with the student. However we have returned to using 'supervisor' because it best represents both the role and students' expectations (Sanders et al., 2011). Outside of the UK, for example in the USA, 'advisor' is the title used by the academic director of studies whilst 'supervisor' is used for the person who supervises the research work in the workplace.

Some see the supervisor's relationship with their students differently, as more of a partnership (Clarke et al., 2012), or in the role of a coach (Fillery-Travis and Robinson, 2011) or a mentor. This controversy does not imply that your supervisor will be unable to fulfil the normal appropriate supervisory role that you expect, but it sometimes creates problems for supervisors who are unused to professional doctoral students. Some students have even reported that potential professional doctorate supervisors turn down the role because they have anxieties about their own knowledge and abilities to supervise appropriately (Anderson et al., 2010).

Although you have already acquired subject expertise and professional knowledge, this knowledge is often 'territorialised' (Baumard, 1999). Your knowledge, and therefore your strategic approach to your professional practice, is bounded by the cognitive map that you have created through personal experience. This could be a barrier for you because you need to create new knowledge in different professional situations within your community of practice to demonstrate your contribution. It may also make you reluctant to adopt new theoretical approaches in place of your well-rehearsed techniques (Sanders et al., 2011). Territorialisation may also hinder your decision-making in professional practice. There is a growing trend towards interdisciplinary working, and increasing complexity is requiring practitioners to solve problems at a high level with an increasing need for an analytical approach to professional knowledge, work and roles (Taylor, 2007).

Much of the tacit professional knowledge that you possess is gained from your post-academic practical experience (Wagner, 1987) and is often difficult to express in explicit terms. Because the knowledge is tacit, it is more difficult for you to acknowledge it and to demonstrate how you have applied it to specific problems elsewhere within your profession. This makes it hard for you to identify your specific contribution to your profession. One of the vital roles of your supervisor is to help you to do this. They should also advise you on how to locate your Mode 2 knowledge within the academic literature and how to develop it further so that it becomes more 'trans-disciplinary and trans-professional' (Fell et al., 2011, p. 21).

Trans-disciplinarity is an 'intentional approach to boundaries of discipline and practices to create a new knowledge synthesis within the individual or domain of practice' leading to another way of knowing called '*metanoia*' (Maguire, 2012, p. 81). Using trans-disciplinarity allows you to develop new Mode 2 knowledge in the context of existing practice in your workplace, as well as new Mode 1 knowledge (Gibbons et al., 1994) in the context of the academic literature, and thus fulfil the novelty requirement of the doctorate.

As with a traditional PhD student, the key areas where a supervisor most influences you are in the provision of academic rigour through honing your formal writing skills, developing your criticality and advice in the processes of research design and methodology. A good doctoral supervisor should focus on these skills so that your doctoral journey of personal and professional growth and increasing practical wisdom (Jameson, 2012) leads to a successful personal transformation on completion of your doctorate. Some of our doctoral students have called this process:

"life-changing"
"enabling and empowering"
"liberating."

However, maintaining traditional PhD supervisory practices with a professional doctorate student can create tensions in the relationship, with differing and perhaps unrealistic expectations from both sides. As stated at the beginning of the chapter, a successful relationship between you and your supervisor is the key to your success, so it is understandable that when you start your professional doctorate you will have some concerns about your supervision.

8.3 Students' concerns about professional doctorate supervision

In doctoral programmes that start with a taught element delivered to a co-hort, the individual student does not spend much time with their supervisor. This situation is completely reversed once the taught element is completed and the doctorate moves on to the research phase when the student only sees the supervisor in one-to-one sessions and previous peer support may appear to be lost. Malfroy (2005) found that many mature professional doctorate students expressed a feeling of awkwardness at this point. They were perceived as a student in a relationship with the supervisor, with the unequal power balance making them feel vulnerable. In a face-to-face session with your supervisor there is nowhere for you to hide and you must be able to answer the questions asked of you. Some students may feel anxious and exposed by this. They talk of initially feeling *"frightened of academic staff"* and *"worried and fearful of the research"*. Students who are used to being in a senior position in their workplace struggle to cope with being asked to defend and justify their actions or responses (Evans and Stevenson, 2011). For example, some of our students have said that their supervisor was *"very challenging"* and asked *"what makes you think that?"* or *"how do you know that?"* and told them *"to go away and read about it"*. Blair (2011, p. 93) describes this conflict of being a leader in one area and a learner in another as an attendant anxiety which can be either 'a powerful motivator or a paralysing constraint'. We have found a similar dichotomy of opinion amongst our students, with some who just want to be *"taught"* and told what to do with clear straight forward answers (*"I want a structured programme"*) whilst for others *"the consistent focus on the need for your thoughts ... is really important"* (Smith et al., 2011). The problem with the *"I am being taught"* attitude is that it can make students become passive, and hence they may not question their supervisor. This can lead to a lack of ownership of their work (Petty et al., 2012) and insufficient criticality in their writing and research.

Although you may feel threatened by your supervisor when they start to question you about your work, you have to realise that academic staff are used to engaging in critical debate. That is their job and that is what they have been trained to do. They have been taught never to accept anything on face value and their frequent questioning isn't about undermining your personal ability. They are not being vindictive. They have learned to reflect on issues and question why events happen in such a way and to postulate hypotheses to test their assumptions. They have to evaluate evidence objectively and see how the evidence supports or contradicts a hypothesis or proposal because this is the way that new knowledge is created and learning takes place. This is the skill that they want you to develop as part of your professional doctorate so that you can construct a balanced argument and back up your discussion with objective evidence to support your conclusions. This is known as a Socratic dialogue or questioning. It was first developed by the philosopher Socrates in Athens in 400BC and the technique is still being widely used today to develop critical thinking skills. So when your supervisor says, *"how do you know that?"* and *"go away and read about it"*, they are not simply being difficult. They are deliberately making you question your assumptions and encouraging you to evaluate objectively the evidence from your personal experience and the academic literature. In this way, you are creating new knowledge and understanding, and that is what lifts your work to doctoral level. These higher-level skills are exactly what will be tested by the external examiner in the *viva voce* when you complete your professional doctorate and you have to defend your thesis. These skills are also transferable, and developing your criticality will become one of your key personal and professional achievements as you progress through your professional doctorate. You will achieve an epiphany with this at some stage and, when that light bulb moment suddenly occurs, you will look at the world differently. It is this process that makes students say that professional doctorate is "*life changing*" and "*empowering*".

An experienced doctoral supervisor will be able to develop these skills in you. But that is not all that you require from a supervisor. You will have a list of requirements and expectations of what you want to see in your supervisor in order to make them a good match for you, and you need to discuss them with the programme leader when you first enrol on your doctoral journey.

8.4 What should you expect in a supervisor?

Lee (2009) suggests that there are four areas to consider in relation to selecting a supervisor:

1 The subject/research interests of the supervisor and their methodological interests.
2 Your learning styles and preferences.
3 The professional experience/professional insight of the supervisor.
4 Their knowledge of doctoral requirements. (Lee, 2009, p. 90)

Armsby and Fillery-Travis (2009) would argue that you are the 'expert in terms of the context and the goal of the research' whilst the supervisor or advisor is the 'expert in terms of the process of research and enquiry'. The aim of the work-based research project is not to generate Mode 1 academic knowledge, as with most PhDs, but Mode 2 knowledge (Gibbons et al., 1994) that is 'theoretically sound, original, and of relevance to their practice area' (Carr et al., 2010, p. 279). It may seem obvious that your supervisor has to have the same subject or research interest as you, but the very nature of the professional doctorate makes an exact match very difficult to achieve in practice. Usually your supervisor will have a similar subject interest to you but not an exact match. Similarly, trying to match a supervisor's professional experience to your own will be difficult because the supervisor may have been out of professional practice for some time. Indeed, their practical experience may be dated, or even non-existent if they have always worked in academia. In this case, you should consider having an additional supervisor or mentor in your professional practice or workplace who can provide you with this vital support and who can critically evaluate your contribution to your professional practice. In some EngD programmes, for example, students have a work-based mentor who supports them in undertaking industrially-relevant research (Barnes, 2011). Critten et al. (2010) suggest that the work-based supervisor should develop your thought leadership agenda and the role of the academic supervisor is to underpin this process with sound research methods.

If you do have more than one supervisor then it is open to discussion how the relationship within the supervisory team works in practice. Some would advocate a collaborative approach (Maxwell and Shanahan, 1997) whilst others acknowledge that this is a challenge (Evans, 1998). This is something which you need to clarify at the learning contract stage (see Section 8.5), otherwise you may have problems trying to manage the expectations of both supervisors and their (possibly conflicting) advice. Your academic supervisor needs to understand the language and needs of business, industry and the professions, whilst your work-based supervisor needs to understand the value of academic literature and research.

Whichever supervisory approach is adopted, the key role of both supervisors is to support you in identifying a suitable research topic in your workplace. In this regard you are all co-learners in surfacing and sharing contemporary problems of professional practice (Ashford et al., 2012) in order to achieve what Plowright (2012, p. 37) calls 'theorising professional practice'.

Your experience of supervision will be influenced in terms of:

- your supervisor's style and behaviour;
- collaborating with different organisations;
- identifying a research topic in the workplace;
- where your academic research is published (see Chapter 9).

In PhD studies, Vitae (2012a) suggests a pattern of phased supervisory behaviour based on the situational leadership work of Blanchard and Hersey (1986). This has been adapted by Clarke et al. (2012) to include the supervision of professional doctorate students. The pattern identifies four types of behaviour which your supervisor should adopt with you:

1 Directing
2 Coaching
3 Supporting
4 Delegating

This is a continuum of behaviour rather than a series of consecutive phases. Your supervisor should aim to be flexible so that they adopt different behaviours at different times of the supervisory process. In acknowledgement of the parity of knowledge between you and your supervisor, it is preferable that directing is kept to a minimum. Using such behaviour can create tensions in a relationship which is likely to be characterised by differing, and perhaps unrealistic, expectations from both sides (Sanders et al., 2011). Malfroy (2005) found that many mature professional doctorate students expressed a feeling of awkwardness in their positioning as 'student' in a relationship with a 'supervisor', in particular commenting on their perception of an unequal power balance that made them feel vulnerable. However, in the same study, supervisors expressed some frustration with their doctoral candidates, finding them unwilling to be independent in their learning and research development. Malfoy (2005) argues that these tensions can in part be attributed to the retention of traditional PhD supervisory practices by the academic supervisor, and shows that some of these stresses can be dissipated by 'opening up' supervisory practices into a more collaborative learning environment. This is something that you will need to take into account when you establish a learning contract with your supervisor.

As discussed earlier, any good doctoral supervisor should be able to engage in Socratic questioning (Paul and Elder, 2006). This is a generic technique which is independent of the subject area, and it could be argued that the requirement for the supervisor to have exactly the same subject interest as you is less crucial (Delamont et al., 2000). Some students prefer to utilise their professional support networks, rather than their academic advisor, to address professional issues (Lee, 2009). Whichever approach you prefer, it is important to ensure that at least one of your supervisors is experienced in your methodological approach. This is a key component of your research and one which you will have to strongly defend in your viva, so you must have a supervisor, or easy access to someone, who has a sound working knowledge and understanding of your research design and methodology and can guide you through this process. For example, your supervisor may be a subject expert who has always used quantitative methods to statistically analyse their research data, but you may wish to take a qualitative approach by garnering rich deep data from fewer but more representative sources rather than less detailed data but from more sources. You will need explicit support and guidance early on in the research design stage, perhaps involving an additional advisor, to ensure that you use the mode of social enquiry which best fits your research, as well as applying adequate statistical rigour to the results.

Similarly, you need a supervisor who understands the formal process of the professional doctorate programme and can navigate through your university's structures, systems and procedures to ensure that you are appropriately supported during your doctorate, and particularly when the time comes to submit your work. It is important from your perspective that your supervisor has a working knowledge and understanding of the professional doctorate and appreciates the subtle but important ways that it differs from a traditional PhD. These specific differences will vary between subject disciplines, institutions of higher education and countries so they are not discussed here (see Fell et al., 2011 for further discussion). Ideally, your supervisor will be experienced in working with professional doctorate students and understand exactly what needs to be done in terms of university processes.

Lee (2009) suggests that your learning styles or preferences are important when considering your supervisor. This may be so, but it is most important that you feel comfortable with your supervisor and that there should be mutual trust and respect between you. You will make a lot of emotional investment in your professional doctorate, as will your family, friends and work colleagues, and there will be many powerful external pressures on you to complete, or sometimes even to abandon, your work. As you proceed along your doctoral journey you will be spending a lot of time with your supervisor. This is particularly true towards the final stages when the doctorate will be occupying every conscious and unconscious moment of your time. Your supervisor may be telling you things that you don't want to hear, such as saying that you haven't analysed your data correctly, that you need to write another chapter or that you are not finished yet and are not ready to submit. Don't forget that your supervisor also has an incentive for you to pass as it affects their research status within the university. You must be able to trust your supervisor's judgement in these matters, and vice versa, so it is important to establish a good working relationship with them. However, you must be wary that this relationship doesn't become over-familiar or there may be a tendency to adopt less challenging behaviour, which could negatively impact on your work.

These are the explicit requirements of a supervisor, but there are also implicit requirements which make up the psychological contract between you and the supervisor (Clarke et al., 2012). The implicit requirements need to be made more explicit if your relationship is to be positive and productive. For that to happen, right from the beginning of your relationship you should adopt certain strategies which will help you to establish a pattern of behaviour for the whole of your supervision.

8.5 Establishing an effective relationship with your supervisor

Effective communication is the key to any successful relationship, and the relationship between you and your supervisor is no exception. It is worth spending some time reflecting on your expectations of the behaviour of your supervisor before you have your first formal meeting, and the previous discussion should help you to clarify some of the issues which you may wish to consider. Once you have done so you should discuss these with your supervisor at one of your early meetings. Apart from the obvious advantages of doing this, it will help to remind your supervisor that the power balance between you is more equal than between most PhD students and their supervisors, and that you are colleagues in this endeavour. This will produce a more satisfying relationship for both of you. Expectations of supervision are often strongly influenced by your past educational experiences, and this may be particularly problematic if your culture expected you not to question your teachers (Evans and Stevenson, 2011). Reflecting on your expectations of supervision and communicating them to your supervisor is the first step to overcoming previous barriers.

In discussing your expectations of your supervisor, do not forget that communication is a two-way process. Your supervisor will also have very clear expectations of your behaviour. If you want to achieve mutual trust and respect then both of you will need to articulate these expectations and agree on how you can achieve them. This should form the basis of a learning contract which will help to both formalise and make explicit your working relationship. Figure 8.1 shows an example of a learning contract.

As described in Section 8.4, many professional doctorate students are not supervised by a single person and often have a team of two or three supervisors, including someone from the workplace. The first or principal supervisor is the main point of contact for you and for the university in terms of its procedures. The second supervisor often has a different knowledge or skill base from the first supervisor and can provide you with additional support in specific areas of your work. If you also have a work-based supervisor then this person can provide you with specific support and access to resources in your workplace. Depending upon your experience and position in the workplace, you may not need a work-based supervisor, but you may find it useful to have a work- or profession-based mentor who can guide you, particularly when you have to demonstrate your contribution

Supervisor expectations of the student

Student expectations of the supervisor(s)

Frequency of meetings

Who should be attending the meetings?

Acceptable behaviour in meetings:
- Having a meeting agenda
- Keeping records of the meeting
- Completing the PDP
- Identifying the student's training needs (see below for example)
  - Academic writing
  - Research methodology
  - Information retrieval skills
  - Referencing software
- Planning the work and identifying milestones
- Meeting deadlines (both parties)
- Submitting written work
- Receiving timely balanced and constructive feedback
- Publishing and presenting the work

Figure 8.1   An example of a learning contract

to your community of practice. Your professional mentor should be someone who is experienced and reputable, and can provide moral support and guidance in your professional role. Some universities insist on you having a professional mentor and have specific requirements in terms of their competency and experience.

Whilst having a team of supervisors is very valuable for you as a student, and ensures that all aspects of your work are covered, there are downsides. The main issue is what to do if they give you conflicting advice. This situation will arise if you see your supervisors separately because each will have their own opinion of your work. Consequently, as part of your learning contract and your expectations of your supervisors, you should clarify whether meetings will involve all of the supervisory team. If this is not possible, then formulate a mechanism whereby the key actions from the separate meetings are logged and made known to all members of the team. A multi-party discussion should be undertaken so that each person understands their individual role and how their contribution to the relationship will be effected. For example, should all meetings require all supervisors to be present? Will different supervisors adopt different roles during the research project?

The frequency and length of your meetings should be decided at the beginning and regularly reviewed as you may need to meet frequently to help to maintain the thrust of the work. The frequency will depend upon when you envisage the doctoral work to be completed. Whilst both you and your supervisor would like the doctorate to be completed as quickly as possible, you must remember that you are undertaking this work as a part-time student and probably also working, so you are likely to have many other commitments. The more that your research is linked to your practice in the workplace then the easier it is to undertake and the sooner the output will be achieved. Whilst our students have said that they liked the *"flexibility as to how long it takes to complete"* and the *"freedom to work at your own pace"* they also liked to be set deadlines to help them move the work forward (Smith et al., 2011). So, setting the dates for your meetings over the first year of the doctorate, and ensuring that you both put these dates in your diaries, will help to structure a working plan for your doctorate and an action plan of what you should be doing at each stage. This may appear to be very regimented but it will help you to meet deadlines and reinforce your time-management skills. Professional doctorate students and supervisors are all busy people with multiple demands on their time and slippage can easily occur on all sides. How often you meet will depend on the stage of your project, but it is probable that you will meet frequently at the beginning of the research process to discuss the structure of the work, less frequently during the research phase as you become more independent and more often during the final phases when you are close to submission. At the beginning, you will want to talk through your ideas to see if they are feasible and sufficiently novel, and this may require a lot of discussion. In the middle stages, you will be working more independently so you will need to spend less time in meetings. However, reducing the frequency of meetings could also mean that you lose your focus and get side-tracked. To avoid this, don't allow big gaps to occur. Try and meet as often as you can, but perhaps shorten the length of time that you meet. Remember that you don't always have to meet face to face, and it is often very simple and equally effective to have virtual meetings. These are particularly valuable when all of you are busy with conflicting work schedules and unable to meet in person. A video conference, using Skype for example, can be very useful and informative, particularly when you have a specific problem which needs a quick resolution. Virtual meetings tend to have the advantage of making you focus on the topic in hand as it is less likely that you will have an informal chat. Similarly, sharing access to an online drop box is a useful way to ensure that documents can be shared whereever you and your supervisors may be.

When agreeing the frequency of your meetings or your plan of work, don't underestimate the lack of control that you may come to have in your professional life. Over the course of their projects, many professional doctorate students experience massive changes in their role within their organisations, their organisational structures and the resources available to them. Some students experience a change in the level of support from their employer, perhaps because a particular manager, who has supported and championed their case, has left the organisation. In other cases, this is purely a result of financial restrictions and occasionally students may be made redundant. In challenging times you may need to explore how your research can transcend your work with an individual employer. By focusing instead on your impact upon your community of practice (Smith et al., 2011) you will be able to demonstrate more 'transdisciplinary and transprofessional' work (Fell et al., 2011, p. 21).

From the beginning, you need to consider the tone of the meetings and what behaviour patterns you all need to adopt in order to achieve this. You will want the meetings to be open and friendly, but not necessarily informal. These are not social occasions and you are all busy working professionals so none of you can afford to waste your precious time. Agreeing to be open and frank in your meetings will help to develop an effective relationship where mutual constructive criticism can take place. Setting the tone of the meeting from the outset is important because the behaviour patterns of all the participants can be established, and maintained successfully throughout the relationship. The tone needs to be relaxed and friendly but remain professional. This is something that you will all need to work on, it will require time, consideration and commitment from everyone if it is to succeed. The relationship needs to be sufficiently robust to allow reciprocal, open and constructive criticism without meetings deteriorating so much that your progress is affected. You both need to create a safe atmosphere where you are not afraid to ask questions, even if they are questions to which you should know the answer. You should be able to use your supervisor as a sounding board for your ideas about your research project and to establish whether they are achievable within a reasonable length of time.

You need to be sufficiently prepared and organised to go into your meetings with an agenda. Ideally, you should agree this with the participants before the meeting (perhaps by email) so that you are all clear about the nature of the discussion, expectations of the work to date and what all of you want out of the meeting. Setting an agenda will focus your mind on what you personally want to achieve from the meeting and can help to bring up issues which you may find difficult to raise in a conversation. You should have work that you can bring to the meeting, as previously agreed with your supervisor. This will allow you to demonstrate your progress so far and your ability to meet deadlines. If progress has not been achieved, then a discussion of the reasons for this should help to remove the barriers to your progress or offer an alternative solution to any problems.

You should personally keep records of all of your meetings with your supervisor. Do this during the actual meeting and finish them off immediately after the meeting has ended, when it is still fresh in your mind. Send the notes and agreed actions to your supervisor as soon as you have completed them, and ask for confirmation of their accuracy so that you both have a clear and shared understanding of the meeting and its agreed follow-up actions. There are a number of good reasons why you, rather than the supervisor, should take the notes of the meeting. Taking that responsibility will:

- Empower you.
- Give you ownership of the process.
- Clearly articulate the agreed actions from the meeting.
- Demonstrate that you have understood what is being asked of you (Clarke et al., 2012).
- Act as an aide-memoire for your work.
- Keep you on track.
- Help you and your supervisor to monitor your progress.
- Provide evidence if there is any dispute about your work, your progress or your supervision.

Your training needs should be analysed as part of the learning contract and inform a professional development plan (PDP). Your formal requirements for training will vary with different universities, as many professional doctorates programmes begin with generic training in information-retrieval skills, identifying resources, academic writing, reflective practice, research design and methodology, ethics and so on. If your professional doctorate programme does not include some of these as taught components then they will form the basis of your key training needs, under the headings of subject knowledge (research methods and information retrieval) and generic skills (critical evaluation and constructing an argument).

All of our professional doctorate students found undertaking the programme to be much more challenging, exciting and motivating than they had initially envisaged. Many students join the programme with unrealistic expectations of the amount, nature and level of the work involved, especially in the process of research, and struggle with the practice of academic writing. In particular, they are often ill-prepared for the level of criticality that they are required to exercise when exploring and interrogating their own familiar work-based issues. They are sometimes looking for clear, straightforward answers which may not exist and can become frustrated with this, and with the supervisor for pointing it out. Thus developing your academic writing ability and the skill of critical enquiry may be a real issue for you, and you may need to work hard with your supervisor to improve your competency in these areas.

Your training needs may include additional requirements, for example in the use of software or specialised research methodology specific to your project. The analysis of your training needs should occur annually and may inform part of the annual monitoring process for your programme, so it is important to keep records of the training.

A key purpose of the supervisory meetings is to plan your individual research and to identify reasonable milestones to drive your work forward and allow you to demonstrate the achievement of your objectives. Some supervisors like you to use project management software to keep your research on track, others prefer to see you use a Gantt chart, whilst some think that an action plan with deadlines is sufficient. Whatever approach you decide to use, you must all agree that the deadlines are reasonable and that you can address any subsequent slippage which may occur on all sides. One of the reasons for creating milestones is to control the project by identifying different stages of the work, planning what each stage will involve, how one stage may depend on another, and predicting how long it will take to achieve each stage. You don't live in an ideal world, and neither do your supervisors. There are many factors which can affect the achievement of each planned stage, and the more responsibilities you have in your professional and personal life the more complex it can be. The more factors that are outside of your personal control, the greater the likelihood that there will be slippage within your project plan. If slippage does begin to happen on either side, then don't try to deny its existence. If a problem is ignored it will quickly get out of hand and be more difficult to address. Your relationship with your supervisor should be based on sufficient trust and honesty to ensure that any problems can be openly discussed. All of you need to agree to meet deadlines, and if they prove to be unrealistic then a frank discussion about targets should be instigated and the project plan reviewed by all of you to take these problems into account.

One of the most important parts of a supervisor's role is to provide you with feedback on your written work so that both of you can judge your progress on the achievement of your thesis. Obtaining feedback on written work is an area of supervision which benefits from the clear articulation of the expectations of both student and supervisor. Supervisors will expect that you are able to express yourself clearly and correctly, both orally and in writing. It is your responsibility to acquire the appropriate writing skills because supervisors won't expect to be correcting your spelling or your grammar. If you are communicating in a language which is not your first language then you need to ensure that you attend writing classes and that you have some support system to ensure that the standard of your writing is adequate. Your supervisor may expect you to have some initial difficulties with the academic style of writing which is appropriate to your subject or discipline. However, in response to your supervisor's feedback, and as you systematically proceed through the writing of your thesis, you soon learn how to address the feedback and your writing will improve. In order for you to get the best feedback from your supervisor when you submit your work you should specify the areas of the work in which you most require feedback: the writing style, the ideas, the evidence, the presentation, the data analysis, your interpretations, the structure of the work, the logic of your discussion and so on. By doing this you have articulated your expectations to your supervisor, and this makes it easier for the supervisor to meet them. If the feedback you receive is unclear then clarify what your supervisor meant by asking specific questions which relate to the points that they raised. Don't be afraid to ask your supervisor for feedback, that is one of their primary functions and they will be expecting it. Don't put off submitting work because you worry that it may be academically incompetent. If you have been out of academic study for some time you are bound to feel this way and your supervisor will anticipate it. They will know that this is an area where you will require a lot of additional support. It is much better to get constructive criticism and support early on when you have lots of time to practise and develop your writing style, rather than at the end of the research when you have a deadline looming and little time to learn a skill you should have already mastered. So, submit written work such as progress reports or draft chapters early on in the process to get the feedback you need as soon as possible. If you feel that your supervisor has only provided feedback on areas that need improvement, and not on areas that were good, then you should ask for more balanced feedback so that you can gauge what you can do well in addition to what needs further development. Similarly, if the feedback is too brief then clarify this by asking questions so that the response is sufficiently expanded. Don't be complacent about sparse feedback, it is important that you are given the full picture because this is how you learn.

One of the ways in which your supervisor can help you to improve your communication skills is by encouraging you to present your work to others. This may sound like a frightening prospect but it serves many useful functions:

- It will improve your personal confidence.
- It provides you with an opportunity to practise structuring and explaining your work.
- It improves your communication skills.
- It will demonstrate the rigour of your work.
- It allows you to receive feedback on your work and can influence your ideas.
- It develops your ability to answer questions about your work and is good practice for your viva.
- It allows you to demonstrate your contribution to your community of practice.

The initial presentation could be a small report to your fellow students or a departmental seminar. Once you have gained confidence with this, then you could submit an abstract to a conference in your field for either a poster display or a short oral presentation. Later, this could be worked up into a full research paper which you could submit to a recognised academic or professional journal or as a chapter for a book, providing the information from your workplace is not sensitive and would not confer a business advantage to others. You will need the agreement of your workplace to do this, and you should include the names of all your supervisors as co-authors as an acknowledgement of their contribution to the work. The more your work is presented to others, and the more external validation your work receives, the more it improves your chances of successfully achieving your professional doctorate. So, when your supervisor suggests that you present your work, don't make excuses not to do it. The undertaking may be painful, but it is worth the effort and your supervisor will help you with it.

It should be clear now what your relationship with your supervisor should look like. In common with any other relationship it will have its ups and downs, but it should always be developmental. The key fact that you must appreciate is that your supervisor does not want you to fail because that may negatively impact on them personally in terms of their research career. So it is in the supervisor's own best interests, as well as yours, to make the relationship work. However, what should you do if the relationship between you and your supervisor breaks down?

8.6 What happens if I disagree with my supervisor?

You must acknowledge that there will be times when you disagree with your supervisor about your work. This could relate to your written content, the amount of research you have undertaken, your data interpretation or your critical evaluation of the work. You have made a massive emotional investment in your professional doctorate and you will have made many personal sacrifices to undertake the work. It means more to you than it does to anyone else and you are more sensitive and protective about it than your supervisor may expect. It is very likely that there will be occasional disagreements between you and your supervisor, and you must try to overcome them by continuing to engage in frank and objective discussion and by keeping a sense of perspective. If there are disagreements, then your supervisor needs to be very explicit about the problems and why they are important so that you can clearly understand the issues and how to resolve them.

If the situation does not improve and you think that your supervisor is being unreasonable, then it is perfectly acceptable to get a second opinion. However, be prepared for the possibility that the second opinion may reinforce the first. If this happens you need to appreciate that you may be wrong(!) and that you need to calm down and look at your work more objectively. Your supervisor is trying to ensure that you achieve the best possible outcome and will have a lot more experience of these things than you have, so you might have to do some more work in order to get a positive outcome. The last thing that you want is for the same issues to come up at a viva and you find that you are not able to defend your work.

If the second opinion supports you and not the supervisor then the situation is more problematic. Your graduate school or professional doctorate team can help you with this and they would be the first port of call in identifying someone who can provide a second or even third overview of your work. If the situation between you and your supervisor deteriorates so much that it cannot continue then the university will have formal procedures which will allow you to change supervisors. However, if you have followed all of the good advice in this chapter then this situation should never develop and your relationship with your supervisor will be a positive and productive one.

Finally, if your supervisor leaves the university unexpectedly then you will need a replacement. It isn't your task to find a new one and your university will have procedures in place to allow for this. One of the advantages of having a supervisory team is that there is a reduced effect on your work during this hiatus in supervision.

Summary

In this chapter we have discussed how to develop an effective working relationship with your supervisor. The key to this is agreement on a learning contract between all parties so that the expectations of all concerned are clearly articulated and everyone understands their role in the process. The learning contract largely relates to what you should expect from your supervisor and what your supervisor should expect from you. One of these expectations relates to the dissemination of your findings and demonstrating how you have influenced your community of practice, which is covered in more detail in the next chapter.

9 Dissemination and Influencing your Community of Practice

On completion of this chapter you will:
▶ be able to identify strategies for disseminating your work
▶ be able to examine the practicalities of particular dissemination approaches

9.1 Introduction

A primary aim of the professional doctorate is to demonstrate an impact on practice. In order to make an impact people need to know what you are doing and why you are doing it. This might seem an obvious thing to state but it is something which is overlooked by many. It is not just a case of disseminating everything you have done. The dissemination needs to be achieved in a focused and planned manner, and this means publishing in appropriate journals and other literature. Some form of dissemination should be considered when you have produced something which you think might be of interest to other practitioners and which could open a discussion leading to a change of views. The product can be an original research study, a series of reflections on the research activities or a novel way of presenting or synthesising material. Usually, it is about something which has worked particularly well, but it could be based on something which has not worked and from which a lesson can be learned. Often a really positive message and strategic approach can come out of something which was an apparent failure. The overriding principles are that people need to know what has been done and that the information is presented in an efficient and effective manner. This chapter will explore appropriate ways in which this can be achieved.

Dissemination is an integral part of a professional doctorate programme of study. As circumstances and professions can differ greatly, there is no one clear or obvious approach to dissemination, but the common factor is that all dissemination involves a strategic approach. In many professional doctorates dissemination is integral to the entire process. For example, the doctorate may be built around action research in which there is a continuous cycle of dissemination or it may be built upon innovations which the candidate has introduced to their individual practice. Whatever the scenario, it is important that the innovations and experience are disseminated to the wider community of practice. In thinking of dissemination, it is very important that a strategic approach is followed. Dissemination can happen in an unplanned manner, but it will be considerably more effective if it is properly planned and focused.

9.2 Dissemination at a local level

The first, and perhaps most important, area is dissemination at a local level. This is integral to the professional doctorate which, by its very nature, is concerned with the development of practice and necessitates working with other people from the outset. Chapter 11 outlines some of our candidates' stories and details their particular projects and the ways in which this issue was addressed. Most have one thing in common: the need to bring others on board and to do it right from the start. Dissemination of the ideas, at least, is an important aspect of the professional doctorate. In action research projects, dissemination of the development at each stage is quite formally built into the project. In others, points of feedback are planned at systematic intervals.

Once the professional doctorate is complete, perhaps a more formal dissemination strategy is required. This dissemination of findings can be written or oral, printed or electronic. Usually in the case of work-based projects, a report is required and the requirements of the project tend to structure the report. Reports commence with an executive summary in which the key points are laid out and discussed. As in all publications it is important to determine who the audience is and to tailor the report to meet their particular requirements. It can be useful to introduce visuals in the report and diagrams can be an effective means of putting across ideas. The structure can vary quite considerably from a journal paper because points tend to be made succinctly. Oral presentations are another means of dissemination; PowerPoint® presentations can be included in your portfolio of evidence.

It is important, particularly in work-based dissemination, to demonstrate the impact that your work has had on practice and, when possible, you should link your reports and presentations to a tangible outcome. Feedback is beneficial and important, and it is useful to collect and correlate any feedback or dialogue you have been having about particular projects. This can be difficult when you have published a journal article and you are relying on feedback from other people, but at a local level it is more straightforward and you should see dissemination very much as part of your project.

9.3 The importance of dissemination

Before thinking in any great depth about your own dissemination strategy, it is important to ask the question: who comprises my community of practice?

This may seem obvious, but it is worth bearing in mind that your community of practice may not be the same as your profession or those sharing a job title. For example, someone with a nursing background may be involved with quality management and quality managers from a range of backgrounds are the community that they are trying to influence. So, it is worth considering who or what groups would be most interested in your work.

Once you have established who the community comprises, it is useful to ask whether there are any segments or further sub-groupings. A group of academics may be interested in the innovation, but there may also be people in managerial positions who have the power to implement (or allow implementation of) the changes. Apart from the practitioners, in some instances the general public may be interested in what is happening in practice. All of these segments of the community will require quite different dissemination approaches.

Activity 1

Spend some time thinking about your community of practice.

⬤ Who does this community comprise?

⬤ Are there any sub-groupings?

Jean, a professional doctorate candidate, is a nurse involved in bringing about innovation in clinical practice. She determined that her particular community involved academics, who were interested in the area of practice, senior nurses in managerial positions, who could appreciate and influence policy decisions, and practitioners, who would bring about the changes in practice which she suggested. The activity was useful to Jean because very different dissemination strategies were required for the different groups.

Once you have made the decision to disseminate your work and you have identified your particular community or area of practice, you need to consider where it should be presented. That is why it is important to think of the different areas or segments of practice. For example, the academic community publishes in particular journals, whereas practitioners may look at the academic journals but will more regularly read a trade or professional paper. For example, teachers have numerous academic publications but many teachers (practitioners) in the UK will turn to the *Times Educational Supplement*. Similarly for nurses, there are several academic journals but many UK practitioners will regularly read the *Nursing Times* or *Nursing Standard*.

If you wish to reach a large number of professional people, rather than a more specialist audience, you might consider publishing in a popular journal. However, if you wish to reach the public then the general press might be more appropriate. Relevant questions are:

- What journals do people working in the area consider?
- What are the top-rated journals?
- Is there a standard trade journal aimed at practitioners rather than journals aimed more at academics?

The paper or journal that people use when looking for jobs is a good example of where to turn for a publication with a wide dissemination. As well as the formal means of publication, internal reports or widely-used teaching materials are very powerful means of communication and dissemination. Written communications are important, but do remember that communication also takes place via speech. Conference publications in particular can be an important means of dissemination.

Another important question concerns when to go public. This also needs some careful consideration. If you publish too soon your innovations may not have been tested, and if you leave it too late you may lack the evidence of impact which is vital for the professional doctorate – your innovations have already become part of accepted practice. That is why it is important to plan the dissemination from the beginning of your study.

In this chapter the following areas will be considered:

- Academic peer-reviewed journals
- Conference presentations
- Poster presentations
- Professional journals and magazines
- The media
- Internet-based material
- Local dissemination
- Books.

This list is by no means exhaustive; rather these suggestions are an indication of the range and types of publications which can facilitate dissemination to a wider audience. It is also useful to bear in mind that the first three would be directed predominantly to the academic community; the remainder are more appropriate for a much wider range of people, including your professional community or the general public.

9.4 Academic peer reviewed journals

Academic peer reviewed journals are the pinnacle for people striving to publish within a particular discipline or community of practice. It is therefore important that any papers submitted represent fully-formed work. This is not to say that you need to have finished your professional doctorate, but any papers submitted should represent a substantive piece of work. In addition to an editor and editorial board the journal has a team of reviewers who are active in publishing and in researching the particular area or discipline; hence the term 'peer reviewed'. The reviewers are called to comment on submitted papers, and they do it 'blind', that is they do not know the identity of the author. Rather than using a regular team of reviewers, the editors ask people who are considered to be experts in the area of the paper's content to review it. This ensures rigour in the process.

Most journals will accept an electronic copy of the paper, some by email whilst others will have a website using specialist software to facilitate the electronic submission. Using an online system to submit a journal paper is daunting for the novice, but it is another opportunity for learning more about the process of publishing your work. It is important to read the instructions very carefully and to follow them step by step. A key principle to the whole process is the anonymity of the review, and you are likely to be asked to submit your biographical details in a separate file. Although initially time-consuming, once the paper is submitted that's it (!) and a confirmatory email is quickly sent. Although the submission itself is fairly quick, the time it takes to get a response from the reviewers should not be underestimated. Most journals are committed to a speedy turnaround time of one to three months, but you can sometimes wait much longer.

On receiving a paper, and before sending it out for review, the editor will consider whether it is appropriate for the journal, both in terms of standard and subject. If it is deemed suitable for possible publication, it will go out for peer review to two (and sometimes three) people who will comment on the work and decide on its appropriateness for publication. The reviewers will make this decision independently and anonymously; they do not know who the author is or who else is reviewing the paper.

The decisions reached will be in one of the following categories:

- Accept – the paper is accepted with no changes
- Accept subject to minor amendments
- Resubmit with major amendments
- Reject—the paper is deemed to be inappropriate for the particular journal.

Acceptance with no changes can happen, but is comparatively rare. More commonly, the paper needs to be resubmitted with minor or major amendments. The author will receive these comments, and the reviewers will clearly indicate the amendments which they would like to see. Sometimes the comments are supplied line by line or they can be more general references to sections which are required to be rewritten or refocused. The important point here is that egos should be left to one side, the reviewers do not know the identity of the author and the suggestions are about improving and developing the paper. The work will benefit from these comments.

When selecting a journal, look at its rating. Journals are rated according to their impact, based on the number of times articles from that journal are cited in other people's work. The higher the impact factor the more people will want to publish in the particular journal and, naturally, the aim of most researchers is to publish in a high impact journal.

An additional factor to consider is appropriateness – whether your topic is appropriate for that particular journal. It is helpful to have a journal in mind before writing, or certainly finishing, the paper so that you can ensure the content and style are in keeping with the requirements of the particular journal. Most journals have a website which details issues such as house style, referencing system and preferred length. It is also good practice to look at an edition of the journal and analyse the style and content of published articles.

Open access publications are on-line journals which are scholarly and subject to peer review. Their main distinction from other journals, newspapers and magazines is that readers do not pay for the journal. There are different costing models: open access journals may be subsidised by academic institutes or writers may pay for publication. Papers are still subject to peer review and can be rejected, and open access publications are comparable to traditional journals in terms of their quality.

If the article you have written is rejected (which may be done at editorial level) it's not necessarily negative. It could be because the paper is not appropriate for that journal or because the journal has recently published several articles on that particular topic area. When rejected, feedback is given on the reasons why and these can be taken into account in the subsequent revision.

9.5 Conference presentations

Most subject areas (or communities of practice) have conferences where people can familiarise themselves with recent innovations. Conferences are usually held annually in fairly nice venues. Once you have identified the appropriate community of practice, check out which conference is suitable for presenting your work. Details of upcoming conferences can be found in journals and, perhaps more effectively, on relevant websites. It's always a good idea to attend these conferences, or as many as you can! Certainly you should try and attend the one most relevant to your work. It is a very good way of meeting people and networking, but it is also an excellent opportunity to present your ideas in a public forum and to see other work in progress.

When a conference is first announced there is a 'call for abstracts' by which people are requested to submit a summary with a view to either presenting a conference paper or a poster presentation. Sometimes there are also categories asking people to run a workshop or seminar, but the first two categories are the most likely.

The first thing to note about a conference presentation is that (usually) this will not be a presentation to the entire conference of several hundred people! It will be given to a small sub-section of attendees, 20 or so people, at most. As there will be several sessions running concurrently your audience will have actively chosen to attend and will be particularly interested in your area and your presentation. Many conferences aim to be inclusive and to give everyone who applies a chance to present, provided their abstract is appropriate and of the required standard.

Once the abstract is accepted, the next step is to prepare the actual presentation. Some conferences ask for a paper which is published in book form, but more commonly they publish the collected abstracts. You will be told the timing of the presentation, which is usually a half-hour slot with 20 minutes for presentation and 10 minutes for questions. There will be IT facilities, and it is usual to make a PowerPoint® presentation. It is sometimes difficult to condense all that you want to say into 20 minutes, so your slides will need to demonstrate impact.

It is useful to present your ideas in a format that enables you to gauge the reaction of your audience because the feedback can be helpful and give future directions for the work. People will be interested in your ideas and often discussion goes on after the session is finished. It is, therefore, useful to bring business cards or some other means of giving your contact details as people often wish to contact you afterwards for more information.

It is common for presenters to bring 'hand-outs' or copies of their presentation. However, it is always difficult to foretell how many people will attend your session, and inevitably you will either bring too many or too few hand-outs, so it is best to give your email address or produce web-based materials that people can easily access.

It is also important to emphasise that attendance at conferences is not just about you presenting your work. It is also an excellent opportunity to hear about recent developments in your field of practice, as people at conferences will discuss their work in progress. The usual format for conferences is to have keynote speakers, who are prominent people in the domain of the conference and will deliver an address to the entire conference. Their presentation will be followed by a series of concurrent sessions, and you will probably present as one of these speakers. It is very useful to go to other sessions as this gives you an opportunity to see work in progress and to get a feel for other people's work. You will not be able to attend all of the concurrent sessions, so you will need to choose carefully. Often the conference programme is sent to participants well in advance so that you can choose the most relevant sessions.

Conferences are also useful networking occasions and provide opportunities for informal discussions. Often people are working in comparative isolation, with immediate colleagues who are not directly related to the same area of practice. At conferences many attendees are working in a similar area, and it's an excellent opportunity to meet and discuss issues with fellow researchers. This is why it is important to spend your time wisely. Planning is very important and, as well as pinpointing the sessions you wish to attend, it can be helpful to look at the list of delegates to see if there is anyone who would be useful to meet. Of course, there will also be chance encounters with people, and the opportunity to discuss and ask questions about issues raised at the concurrent sessions.

9.6 Poster presentations

Most conferences have sections for poster presentations, and this gives people the opportunity to exhibit their work in a public forum. The poster will reach a lot more people than the concurrent session, but not in the same degree of detail nor with the opportunity for issues to be explored to the same extent. Nonetheless, a poster presentation is an excellent way of bringing your work to the attention of many interested people.

Conferences will have an area for posters which people can view during coffee and lunch breaks. It is important that you are standing beside your poster and are available to discuss it with interested parties. It is also worth bearing in mind that many conferences have prizes for the best posters and any special effort in preparation can be worth it!

There is an art to making a poster and the key principle is accessibility. The viewer should easily grasp the key points and get a good sense of the work on which the poster is based. The poster should not bombard the viewer with information, and it should be visibly appealing and engaging without being sensational. Most commonly, the poster is divided into sections, and each section has one or two paragraphs. Where possible a diagram should be included because this is an easy way of getting many points across. If the poster is based on a research study than it should be designed around the usual headings of aims, literature review, methodology, results and discussion, and the key points of each section should be succinctly summarised. It is useful to use colour as this can make points stand out and get viewers' attention very quickly. It also worth mentioning that references should be included on the poster.

The conference will give details about the expected layout and format of the poster, usually A1 in size and laminated. It is a good idea to look at the posters presented at other conferences to get a sense of the format. There are a number of IT packages which can help with the preparation of the poster and the reprographics department in your university may be able to assist, as will a number of commercial graphic design and printing organisations.

9.7 Professional journals and magazines

In some communities of practice academic publications are an excellent means of disseminating material. In the case of the professional doctorate, where the attempt is to disseminate to a wide range of people within the community of practice, bear in mind that not everyone will read academic journals! For this reason you might consider publishing your work within a professional journal.

Most professional groups will have a journal aimed at practitioners, which may contain a synopsis of recent research and news about developments within the profession. One student, who is a personal trainer, wished to disseminate his findings to as large a range of readers as possible. He planned to publish in an academic journal but he also wrote a shorter article for publication in a more popular journal such as *Men's Health*. A useful means of identifying the appropriate journal or magazine is to consider which is most commonly read and/or which one people turn to when they are looking for a job.

The style of writing may be different from the more formal academic press, and it is worth looking at the journal to ascertain its particular style. It is also important to read carefully the instructions for authors, which can be obtained on the journal or paper's website. Once the article is written, your first job is to get it proof-read for any typographical mistakes or errors of expression. It is also worth getting a friend or colleague working in the area to read the article to pick up any technical errors or ambiguities. When submitting an article to a professional journal the same principles apply as with an academic journal.

9.8 The media

Another area for presenting your work is the media. Unlike the professional and academic press, some skill is required when dealing with the general media. It can be useful to disseminate via the media if your work is likely to be of interest to the general public. Public opinion may be important as feedback or in gaining acceptance for your innovations, and this may be gained through the local or national press. The press are always looking for stories, particularly those which have a human interest or tie in with a key issue. Your university will have a press office that will be very happy to give advice. They will be able to advise on whether or not your work will be of interest to the press and, if so, they can help with the process. It is best to contact the paper's subject editor (such as education or health) by telephone or email, and prepare an outline of the issues in case they wish to hear more. Sometimes this is enough, or they may contact you for an interview by telephone or face to face. It is important to be realistic and ensure that the item is of genuine interest before contacting the paper. The news editor will be the appropriate person to contact if there is no designated editor for your particular area.

Whilst it is useful to disseminate via the press, and indeed it can be very fruitful, it is also important to emphasise that newspapers want maximum impact. If you are not dealing with a specialist, the paper may go for maximum impact to the detriment of your ideas. They may not accurately reflect what you are trying to communicate, nor are they concerned with building relationships in the subject area in the same way as a specialist journal. Journalists will not falsify or distort stories, but they will go for impact, and this is a factor which should be considered when sending material for publication. Journalists will not take kindly to requests to see articles before publication – they are professional writers and would consider such requests as compromising their professionalism. So, it is important that anything you send to them is accurate and reflects exactly the message you want to get across. It is also important that you gain permission from your supervisors and, if it relates to any work-related issues, your employers.

A useful approach is to put out a news release. These are usually in the region of 300 to 500 words and should be short and snappy, using short sentences and paragraphs and spelling out the issue with maximum impact. Start with the conclusions and put any opinions or quotes from others in inverted commas. This can be sent by email with your release as an attachment or in the body of the email, which should be followed up by a telephone call.

Another approach is to build up a relationship with a paper which is looking for experts on specific issues. This can also make it easier to get things in the press. It is important that you think about the wider implications of your work by looking at related articles in the local and national press and by reflecting on the type and impact of those articles, as the following example illustrates.

Case study

Rob, was involved in setting up a free school in an inner city area. The first step was to state the case for the school and to gain backing from the local community. Rob thought an article in the press would be a good means of gaining publicity and raising awareness of what he was trying to do. He particularly wanted to put across the philosophy of the school. The school wished to establish a very different educational approach from the state schools, which followed the national curriculum. The basis of the argument was that there was a history of under-achievement in the area, which had many social problems. Whilst the teaching in all of the existing schools was excellent, Rob argued that an alternative approach would help a greater number of young people to achieve. The entire *raison d'être* for the school was based on providing an alternative, and not on criticism of the present provision. At his interview, Rob explained this very clearly and logically.

However, the paper's article slanted things in a particular way, with the focus on under-achievement in the local young people and how the Free School planned to rectify these deficiencies. A photograph of Rob, which the paper had on file, showed him standing in front of one of the local schools (its name clearly visible in the background). On a quick viewing of the article and the heading it looked as if Rob was directly criticising (or attacking) the standards of the school, which was far from the case. Needless to say, this particular attempt at dissemination did little for future relations between Rob and the local educational community, and Rob had to write an explanatory letter to all the schools. Whilst it did not in the longer term adversely affect the project, the article certainly did not have its planned effect initially.

The wider political issues should be considered before interacting with the press. The free school agenda was regarded suspiciously by the local school teachers who feared for their jobs and the left-wing council was ideologically opposed to the whole idea, so it is not surprising that the report met with some hostility. It is useful to consider the possible reaction before the interaction with the press, and then the issues can be focused in such a way that the article gives a more balanced viewpoint.

Dealing with the media requires a degree of skill and knowledge of the system, and should be done in a careful and thoughtful manner. If approached in this spirit, it can be a fruitful way of disseminating to a large audience. It is also worth remembering that you should only go to the press if you think the subject is of wide interest. Many projects, no matter how dear to the individual and how good, often are only of interest to a narrow range of specialists.

9.9 Internet-based material

The internet is another useful means of dissemination, and there are many e-journals of the same quality and applying the same degree of rigour as paper-based journals. Many 'issues' (such as medical conditions) have specific websites and are often happy to publish news on developments within the area. Depending on the focus of your work, this can be a useful means of dissemination. However, you need to be careful when publishing in this manner because websites vary in quality and some contain inaccurate information.

Before rushing into producing material for the internet, it is useful to stand back and consider its advantages and the disadvantages. It is relatively easy and straightforward to produce material and many people can easily access it very quickly. It is also fairly easy to keep the material up to date and in many ways, such as a link to email, it is simple to open up channels of communication. One disadvantage is that it can be expensive to maintain, particularly if you wish to be innovative and use multimedia techniques. The internet contains a wide range of 'research' material, from electronically-based, high calibre academic journals to websites which simply reflect a range of opinions. It is worth bearing in mind that this is how your website may be perceived, so you need to spend some time on a design that reflects the significance of its content.

The reasons why you want a website should be given a great deal of consideration before you commence setting it up. People create websites for a variety of reasons: commonly it is to provide goods or services with some form of financial reimbursement in mind, or maybe to gather information (such as in a research study) or to disseminate information and keep particular issues in the public domain. It is unlikely, although not entirely improbable, that you will set up a website for financial gain! However, it can be a useful means of gaining information for research purposes. It is more likely that you are planning to disseminate information, and the remainder of this section will consider this scenario.

The web is a very useful means of dissemination. Setting up a website can be an excellent way of reaching a large number of people and, when talking at conferences or meeting people interested in your work, it can be useful to refer them to your website. There are many websites which offer advice about the development of web-based material, and they can give detailed guidance as well as very useful tips. Many organisations have IT departments who can assist with the development of a website and will enable links for the use of search engines.

Much of this technology can seem daunting to the novice, but it is quite easy to build up a degree of skill and apply the technology in an increasingly sophisticated manner. The key principle and purpose of a website is to disseminate your work to a wider public – it is a means of interaction and not an end in itself. It can be tempting to use a variety of sophisticated techniques, but these can be very expensive and require high-level IT and design skills, and they may not add much to your key purpose of setting up the site.

There are, however, some practicalities to consider in setting up a website. You need a web address, and this is your domain name, which can be bought from several websites, for example 1 & 1 my website.

You then need to find a host. The World Wide Web links computers, as the name suggests, all over the world. Web browsers such as Firefox® can identify your address on the host server and open the website. Again, there are many hosting websites which offer a number of options, and these can be expensive or relatively cheap. Wordpress®, for example, is very popular and has two options: wordpress.com is inexpensive and provides very basic facilities for uploading information, wordpress.org is considerably more complex but will enable you to build a high-quality website. It very much depends on your particular needs and the purpose of your site.

You are now in a position to design your website. There are several points which should be taken into account when planning how to organise your website. The overriding principle is that the website is not for your amusement – it is a means of interacting with other people. This is an important consideration and should guide you when designing the layout. The website should be easy to navigate and user-friendly. When you create the pages you need to consider the content (information should only be included if it has a purpose) and practical design issues such as colours and background. Readability is another key issue, entailing considerations such as font, type size, paragraph length, background and and text colour and so on, to maximise engagement with the viewer. Useful advice on website design can be obtained from the many sites and books on the subject. It is also important to update the website on a regular basis. There is nothing worse than an out-of-date website with inaccurate and misleading information, especially one which was set up to promote innovation and change.

The term 'blog' is short for 'web log' and, as the name suggests, a blog provides a chronological account of your communications. Blogs are much cheaper than regular websites and easier to maintain. Items can be added quickly by the press of a button. So, with minimal work, information can be widely transmitted – the hard part is getting people to read your blog! Blogs can be interactive and it is becoming increasingly common for people to use them as a means of communication by adding comments, although of course you have no control over what people might add. Alternatively, an email address can be added to the blog and people invited to respond via email.

Social networking sites, such as Facebook®, Twitter® and LinkedIn®, can also be used to reach a large number of people. Many businesses and even academic groups are using social networking as a means of disseminating information and interacting with each other. However, as the name 'social' implies, these sites are not primarily for research or business purposes and, no matter how serious your material, it links to a more frivolous site and may not portray quite the image you had in mind!

The leading social networking sites in the UK are:

- *Facebook*® – people can freely and easily interact with others who are signed on; it is used primarily for social communications, although some people use it for more serious purposes.
- *Twitter*® – people post messages up to 40 characters long, known as 'tweets', which other people then follow; there are over 100 million followers of tweets (although not all of the same one); it is relatively easy to operate, and you can set up a free account with twitter.com.

● *LinkedIn®* – popular with the business community, you can set up a page with your details to get you known and create contacts; it is an excellent opportunity for networking although it would be useful to check it is popular with your community of practice before you sign up.

9.10 Publishing a book

Another means of dissemination is to publish a book based on your work. Normally this is something you would do when your work is complete. However, that need not always be the case. For example, as part of the demonstration of impact on practice some candidates may publish a textbook and assess its impact on a specific area of practice. If you decide to publish a book, the first thing to bear in mind is that publishers do not like unsolicited manuscripts, and the second point is that it is unlikely your work will be a best seller and make millions!

It is also worth considering the type of audience you have in mind. Do you wish to present your work in an academic monograph which explores the theory and methods, or do you wish to disseminate your findings to practitioners, perhaps as a textbook in a particular subject area? This will determine the style and scope of the book and the publisher you choose to approach.

Unlike many other methods of dissemination, academic publishing is a purely commercial matter so you will need to convince the publisher that your idea is financially viable.

When approaching a publisher it is best to select one who publishes the type of book you envisage in your area of practice. Publishers usually require a detailed proposal which includes a rationale for the book and a consideration of how it fits into the current market. This proposal will be sent out to experts in the field who will review your proposal and make recommendations to the publisher. If you propose to publish your professional doctorate it will require considerable editing into a different format and style from that of your doctoral submission. Details of what is required can be found on publishers' websites.

Your work can be published as a monograph but an alternative is a chapter in an edited book. If people know you are working in a particular area, they may ask you to write a chapter. Indeed, one of our students was asked to write a chapter for an edited book after someone heard her speak at a conference.

Summary

If you are going to bring about innovation in practice then people need to know what you are doing and what you have achieved. This chapter has outlined various approaches to disseminating that information. It is not exhaustive and you may be able to think of other ways to publicise your findings, but the important principle is to think about your audience and target them directly in the way that has the highest impact. To summarise:

- At the planning stages begin to think of dissemination and identify a strategy.
- Think of dissemination not as something you will do at the end of your study but as an on-going activity.
- Identify your current community of practice and its various segments.
- Think of the most appropriate approach to dissemination for all of your communities' segments.
- Follow the codes of practice for your chosen means of dissemination.
- Do get feedback and capture these responses.

10 Assessment and the Oral Examination

> **On completion of this chapter you will:**
> ▶ understand the practical issues in preparing for the final assessment
> ▶ know how to present a thesis, portfolio and/or artefacts for assessment
> ▶ be able to prepare for your viva

10.1 Writing the thesis

Usually when a candidate begins a doctorate, the final assessment seems a long way off but this doesn't mean that it can be ignored until the work is near completion. Preparation for the final assessment should start on day one of the project. Achieving your final goal of obtaining a doctorate should always be in your mind and your research is the journey that you take to get to that end point. Leshem and Trafford (2002) call this planned approach 'the stepping stones to achieving your doctorate'. This is what our students say:

> *"Top tips to achieving your doctorate:*
> *1 Realistically plan.*
> *2 Realistically plan more.*
> *3 Realistically plan some more again!*
> *4 Stick to the plan, but review constantly and adapt."*

> *"On reflection I began the preparation for my viva I suppose from the outset of the programme. I had to reflect, refine and contextualise throughout the process and this is probably for most people, the most useful thing they can do in business."*

Regardless of how your professional doctorate is assessed or what has been produced at the end of the work, you will be required to undertake a substantial piece of academic writing and undertake an oral examination, also known as a *viva voce*, to defend your work. It is good advice to write up your work as it proceeds, and this writing should develop over the time of your doctorate so that as you reach the end it is as close as possible to the final version. There are many reasons for doing this but the main one is to ensure that your work is completed in the minimum time, and with the minimum amount of post-viva corrections. You are a busy person, working and researching concurrently, and spare time is not something that you have in abundance, so you must use your time efficiently.

Some professional doctoral candidates may think that this is unrealistic when they consider all of the conflicting demands on their time and put off writing until they have a block of time available to do nothing but write. In reality, this block of time rarely occurs and, when it does happen, it isn't long enough. The best approach is to do a little writing every day. Just one hour a day is equivalent to seven hours, or one day, a week spent writing. Everyone should be able to find a free hour at some point through the day and doing a little at a time in this way prevents you from avoiding writing or becoming stale. It also means that there is less to do if you have a large block of time to dedicate to writing.

If you have never written in an academic way before, then you may need to develop and practise an academic writing style. This necessity reinforces the message to start writing early so that you can practise until perfection. Numerous books on the subject are available, for example Murray (2006; 2011). Your university probably runs sessions for doctoral students on academic writing and writing up your thesis. You must endeavour to understand and practise this specialised skill, otherwise your thesis may not be acceptable to your examiners. It is the usual practice in academic writing to use the third person and past tense. However, in professional doctorates it is often acceptable to use the first person in part, or in the whole, of the thesis. Many professional doctorates relate to the development of professional practice and the candidate's role in influencing their community of practice. Indeed in some qualitative research paradigms, phenomenology for example (Laverty, 2003), the role of the researcher and their influence on the research is an integral consideration. It is often difficult or clumsy in these circumstances not to use the first person and Hyland (2001) argues that using the first person pronoun is significant for evidencing that it is your research and your scholarly identity. The selection of the style of academic writing that you wish to adopt should be made after discussion with your supervisor.

Drafts of sections or chapters should be given regularly to your academic supervisor for feedback, and that feedback should be addressed as soon as it is returned. It is through this developmental process that learning takes place, and academic writing style improves quickly early on in the research phase when there is still time for you to work on it. This may seem to be an onerous task at the beginning, but the benefits are huge and will be greatly appreciated when the end point of the research is in sight and time is running out. It also means that you are not overloading your supervisor with several chapters at once near the end of the project when they are trying to give you feedback quickly so that you can submit you work on time. If everything is left to the last minute then the feedback may lack detail and you may miss an opportunity to enhance your work.

Your university will have a set of requirements which relate to the physical structure and layout of the thesis, for example font size, line spacing, page set-up. Find out what these are and set up a matching template on your computer so that you use this format from the start and don't have to spend a time reformatting your writing at the end. A good tip is to use stylesheets, especially for chapter headings, headings and sub-headings. These icons are located in the tool bar of your word processing software. Using specified heading styles will enable the word-processing software to automatically generate a table of contents when your thesis is finished. Ensure that you set up your computer to autosave your documents every five minutes and copy your files to an external device such as a memory stick at the end of the session. That way, if you do encounter a software/hardware problem then you should not lose much work. Ensure that you switch on the auto-speller to reduce typographical errors and that it is set to the correct version of whatever language you are using.

If you would like to use diagrams, figures, tables and so on, consider first why you want to include them and how you will use them. Diagrams are a very useful method of, for example, presenting data, specialised equipment, plans/layouts, summaries or the relationship between concepts. They should be used when they are the only possible vehicle to demonstrate the point in question, and shouldn't be used as illustrations. Don't use diagrams if they don't add anything to the writing or if you are replicating in a diagram what is already in a table. They should have a clear legend so that the reader can understand the diagram without having to go to the text to read about it first.

Your thesis must be well structured with clearly laid-out chapters which have a logical flow from one to another. The aims and objectives should be clearly stated at the outset, followed by an account of how they came to be developed, either through personal experience and/or through a literature review or both. The aim is the overall goal of the work and should be stated in broad terms. The objectives are the ways in which you intend to achieve the aim and again are stated in broad terms. Your objectives will show each logical step that you have undertaken in order to achieve the aim. The research questions are derived from the aim and objectives, and are clear questions that will be asked and specifically answered by your research. Most importantly, the external examiner will be able to see from reading your thesis that they have been answered. One student's aim, objectives and research questions are given as an example in the case study opposite.

The aim, objectives and research questions don't have to be set in stone at the beginning of the research; you can go back and change them as you come to the end. You could liken your work to a journey. Before you start, you have a rough idea of where you want to go but you don't know exactly where you will arrive or how you are going to get there. Remember that your research is novel; no one else has done this before and therefore you can't know when you start off where exactly you will end up. You may predict where you are going but you won't know specifically. As you complete

Case study

AIM

The aim of the research is to look at the impact of mandatory health and safety training on small businesses in the automotive engineering sector.

OBJECTIVES

I will do this by:

- *identifying the rationale of the large multinational car manufacturer for specifying mandatory health and safety training to its suppliers;*
- *evaluating the nature and extent of the training requirement;*
- *determining the impact on five small suppliers to the automotive industry of a mandatory and specified health and safety training requirement by a large multinational car manufacturer.*

RESEARCH QUESTIONS

This will be achieved by answering the following research questions:

- *What was the rationale of the large multinational car manufacturer for specifying mandatory health and safety training?*
- *What are the advantages and disadvantages of the training programme to the five suppliers?*
- *What changes need to be made to the working practices of the five suppliers in response to this requirement?*
- *What was the overall impact of the training requirement on the financial performance of the five suppliers?*

each stage of the research, you will know exactly where you have got to so you can go back and revise your aim(s), objectives and research questions to reflect this. This provides a clearly defined and planned structure to your work, which is known as a conceptual framework.

You need to be able to clearly demonstrate this conceptual framework, which overtly articulates your theoretical overview and how you have logically structured your research (Leshem and Trafford, 2007). Your writing should make this conceptual framework fully explicit. Every chapter should start by stating what was achieved in the previous chapter and how these findings have led on to the next logical step in the process, which is the stated objective of the current chapter. The end of each chapter should include a summary of the main findings and how the objective has been achieved. The introductory paragraphs and final summaries serve to link the chapters together and act as sign-posts for the external examiner to remind them of what you are trying to achieve. In this structured way, you are guiding the external examiner through your work, demonstrating that you have reflected on your findings and have logically planned and progressed through your research (Doncaster and Thorne, 2000). Although the final assessment outputs will vary with different types of professional doctorates – for example, a portfolio, an artefact, a collection of published works – you will still be required to undertake a large piece of reflective and evaluative writing. This writing should refer constantly to these additional elements, such as the artefact or portfolio, to show a clear articulation of how one has informed the other.

The writing should be referenced and an accurate reference list generated and stored in parallel with the main text as you write. This will ensure that the final preparation for submitting the thesis isn't spent searching for an elusive but vital reference which you read years earlier and subsequently lost. You must use your university's designated reference style, and you must use it consistently through your writing. Get into the habit of citing each reference correctly in the separate reference list as you write because it is a long and painful task to check and re-write every single reference. New literature pertaining to your topic will be published over the time period of your professional doctorate, so don't assume that you have finished your literature review once you have written it. Your work must be updated as you go to incorporate the research literature on your topic that you should be reading as you research. This stops you getting stale, demonstrates that you are aware of what is being published and, most importantly, enables you to confirm that your work is unique and novel. The research papers which are absolutely fundamental to your work should be mainly discussed in your discussion chapter rather than the literature review. They can be cited in the review at the beginning of the thesis, but save your most in-depth discussion, which will place it in the context of your own research, until the discussion of your findings in the final chapters. If you discuss your research question in great depth at the beginning of your thesis, there is a danger that you will answer the question before you have begun to report on the research. The literature review should provide the context to your research question. It should demonstrate to the external examiner that the question is worth asking, that you understand the background to your research field and that you have considered it before undertaking the research.

As you write and re-write your work, try and correct typographical errors as you go along. Although you may miss some, you should really endeavour to keep them to a minimum. When an external examiner reads a thesis and finds it to be full of mistakes, then several subliminal messages are transmitted:

- The work has not been properly finished, what else has not been done properly?
- This person is careless; does that mean that the research is careless?
- This person is not taking this work seriously, so why should I?
- This person seems to think that I am a proof-reader not an external examiner.

The last thing that you want when you go into a viva is for the external examiner to have a bad impression of you and your work, so take proof-reading very seriously and if possible have someone else second-read it just to check for errors.

You must keep multiple back-up copies of your writing as you go and these should be stored on separate devices and in different locations. It is quite shocking to hear of the number of people who lose years of hard work because they have misplaced the laptop which contained the only copy of their research or who were burgled and had their laptop and adjacent memory sticks stolen.

10.2 What makes the work doctoral level?

There are numerous national (Vitae, 2012a, 2012b; QAA, 2012) and international bodies (European University Association, 2005; Council of Australian Deans and Directors of Graduate Studies, 2007; Council of Graduate Schools, 2008) that govern qualifications at this level and specify descriptions of what a doctoral level piece of work should look like. All of them emphasise the critical evaluation of the original findings presented in the thesis in the context of the literature, and originality in the context of your research. Critical evaluation doesn't just mean describing what you found or quoting back what is said in the literature. You must demonstrate that you have looked objectively at your findings and those of other published research to see if there are any flaws in the design of the research or in the interpretation of the data.

At this level of work, it is expected that you should be able to independently construct arguments for and against the findings and to use evidence to support your interpretation (Vitae, 2012a, 2012b). Try to ensure that, as you evaluate your findings, you include what changes you would make if you were to repeat the research. Even the most well-constructed research methodology will include flaws which will only become apparent once the findings have been analysed. Before you undertake your research you can only predict what your research data will tell you. It is only after you have collected, analysed and interpreted the data, and fully understood what it means, that you might realise that the research design should have been different. You have posited a research question but the answer may suggest that you should have asked a different question; that is the basic function of the research process. Theoretically you could go round and round in a circle until your predictions perfectly match reality, but this is rarely achieved because the circumstances and the environment in which you have undertaken the research are constantly changing.

When you start to undertake research at this level, you will, like most other students, focus on the outputs of the research and believe that the actual research findings themselves are the important thing. At the end of the doctorate comes the self-realisation that actually it was the research process that was important, not what you found. Some call this a journey, some call it an apprenticeship. Your ability to design your research objectively and logically and then to critically review and evaluate your findings is what makes it doctoral level, not the actual findings themselves. This doesn't devalue your research work in any way; researchers very rarely have a Eureka moment which produces a fundamental change to how they view the world. You, like everyone else who does research, are undertaking an iterative cyclical process and you are standing on the shoulders of the giants who have gone before.

You have moved our understanding of the world forward. It may be only a small step but it is a step forward nevertheless, and someone else will pick up where you left off and take the next step in the research cycle. Your external examiner understands this and will accept your retrospective identification of flaws in your approach as long as you have acknowledged the limitations of your work and used them to inform the next stage of the research. If that is not possible then you must clearly and objectively state the flaws that you have identified in the design and what you would do differently if you had the opportunity to repeat the process. After all, if you could correctly predict the findings of your research then it wouldn't be that novel, and your literature review would probably have revealed that someone else had already undertaken the research.

There should be demonstrable evidence in the thesis of how you have synthesised your ideas in the light of your experience and in the context of the academic literature, and how this has created new knowledge. Your personal and distinctive voice and opinions should be clearly heard when reading the thesis but everything you say should also be backed up by evidence, and your interpretation must be objective and balanced. This is particularly important for professional doctorate students because many universities will accept candidates on the basis of their professional experience and the fact that they are in a position to influence their community of practice. If you don't have a distinctive voice then it is difficult to evidence this.

As described in Chapter 3, there are two concepts relating to the production of knowledge: Modes 1 and 2 (Gibbons et al., 1994). It could be argued that the literature review generated by the academic and theoretical content which underpins your research represents Mode 1 knowledge production, whilst Mode 2 knowledge production refers to your novel research by which the application of theory to your professional practice generates new knowledge (Lester, 2004; Chynoweth, 2012). By definition of Mode 2 knowledge production, your research must create new knowledge. This new knowledge doesn't necessarily have to be a ground-breaking new theory or hypothesis, it is acceptable to use an existing theory or hypothesis but apply it in a new context. By doing so you have created new Mode 2 knowledge. To go back to our example, researching health and safety training isn't particularly novel or innovative. However, doing it in the context of a small number of specific suppliers to the automotive industry is novel because no one else is likely to have done such a project in such a way, in such a place – this makes it an original contribution. The difference between a PhD and a professional doctorate is that you also have to demonstrate that your Mode 2 knowledge has made a significant contribution to your profession, and this can be more problematic.

O'Mullane (2005) clearly articulates two forms of profession: institutionalised that have professional bodies associated with them such as teaching, nursing, law; and non-institutionalised such as management or leadership. He discusses the dilemma of defining 'a significant contribution' in the context of diverse professions. There are various approaches as to how universities define what outputs can be used to specify a significant contribution (see next section). O'Mullane (2005, p. 16) attempts to classify them into 'active' or 'inactive' in terms of contribution to the profession(s). An active contribution generates 'new significant, knowledge ... which results in a significant improvement in practice', whilst an inactive contribution refers to 'significant knowledge which is not readily available or accessible to the profession because of its location and because the "discovery" has not been adequately disseminated although it has been judged as significant' in the context of the viva. Both active and inactive contributions rely on you having already disseminated your work from your professional life before and during the professional doctorate programme and captured the evidence in your portfolio. Otherwise, how can you demonstrate influence? The value, and hence the significance, of that contribution in terms of influence is the critical question here. It will vary with the length of your experience in that profession and your position or the opportunity you have had to influence it.

In an attempt to clarify this, O'Mullane (2005) ranks the actual achievements of the professional doctorate in terms of recognition from the profession:

1 'Findings' incorporated into professional practice
2 'Findings' incorporated into professional knowledge repertoire
3 Dissemination of outcomes to members
4 Outcomes acknowledged by profession
5 Profession informed about outcomes from a particular project
6 Profession aware of doctorate and aims

Once you have finished writing up the work and compiling your evidence of contribution then the next question is how you know that you are ready to submit. You are ready when you can demonstrate that you have done sufficient high-quality research to satisfy peer review and that you have made a significant contribution to your profession.

You should be ready if you have covered all of the areas which you intended to cover when you planned your research, it is evident from your portfolio, for example, that you have made an original and significant contribution and you have critically evaluated your work. You personally may not know this, but your supervisors should and you must trust their judgement on the state of readiness of your thesis. Although university regulations usually allow students to go against the judgement of their supervisors and submit their theses without their approval, you would be wise to take your supervisor's advice, no matter how painful it may be to do so.

10.3 Differing elements for written assessment

One of the major differences between a PhD and a professional doctorate is the element of assessment which is embodied in professional practice 'materially mediated by artefacts, hybrids and natural objects, centrally organized around shared practical understanding' (Schatzki et al., 2000, p. 2). O'Mullane (2005, p. 14) describes the different outputs used by universities to demonstrate a significant contribution to a profession in order to award a professional doctorate:

- Thesis or dissertation alone or combined with a number of subject areas.
- Combination of different subject areas and a portfolio and/or professional practice and analysis.
- A reflection and analysis of a significant contribution to knowledge from different previous scholarly achievements over time or from one major work.
- More significant published scholarly works recognised as a significant and original contribution to knowledge.
- Combination of subjects, portfolio and presentation (such as a performance in music, visual arts, drama).
- Combination of subjects, professional practice and 'internship' with mentors.

As can be seen from this list, the outputs for assessment are many and varied. Although in some universities the major element of assessment is a written thesis alone, a professional doctorate usually has an additional required element of assessment, such as a portfolio, and the relative weighting of each element may vary. There are some exceptions to this accepted practice. For example, in some programmes the whole of the research is submitted as a series of documents in a portfolio and there is no single thesis (Barnes and Stanley, 2012). In some universities the written thesis is the minor element of assessment and the major element could be an artefact or a collection of published works.

The structure of a professional doctorate thesis usually includes the following chapter titles although they may vary depending on your university requirements:

- *Abstract*: a one-page summary of your research findings, always written when the work has been completed and in the past tense.
- *Introduction*: a brief introduction to the work including the aims, objectives and research questions. It should be able to answer the 'so what' question demonstrating why your research is important.
- *Your learning journey**: how you have got to this point in your career and how this has led you to a professional doctorate.
- *Literature review*: this should provide the theoretical underpinning to your research proposal.
- *Methodology*: including your rationale for your methodological approach, the methods that you have used for all aspects of your research.
- *Your findings*: the quantitative and/or qualitative data that you have obtained during the process of your research which is presented in the most explicit way possible but not discussed.
- *Discussion*: this is the critical evaluation of your research findings in the context of the academic literature. This is one of the most important chapters in the thesis and gives you the opportunity to demonstrate your ability to work at the doctoral level.
- *Conclusions*: a final summary of your work which also may include recommendations to others as a consequence of your research and suggestions for further work to follow it up.
- *Personal reflections**: what you personally have gained from undertaking the professional doctorate process.
- *References*: this should be an extensive and current list of academic work which you have read and referred to in the thesis. It should be presented in the required style of your university, i.e. Harvard, Vancouver etc.
- *Appendices*: this optional part could include, for example, original anonymous data, questionnaires, consent forms/letters which you have used in your research.

The structure of a professional doctoral thesis is usually similar to that of a PhD but contains additional reflective elements (*) relating to your learning journey and includes reference to your portfolio.

Portfolios are often used in the professional doctorate as 'a way of tracking and reflecting upon individual learning, a document to analyse career history as a means to determine future direction' (Martin, 2006, p. 4). The portfolio may include, for example, research papers that you have published, projects that you have undertaken in your professional practice or documentary evidence of your professional experience which demonstrates impact and engagement with your community of practice. But it shouldn't simply be a kitchen sink into which everything you have ever done is thrown, because that provides no evidence of synthesis, reflection or critical evaluation. The portfolio should include a well-articulated and reflective commentary which evidences how you have developed professionally over time in the context of the theory and paradigm appropriate to your profession. By linking it to your thesis and vice versa, it will help to support and contextualise the aim of your research. This is the approach adopted by both Middlesex and Sunderland Universities (Doncaster and Thorne, 2000; Fulton et al., 2012). When examiners evaluate your portfolio they will be making judgements about the originality of your work in terms of how you have analysed it, the scholarship, intellectual merit and coherence of your publications, and your contribution to Mode 2 knowledge (Gibbs and Armsby, 2011).

A reflective written element for assessment is still required in hybrid theses where awards are given to candidates who have created a piece of work such a film and performance (Rinne and Sivenius, 2007), paintings, sculptures or installations (Raney, 2012) or where candidates can demonstrate their authorship of projects which have made a significant impact on the public domain such as social entrepreneurship (du Plock, 2012). This doesn't make the assessment less difficult or the award less worthy because most universities normally require a reflective and contextualised written commentary on the published works which can vary in length from 3,000 to 25,000 words. The external examiners will examine the writing, the public work and the performance at the viva before making a decision on its outcome. They will have an expectation of how your experiential learning has led to the construction of Mode 2 situated knowledge (Gibbons et al., 1994) and how it is positioned in relation to your professional identity (Sanders and Kuit, 2011).

Christianson and Adams (2011) would argue that there is a commonality between doctorates that are examined on the basis of the production of artefacts, as in art, compared to doctorates awarded on the basis of published experimental research, as in science. They posit that neither the artefact nor the experimental data can speak for themselves. In order to achieve their significance they both rely upon referral to contextual material and a critical understanding of where the work fits in with that of others.

Whatever the different elements of written assessment required by your university, you will certainly have to make an oral defence of your research. This is usually in the form of a *viva voce*, although in some European countries you may be assessed by a committee.

10.4 Preparing for the viva

Preparation for the viva should start early. Leshem and Trafford (2002) argue that it should start on day one of your professional doctorate. Before you are at the point of submitting your final version of the thesis and preparing for a viva it is useful to know who your examiner is going to be because they are the most 'important arbiter' of the award of your degree (Joyner, 2003). The selection of the external examiner should arise naturally from the literature review. They should be an established researcher in your field of study whose work is known to you, so that they are able to make informed decisions about your academic contribution to knowledge in your area. Joyner (2003) would argue that this shouldn't be the only selection criterion, and that further consideration should be given to the personal qualities of the potential examiner with respect to how well they are likely to empathise with you. Once the external examiner is selected, ensure that you have cited their research in your thesis. This isn't just flattery. If you have selected the external examiner on the basis of their subject expertise then your comprehensive literature review should already include their work, and they will expect to see it.

In some universities there may also be an external examiner from your profession whose role is to evaluate your influence on your community of practice. This examiner may be known to you and the more you have influenced your community of practice, the more likely you are to know each other. Providing that the professional examiner hasn't been closely linked to you and your research, personally or professionally, then this is acceptable. In addition to the external examiner(s), two other people will be present at your viva: one is the internal examiner and the other is the Chair of the panel. The role of the internal examiner is similar to that of the external examiner, except that the internal examiner is a member of the university staff who is experienced in the subject area but is not a member of the supervisory team. If the decision at the end of the viva is that you have passed subject to minor amendments of your thesis, then it is the internal examiner who will re-assess the thesis once the amendments have been made and report to the university's research committee whether the amendments have been satisfactorily completed or not.

The role of the Chair of the examination panel is not to examine you, but to see that you have been fairly examined and that the examiners have not put you under undue pressure. The Chair is an independent member of university staff who is not a member of your supervisory team but knows the broad subject area of the work. The Chair:

- Aids the examiners in their role by advising them on university process and procedures.
- Ensures that the viva is conducted according to the university regulations.

- Attends the private meeting with the examiners before the viva.
- Attends the viva with the examiners and the candidate but does not take part in the examination.
- Informs the candidate of the decision of the panel.
- Acts as a host before, during and after the viva, handling domestic issues so that the examiners are only concerned with the actual examination itself.

In the viva there will be at least three people who are likely to be unknown to you: the internal and external examiners and the independent Chair. There may also be a fourth examiner, if one is required from your profession. This can be quite overwhelming so take your supervisor in with you to provide moral support.

Before you finally submit your thesis, you should ask your supervisor for a mock viva. Some would argue that the mock should take place a week or two before the actual viva so that the questions are fresh in the student's mind. Others would argue that a mock viva should occur before the final submission of the thesis, before it is too late to make any changes. For example, a problem may arise in a mock viva which could be easily rectified before submission. However there is a danger that the examiners in the mock viva may make suggestions for substantial changes which will delay your submission but which the real external examiners may not think to be important. Remember that the viva is a subjective process and some academic staff will disagree with the findings of others. This is known as academic debate, but these differences do not diminish the requirement, laid down by every university, that the viva should be fair and equitable. The timing of the mock viva, therefore, should be decided in consultation with your supervisor. If your supervisor thinks that you need to practise your oral defence of your thesis, then have a mock viva a few days before the actual viva. If your supervisor is concerned about the quality of your writing and you don't concur with them on the readiness of your thesis, then a mock viva before submission may inform this decision. Although the last thing that you want at this stage is for someone to tell you do more work, it is better to hear it in a mock viva than the real one.

Once you have submitted your thesis you must wait for a date to be agreed for your viva. This is usually 6–8 weeks later, but it could be longer depending on the time of year and how busy your examiners are. If the viva is delayed then don't assume that this is bad news and that there is a problem with your work. The examiners will just be busy. It is a good idea not to look at your thesis for a few weeks so you can give yourself a short break. Leaving it alone for a while will help when you pick it up again as you will look at it with fresh eyes. It's at this point that you may find a few typing errors, despite your previous best efforts to ensure perfection. Don't panic, just highlight them and correct them in your electronic version. It is likely that your external examiners will have picked up the same errors and this will mean that you have less work to do after the viva.

Most universities have a wealth of on-line resources which can help you prepare for your viva. These often include videos of mock vivas and materials for developing listening skills, responding to questions, defending your work and so on. Many of these resources will be generic, but they may also include university-specific requirements which you need to be aware of. Try to ensure that you have looked at these resources so that you are prepared as well as possible for your viva.

A couple of weeks before the viva, you should start going through your thesis to ensure that you are able to justify your arguments. You then need to construct a coherent and confident defence of your work and your contribution to practice. The key point is that you know more about your research than anyone else. Remember that you are the world expert on it, and no one else knows or understands the depth of the new knowledge that you have created. However, don't forget that your position does make your interpretation of your data and the synthesis of your ideas more subjective.

This is what one of our doctoral students said about her viva:

"I found the lead up to the viva quite stressful. Having run a successful business for 13 years I was not prepared to find this a daunting experience, but as the time moved closer, it began to feel like an interview which was not only for a job but a judgement of my life. My supervisor was supportive, reminding me of my journey and getting me to consider how far I had come in working academically. A couple of intensive sessions where we broke down the final polishing to bite size chunks with deadlines given was not what I thought I would need at my age and with my experience! However writing academically is a skill and the process of defending my business model in this way was useful as I began to articulate the model's benefits to outside agencies. The viva was not only a defence of my business, which I was not as stressed about, it was going to be a judgement of my choices, my approach to others , empathy, and acumen, it was me!!!! "

Another student wrote a longer piece discussing the importance of preparing for the viva and her experiences of the viva itself, which is presented in the case study overleaf.

Your external examiners won't have the same level of emotional investment in your research as these students or as you, so they will look at it differently. They may criticise your work, but it isn't intended to be a personal criticism so don't take it personally. They will expect to see clearly-presented evidence of a coherent intellectual understanding of the well-designed and

Case study

"'Fail to prepare…..prepare to fail'….. This is a mantra I have become used to in my everyday life. Particularly in leading and managing many projects in my working life. Hence in preparing for the viva I was reminded that this mantra works well. Yet the application of this preparation in this instance was vastly different … for whilst I was the project lead, there was an overarching project executive who would decide on whether the project lead had completed the project in full.

What to prepare? Over the course of the years of research I had read tomes of literature, studied various research methodologies (before deciding on my particular approach) whilst tracking each step of my research journey and outcomes to inform my conclusions and recommendations. The countless hours spent on data analysis, reading and re-reading my data meant that I had an intimate relationship with this data and had come to know it instinctively. But the question I was asking myself now, was not what I didn't know about my work but what I did know and the decisions I made throughout my work to defend it at a viva. So whilst it appears to be pretty simplistic, if you know your work, the viva should not pose a problem, it was not just about knowing your work, but defending and understanding the key decisions you have made in undertaking your work; what other options or methods were available to you that you didn't use and the consequences of those actions.

Initially to me the process seemed like I was the haystack with all this information and insight into my work, and the examiners were coming in with their forks to find the needle! This made me feel quite uncomfortable and question whether my work was at the right level. This was a question, particularly at my write up stage I constantly asked myself: "is my work at the right level … is it at doctoral level?" In the final months coming up to submission, my supervisor had advised that my work was ready, however I was still highly critical and was unconvinced of its readiness at that stage. I did however finally concede that I had reached a point whereby I was satisfied to let it go and to be critiqued by peers.

So in preparing for the viva, I found myself in a perplexed state. I knew my work intimately, yet was very apprehensive of how others would view my work and potentially what areas would be critiqued and questioned. Additionally, there was the compounding effect of the "interview", and some people do better than others in this type of performance.

So I did as my mantra had always guided me….I prepared. I read and reread over my report and portfolio. This helped to immerse me back into the language of my work and how I had presented particular arguments and recommendations. I re-orientated myself to all of my findings and not just the key findings of my work. This required me to know particular facts and figures. Similarly, whilst I had discussed the rationale for the choice of my research methods, I reviewed this section as though it was being criticised so that I was prepared to defend my choices more articulately and rationally. I asked colleagues to read sections of my report and portfolio and ask me questions on it. I wrote out questions for myself and thought critically about the answers to these questions.

On the final week of the viva I marked out the sections of my work into their chapters so that I was ready to refer immediately to a particular chapter under scrutiny during the viva itself. I referred to available literature and tips on the internet and other authors on the viva process itself and how to survive the viva!

On the evening before the viva I had lots of rest, stopped reading my work, had my suit prepared and had a plan for my travel to the viva so that I would be there in plenty of time allowing for unexpected events.

When the time finally came, and I was being escorted into the viva interview room, the nerves kicked in, and unlike going into a job interview, whereby one sells yourself and has to exude confidence, I could instantly feel my confidence drain. However, as soon as the questions began my energy and confidence levels began to rise, as I felt that I was in a position to answer the questions and felt a sense of comfort with the questions being asked, based upon my preparations.

What I was unprepared for was the questioning sequence. I had expected that each examiner would ask their series of questions and then move to the next examiner. This was not the case. The questions whilst initially in this type of sequence drifted to a less sequenced style and more random questioning of the aspects raised in my discussions. This was unsettling for me at that point, as I was unsure of where and when was the questioning was going to end. I felt I couldn't see the end point at one stage in the viva. Yet I continued to be in a position to answer each of the questions asked. What was particularly important in the defence of my work, was my ability to recognise the key points whereby my examiners were highlighting areas for alternative presentation in my work, and to concede that these were valid points worthy of my consideration. In this way my viva as it progressed became more of a discussion. It was at this point that I realised we had potentially reached saturation point on the areas for questioning and were now in a discussion phase on the impact of the work and where it should progress from this stage. It was at this stage that I felt more at ease, just as the viva was drawing to a close.

At the end of the viva, upon being asked to leave the room to allow the panel of examiners to discuss my overall work and my viva performance, I felt a sense of relief coupled with numbness. It was at this point that my supervisor was an essential support. I desperately sought their viewpoint on my performance, knowing that their insight and experience of the process would give me a good indication on whether I had performed well in the viva itself. The viva had been longer than I had expected and the discussion of the panel was particularly extended, even according to my supervisor. This was the element of the viva I had prepared for the least. Whilst my supervisor had advised me that there would be some time to await the outcome of the viva, I had underestimated the time and the experience of this in reality. I began to reflect on my performance only focusing on the negative points rather than the areas I had done well. As the time passed I started to become paranoid that the outcome would be negative and that the panel was deliberating on how to deliver the devastating news to me. At least my supervisor's paranoid button was turned off and so provided the necessary reassurance.

After considerable time I was invited back into meet with the examiners. At the outset I was given positive feedback on my performance and then it was outlined to me some of the areas that required improvement. Whilst I was

continued overleaf

> **Case study continued**
>
> *listening intently to the amendments I would have to make I was wondering if I had actually passed. Obviously my body language spoke volumes to the examiners, who then paused and stated that I was successful and that these were minor amendments I would need to make.*
>
> *At this point I both mentally and physically relaxed for the first time that day. After the discussion on the amendments, there was general discussion on the work which was very light and conversational which allowed me to feel more at ease.*
>
> *On my way home after the viva I cried with relief along with feeling a sense of anti-climax that all my years of research and work had culminated into just 2–3 hours at the finish line. This however soon lifted to elation on the success of the viva and the realization of not having to repeat it again!*
>
> *All in all….the mantra of fail to prepare, prepare to fail…whilst it was essential to prepare…..you can only prepare to a point for your viva in my opinion."*

original piece of research in the context of the academic literature. If they don't see this evidence in your written submission then you will have an uphill struggle in your viva to persuade the examiners that you are worthy of the award of the degree.

10.5 The viva

In some universities, the student is expected to give a brief presentation of the major findings of the research whilst in others this may be optional. If you have the opportunity to give a presentation, you should take it. Practise your presentation and work with your supervisor to ensure that your most important findings are clearly articulated. It should be a logical but critically evaluative summary of your main findings that will help to guide the structure of the viva by providing a natural starting point for the subsequent questions raised by the examiners. The point of the presentation is to demonstrate your ability to reflect on your findings. It is not an opportunity for you to show your competency in making presentations by adding animations, transitions or other gimmicks, and under no circumstances should you exceed your allotted time allocation. Keeping to the point and staying within your time are important skills to demonstrate, otherwise you look rambling and indecisive and this detracts from the importance of your findings.

As well as preparing intellectually for the viva you should prepare personally. You should be smartly dressed because wearing anything informal may suggest that you don't take the viva seriously. Take your personally-annotated copy of the thesis, so that you can demonstrate that you have been going through it after submission. You might also take in a notebook to make notes during the viva. Although you will probably be too nervous to keep your own record of the event, your supervisor may also be there (although they can only attend at your request) and could do this for you. This is really useful later, when you are addressing the issues raised by the examiners, as it helps to identify where in the submission the issue arose and clarify the point the examiners were trying to make.

Go into the viva when invited and look positive, smile and be enthusiastic about your work. This is your opportunity to discuss your work for a couple of hours with a group of people who are really interested in it. You must always be polite and don't lose your temper even if you don't agree with what is being said. Try to relax, and enjoy the discussion and answer confidently. Listen carefully to the questions and, if you don't understand what you are being asked, ask them to repeat the question. You don't always have to answer immediately, you can think about your response before you reply. You don't always have to agree with the comments that the examiner is making but you should provide a logical and considered reason, which is strongly supported by evidence, why you don't agree. If the examiner makes a point about your research which you hadn't considered, then reply that it is an interesting point that you hadn't considered but you will now. This isn't merely flattery; it is acknowledging that the external examiner may have a different viewpoint to your own.

External examiners often find that students have sold themselves short and undervalued their personal contribution, and a good experienced external examiner will be able to bring out the student's strengths with careful questioning. Remember that your oral defence of your research at the viva can make the difference between passing and failing, between minor changes and major changes. One of the main differences between you and a typical PhD student in a viva is that you are a mature professional person who may be at an equivalent level to your external examiners, so think of it as peer review (Costley and Lester, 2012). Your external examiners will certainly approach the viva in this manner. They will expect you to be confident and enthusiastic about your work, but will acknowledge that you may also be nervous and apprehensive. A good set of examiners with a good thesis in front of them will immediately set you at ease by saying how much they have enjoyed your work and that they would like to spend the next couple of hours discussing it with you.

Often in a professional doctorate examination, the viva will start by you being asked about personal transformation, as professional doctorate students are typically transformed by the educational process they have undertaken rather than the research process (Lee and Boud, 2008; Smith et al., 2011). These introductory questions may include:

- Why did you decide to undertake a professional doctorate?
- Was undertaking the professional doctorate what you expected?
- How has undertaking the professional doctorate changed you?

Once you have relaxed and answered these questions, the examiners will start to ask you questions about your research and your contribution to your profession. This allows you to give an overview of your work:

● What do you think are your major findings from your research?
● What is your major contribution to your professional practice?

In terms of the research that you have undertaken, some of the questions asked by the examiners are likely to be:

● How did you come up with the aim of your research?
● How did your literature review inform your research aim, objectives and research questions?
● What was your rationale for selecting your research design and methodologies?
● What methodological approaches did you consider and reject and why?
● Did you have any problems in collecting your data and if so how did that influence your research design?
● Were you surprised by your findings?
● Are you convinced that you have answered your research question?
● What would you change if you were starting again?

This list is not intended to be, and cannot be, definitive. What the examiner is trying to investigate with these questions is your ability to logically and coherently undertake research. The examiner will expect to see that the first part of your research has informed the second part of your research and so forth, and that your research is incremental, building up step by step. The examiner will expect to see that, if the research methodology proved to be flawed and did not allow you to answer your research question, you logically and analytically adapted your approach so that you could answer the question.

The examiner will follow up the discussion about your research design with questions about your findings, your interpretation of your findings and ask you to justify the claims that you make in your final discussion.

If a professional examiner is present they will concentrate on your contribution to your profession and how you have demonstrated it by what you have evidenced in your portfolio or thesis. This will rely on proven past achievements and your analysis and insightful reflections on events. This should be more than an autobiographical study because you must be able to substantiate your claim of being an experienced professional who has made a significant contribution to professional knowledge and practice (O'Mullane, 2005). For example, the following questions could be asked:

● What impact have your findings had on your own professional practice?
● What impact will your findings have on your profession?

- How will you disseminate your findings to your professional colleagues?
- What do you think that the profession should do differently as a consequence of your findings?

Most vivas take about two hours, but they can be considerably longer, particularly if there are controversial areas within your work and you have to make a spirited defence of your findings. The viva will take as long as it takes to satisfy the examiners that you and your work are worthy of the doctorate. The examiners will each start the viva with a list of points that they want to discuss with you and the discussion will come to a close when they are satisfied that you have addressed all of these points. At the end of the viva, the Chair of the examiners will ask if any further questions remain and whether all points have been clarified. They will also ask you if there are any points that you wish to raise and, if there were parts of your responses which you think were vague, then this is your opportunity to clarify your reply. Take this opportunity and make the most of it because it will be your last chance to influence the outcome of the viva. Once you are satisfied that you have provided your best defence of your work, you will be asked to leave whilst they make their decision. You will be in a highly emotional state and very anxious. It is human nature for you to assume that you have done badly and you will be reflecting on what you should have said rather than what you actually did say. If your supervisor has been in the viva with you then they will have a more objective view of how it went and should be able to prepare you for the outcome, whatever that is.

No matter how perfect you think your work is and how exemplary you were in the viva, the panel will almost always ask for changes. Before the advent of software packages when theses had to be typed, it was unlikely that examiners would ask for every minor change to be made. However, now that theses are prepared electronically and typographical errors and other mistakes can be quickly changed, then external examiners rarely miss an opportunity to ask for corrections to be made to the final document.

Formally, there are several options which arise from the decisions of the examining panel. Although these may vary from one university to another they are usually as described below, although the first and last options are the most unlikely:

- Pass with no corrections.
- Pass with minor corrections (typographical errors for example) which may only take a few days to address.
- Pass with minor amendments (expansion on a certain point or inclusion of the work of a specified author) which may take up to three months to address.
- Pass with major amendments (re-drafting or the addition of extra chapters) which may take up to six months to address.

● Re-submission of the work with major changes (more research to be undertaken or a complete re-write of the work) which may take up to a year to undertake and require another viva.
● Not a pass at doctoral level, but an award of a Master's degree can be offered.
● Fail.

When you return to the viva room, the Chair of the panel will announce the result of the viva. It is almost certain that you will have to do more work, so you are not yet in a position to relax because it is all over. The Chair will let you know informally what you have to do next, and this will be followed up with a more formal written set of requirements which have been produced by the external examiners. When you have completed the required amendments and your supervisor is happy with them, they will have to be passed by the examiners. It is good advice to include in your submission to the examiners their original list of amendments, which you have annotated to show the sections and page numbers where the changes have been made. This will help the examiners to quickly see how you have addressed their comments and speed up the process of reaching a final decision on the outcome of your examination.

If the outcome of the viva is that you have to re-submit your work and undertake another viva then this could be a massive shock to you and to your supervisor. You will feel very disappointed and possibly angry about this, and your first reaction may be to walk away from the professional doctorate and never come back. But if you do that, then all of the work you have done and the sacrifices you have made over the years have been completely wasted, and it has all been for nothing. You will regret this decision, perhaps not immediately but there will come a time when you do. You have to be strong enough to bounce back from this disappointment and do whatever it takes to ensure that you achieve your professional doctorate. This is a worthy title. It is the highest level that you can achieve and it isn't given lightly, so if your work is lacking in some area then you have to accept that and respond appropriately. It may take more work to finally achieve the doctorate but you will know that you really have given it your best shot and received the recognition that you deserve for your efforts.

Once the amendments or re-submission has been accepted by the external examiners, the decision is submitted to your university's research committee for final approval. When you have formally received the final outcome from the research committee your work can be bound and submitted to the university library, but don't forget to give your supervisor a copy. Make sure that you go to your graduation ceremony and enjoy it because it is a public acknowledgement of the value of your accomplishments. Now it is all over and it is at this point that you get your life back.

Summary

In this chapter we have discussed the issue of preparing for your viva and have made the point that this preparation begins at the start of the professional doctorate process, not at the end. The chapter provides practical advice for you to follow in terms of the structure of your submission, what to do while waiting to hear the date of your viva, putting together an oral presentation of your work, your behaviour in a viva. It attempts to demystify the viva by discussing some likely questions and describing the range of examination decisions which can be made and what they mean in practice.

The next chapter includes some case studies from actual graduates of a professional doctorate programme and describes their personal experiences of their examination.

11 Case Studies

On completion of this chapter you will:

▶ have an understanding of real professional doctorate projects
▶ be able to place your own doctoral project in the context of these projects
▶ understand something of the motivations of candidates for studying a professional doctorate
▶ have an understanding of the range of backgrounds that professional doctorate candidates can have

11.1 Introduction

This chapter presents eight case studies of successful professional doctorate projects. These are drawn from students who have been supervised by the authors and have recently graduated from a professional doctorate programme. The case studies present the candidate's project, their professional and academic background, the methodological approach taken, the impact of the project on their community of practice, their view of the examination process, and the impact which studying the programme has had on them as an individual.

The eight case studies are:

● Case study 1: Claire
A pharmacy lecturer who explored different models of inter-professional education in her teaching.

● Case study 2: Ian
An equality and diversity professional who developed a model for corporate social responsibility.

● Case study 3: Max
A local businessman who followed a doctoral project in the area of quality and management information systems.

● Case study 4: Siobhan
A senior member of staff from a local college who undertook a project in the area of shared services.

● Case study 5: Fiona
A healthcare professional who developed a commissioning framework.

● Case study 6: David
A senior administrator from a university who explored the area of research administration systems.

- Case study 7: Hamid
  An internal auditor for a major international bank who explored financial auditing approaches.
- Case study 8: Liam
  An information specialist working in the health industry who explored a new model for integrating risk, audit and incident management.

Through these case studies we hope you can gain a deep understanding of the whole professional doctorate process, what drove the students to study for a professional doctorate, their professional background, the methodology they used, the impact their work made and something of the examination process. Each case study has the same structure, and has the following sections:

- *Professional and academic background*: the background of the candidate and their professional experience.
- *Motivation for studying the professional doctorate*: the candidate's reasons for choosing to study a professional doctorate programme.
- *The project*: title of the project and a short description.
- *Abstract*: the actual abstract of the project, as taken from the candidate's project report.
- *Project aims*: the aims of the project.
- *Methodological approach*: the approach taken by the candidate.
- *Impact on the community*: a summary of the contribution that the work made to the candidate's community of practice.
- *The viva*: a summary of the candidate's perspective of the oral examination.
- *Personal experience of the doctoral journey*: the candidate's view of how the doctoral process has impacted upon them as an individual and a professional.

Much of the text is taken from the candidates' own words with their permission. The names of the students are not their real names, and the case studies have been anonymised for ethical reasons. The italicised text is taken directly from the candidates' doctoral reports.

11.2 Case study 1: Claire

Professional and academic background

Originally a hospital pharmacist for many years, I have also worked as a community pharmacist, in industry and academia. Most recently, I worked for 4 years in a research team, before 8 years as a lecturer within a university. For the last 5 years I have worked freelance mostly in the pharmaceutical industry, as well as following some academic pursuits.

"I registered as a pharmacist in 1975 and spent the next three years gaining all round experience as a community pharmacist and as a junior hospital pharmacist, and then undertaking a master's degree by research. In 1978 I began work as a Staff Pharmacist (section leader) in a hospital manufacturing unit. I managed a team of ten staff who undertook various work from qualified staff duties (junior pharmacist and senior technician) to ancillary staff (bottle washing, filling and heavy work). This work was varied and enjoyable. I learnt transferrable managerial skills in this post including: project planning, operational and organisational management. My aim was to manage and run a happy and effective team.

These were the early days of the aseptic dispensing era and beginnings of parenteral nutrition which is further described in my portfolio section one. By 1979 I had personally developed the skills and abilities to mix intravenous feeding solutions together, in the aseptic facilities, according to the requirements of each individual patient. This was the first service of this kind in the North of England. I presented this innovative new development for a pharmacy-led improvement of patient care at an educational event for healthcare professionals (see portfolio section one).

I expanded the aseptic service to include preparation of intravenous feeding for neonates and small children at neighbouring hospitals. My developmental work extended to providing individual patient intravenous admixture services to wards such as maternity and oncology wards. I planned and developed a near-patient chemotherapy preparation service in purpose built facilities in the oncology ward block. It was an important development to be able to provide such facilities, near the patents for swift aseptic dispensing to meet clinical needs. These facilities could also be used by nursing and medical staff in an emergency when the unit was not staffed by pharmacy staff because of their ward location. This was important because the very nature of these chemotherapeutic agents posed a Health and Safety handling risk to staff (and any visitor) if mixed on the open ward.

My department also produced sterilised products for use by patients in the hospital (eye drops, ampoules and large volume products) as well as sterile products which were sold to other hospitals (such as metronidazole injection packed in 100ml infusion bottles). The regulations surrounding manufacture of pharmaceutical products was tightened following reported adverse reactions and manufacturing disasters in the 1960s and as such my unit was required to meet the same standards as in any commercial pharmaceutical manufacturing industry. My unit was the first in the Northern NHS Region to gain this 'Specials Manufacturing Licence'. In recognition of attaining the high level of specialist expertise, I was invited to be the first representative of the Northern Region at the National Production Pharmacist's sub-committee of the Department of Health in 1981 (portfolio section two). In 1983 I joined the register of those persons eligible to be a 'qualified person' in the pharmaceutical industry under the transitional requirements as part of the then new European Union Directives (portfolio section two).

Working at a general hospital in the clinical and pharmacy manufacturing role gave me the opportunity to work as a teacher-practitioner at university. This role gave me the 'taste' for academic life and my reflections led me to realise my desire to share my experiences and view of the importance of preparing medicine for the patient in a timely, efficient and cost-effective manner and for working in a multidisciplinary team for the benefit of patient care with the university students (portfolio section three).

During the mid-1980s whilst my two children were small I worked part time in community, hospital and industrial pharmacy. Working in this variety of roles gave me a wider view of the practice of pharmacy which I have utilised in my later work. One such role developed my interest in teaching other healthcare professionals (portfolio section four).

In 1988 I had the opportunity to plan and work on a novel project for the National Health Service (NHS). The role was to plan and then to deliver a pharmaceutical service to a private hospital which was both efficient and effective for the customer and also designed as an income generation project for the NHS. The service was operational in less than six months and quickly was established in temporary accommodation at the private hospital. The service became the largest single income generation project for the NHS at that time. I planned a new purpose built on-site pharmacy which included cytotoxic admixture facilities and an out-patient dispensary. During this time I undertook a management role, with budget and staff control. This work was discussed in two publications (portfolio section five).

1996 saw a move in a new direction with the opportunity to join a research team at a local university working on a Department of Health funded project to prepare clinical guidelines for use by doctors as part of their clinical practice computer systems. This work necessitated learning new skills including advanced computer skills and the ability to excel at evidence-based medicine; to be able search the literature, critically appraise evidence, condense results and write in a particular format which could be uploaded onto computer systems used in the doctor's surgery. I was a clinical author for guideline content. One of my responsibilities was to lead the development of the methodology for choosing the particular medicines to be included in the guidelines, which I presented as a paper at the British Pharmaceutical Conference. The poster and paper together with other explanatory information and links to the website to obtain the guidance is in my portfolio section six.

Whilst working with the research team, as well as working on this project, I was involved in other IT (Information Technology) projects. One such national project was the underpinning and planning work to enable the *production of a UK Drug Dictionary and to prepare for electronic prescribing in the NHS (portfolio section six).*

This work with the multidisciplinary research team was interesting and varied, as well as considerably updating and extending my clinical knowledge about the treatment of a number of medical conditions commonly encountered in primary care. Further reflection served to endorse my earlier beliefs about the importance and usefulness of inter-professional working especially in healthcare environments, because staff from the various professional groups each had a different underpinning knowledge base from their education and together with their work experiences brought different abilities and knowledge base to the team. The whole team worked together to produce the clinical guidance. During informal discussions with medical and nursing colleagues I realised that preregistration (undergraduate) education was changing in many of the healthcare professions but that this was not yet the case in pharmacy. Upon investigation I found that pharmacy was different from most of healthcare education in that pharmacy has remained a science-based degree with little or no inter-professional or clinical practice-based learning.

This led me to the desire to return to academia in a role where I could offer back to the professionals of the future my own experiences and knowledge of the practice of pharmacy. In 2000 I took a post as Senior Lecturer in Pharmacy at a local university. My initial tasks were to redevelop the undergraduate MPharm clinical pharmacy module and to lead the taught components of the postgraduate pharmacy provision. Section seven of my portfolio outlines my personal development as an academic.

As part of my growing professional and personal development I began to undertake research and development roles within my working role. Section eight of my portfolio outlines further the development of training courses for pharmacists and healthcare professionals. This was made possible by funding received for a university Fellowship (portfolio section eight). Portfolio section nine shows my high level of achievement as an academic by attainment of personal promotion to Principal Lecturer Pedagogic Practice. Research is a key part of the academic role and portfolio section ten contains examples of my research output."

Motivation for studying the professional doctorate

Originally I wanted to do a PhD, however when I learnt about the possibility of a professional doctorate I realised that my career achievements were actually well suited to the professional doctorate route. At that time I had what is best described as an eclectic mixture of publications, and, only when I really analysed the basis for them all, was I able to see the common thread through the years and this led me to the basis for my thesis.

The project

Title: A Contribution to Pharmacy Practice Education.

I explained, using examples of various newly prepared academic educational programmes and publications, how pharmacist education needed to change to meet the needs of the NHS and the pharmacists themselves.

Abstract

"This integrative doctoral report describes how my underpinning experience as a practising pharmacist has been utilised to allow me to make a substantial contribution to pharmacy education. Using separate models for undergraduate and postgraduate students I have shown how I succeeded as an educationalist to plan and deliver high quality innovative programmes. The aim of this work was to prepare undergraduate pharmacy students for practice and postgraduate professional students for advanced practice.

Using an action research methodology in postgraduate education, I have planned and led my team to develop a suite of MSc programmes (modular master's degrees) which matches stakeholder requirements (i.e. the students and their employers). These programmes offer flexible learning opportunities requiring limited contact. With support systems in place, this model allows the busy healthcare professional to keep working in a full-time capacity whilst studying for a postgraduate qualification. Using this model I have developed short courses and led my team to successfully operate them both in the UK and in Hong Kong. Taking an early lead in the development of supplementary, and then independent, prescribing courses has allowed our graduates to develop to meet their potential and allow these practitioners to specialise in their chosen clinical field.

I have outlined my work with the Centre for Excellence in Healthcare Professional Education (CETL4HealthNE), what is perhaps one of the most important and major suggested changes to pharmacy undergraduate education for many years. This is the introduction of Inter-professional Education (IPE) and practice-based learning. I am a firm advocate for IPE and practice-placements being at the heart of, and becoming a substantial component of, undergraduate pharmacy education. This allows clinical patient-focused teaching to be maximised. I believe that this is of critical importance to ensure that new graduates have the underpinning theoretical knowledge and practical application ability. This will enable students to be able to successfully undertake their period of preregistration training and go on to become successful practitioners in their own right. This is all with the same goal: for the safe and effective care of the patients.

From my own experiences gained from my collaborative research work and CETL4HealthNE I propose a model where pharmacists work together with other healthcare professionals, both in practice and in IPE, for the benefit of patient care. "

Project aims

"The first aim of this work has been to provide undergraduate pharmacy students with a learning experience which will prepare them for practice in a multi-professional environment and help them to improve patient care. This will be achieved by using an inter-professional educational approach to deliver educational programmes across professional boundaries which will have a positive impact on patient care. The second aim was to offer a postgraduate educational provision which will help qualified students to build upon the basis of their undergraduate education and initial working experiences. These programmes will prepare them for advanced practice as clinical pharmacists, anticoagulant clinic specialists, and supplementary and independent prescribers."

My overall plan was to use my previous experiences as a practicsng pharmacist and to build upon this basis by personal development in academia. My own particular personal and professional development has allowed me to make a substantial contribution to pharmacy education. In preparing separate models for undergraduate and postgraduate students I have shown how I have succeeded as an educationalist to plan and deliver high quality innovative programmes in the fields of IPE, clinical pharmacy education and pharmacist prescribing.

Although the aims may appear broad, my integrative doctoral report and portfolio show how preparation of undergraduate pharmacists for practice and postgraduates for advanced practice has been enabled and underpinned by my own innovation, and my professional experience as a practising pharmacist. The integrative doctoral report and portfolio show how my work has contributed in an original way to further advances of the practical knowledge in this field.

Methodological approach

Action research was my main methodology. This was the thread that ran through the whole work. However, particular (stand-alone) parts of my whole thesis had their own methodology, which could be as diverse as manipulation of large data sets or postal questionnaires, to evaluation of interviews.

My research methodology training has been patchy and is largely self-taught over many years, or in one job or another. Data analysis was largely undertaken within preparation of papers for publication.

Impact on the community

I promoted the concept of multidisciplinary ways of working and learning as well as inter-professional education for pharmacists. These concepts really are widely held as the future for pharmacist education, and some placements are the norm in the MPharm and have become a key attribute of the MPharm programme and are checked in the professional accreditation process. However the whole way of learning together with other healthcare students has been difficult to be fully embraced due to financial limitations in higher education. This remains patchy and is different from one school of pharmacy to another. My contribution was evaluated by feedback from students and their employers. The following section is drawn directly from my doctoral report.

"My major achievements as an educationalist have been achieved during a seven-year period from 2000 to 2007. In this time I have undertaken a rigorous programme of work and research. I have advanced the body of knowledge in the field of development of pharmacy practice programmes of study and in particular the mode of study and content at both undergraduate and postgraduate levels.

The postgraduate pharmacy programmes at this university are thriving, with almost 300 postgraduate pharmacy students studying these taught programmes and these numbers are steadily rising. The income for the university has risen in line with the numbers of students especially with the success of the recruitment of students from outside the European Union who wish to study for a master's degree as full-time students. A whole sub-department has been built up including a suite of teaching class rooms complete with state of the art equipment, full time administrative and secretarial support as well as my team of academic staff both employed by the university and also specialists brought in to teach their own area of expertise.

The innovatively designed postgraduate programmes, updated and modernised to suit practising healthcare professional are fit-for-purpose. The contact time has been kept as low as reasonably possible to suit the needs of the students and their employers. Some contact time has been retained to create a balance to enable peer to peer networks to develop and teacher-student contact.

Use of practice-based education in the workplace has been maximised (with modules such as Clerkship, Therapy Management: Anticoagulation and Prescribing) where students collect real-life examples from their own work to use in their coursework.

My idea to incorporate the new supplementary prescribing module into a master's programme to create a brand new qualification was accepted by the university. Our MSc Prescribing Sciences was the first such Master's degree in the UK incorporating the new pharmacist prescribing module. This allowed students to specialise in their own chosen field by choosing particular options available to them in our innovative programme design.

> *Separately in my undergraduate work, the introduction of IPE into the curriculum for undergraduate pharmacy students was begun at a critical stage in the development of the MPharm programme at the university. The initial developmental work was undertaken as pilot schemes aided by collaboration made possible via the CETL4HealthNE network. This IPE is of critical important to the university as IPE and practice-based clinical contact sessions are important criteria in the accreditation requirements of UK MPharm programmes."*

The viva

I was a student in the School of Education due to the nature and content of my topic. The Chair was a professor from the School of Education. The internal examiner was a principal lecturer from the School of Health. As a former academic member of staff I had two external examiners who were both academics with healthcare qualifications: a pharmacist (principal lecturer in pharmacy practice) and a nurse (DProf programme leader from another university).

I was really nervous about the viva, so I had prepared very well. A couple of weeks beforehand I had a practice viva with my supervisors asking the types of questions that they felt would come up. This process gave me confidence on the one hand, but also made me realise that I had to really revise and read up on the theoretical concepts before the big day. This preparation paid off as indeed several questions on theory did come up. On the day of the viva I met my supervisor and she came into the viva with me for support. My viva lasted for two hours and afterwards I had to wait outside for a few minutes (which seemed like an eternity). Then I was asked to return to the room with my supervisor and given the good news that I had passed, with some minor corrections. After hearing the good news, the examiners did talk to me, but to be honest I can't remember a thing!

Personal experience of the doctoral journey

Looking back on my journey, in the beginning I didn't really understand what was required in the thesis and especially about the style of writing required. I found it difficult to write 'I did... and this shows that I ...' and in this way to write about myself meeting the learning outcomes for the professional doctorate. Basically it was the I ... I ... I ... part which I found difficult, as previously I had held these thoughts in private.

My supervisors were instrumental in keeping me going. Without their enthusiasm and ability to inspire confidence I doubt that I would have completed the work. Your choice/allocation of supervisory team is key to your success.

The whole professional doctorate experience had a profound effect on me and changed me as a person. I am now a quieter person overall. I am also more of a reflective practitioner than I was.

The other change is that I am 'hooked' on research, and I undertake research as a hobby. I am a member of a research team at a local university with a current project under way. We have achieved publications in good quality journals in the last two years and of this I am very proud.

"Looking back at the achievements outlined in this report gives me an opportunity for self-reflection. Which of the learning achievements outlined in this work may be used again? What could be adapted? Would I wish to repeat or extend any of these projects in the future?

The model developed by Kemmis and McTaggert (1988) suggests a cycle of 'plan, act, observe and reflect'. This is particularly suited to the education environment with suggestions from several sources identifying those educationalists, who adopt this action research as a method of self-reflection, will more deeply consider their teaching methods and total teaching ethos than others (Street, 1986; Oja and Pine, 1989). I have used a cyclical method as a tool to aid my reflective practice for many years. The Experiential Learning Method, as described by Kolb in 1984, denotes work or practice as the concrete experience part in the cycle which is followed in this model by 'reflective observation, abstract conceptualisation then active experimentation'. The cycle is completed by a return to 'concrete experience'. The value for me in using this model is that the cycle may be begun at any of the four points or stages and that this method has the added advantage in that it does not require any testable model to be formulated before initiation.

Undertaking self-reflection about the whole of my work, as opposed to each separate task undertaken, has shown that many of my innovative developments have been initiated in response to a practical or workplace need. As such they can be perceived to arise from active experimentation and not from the reflection part of the cycle. For example when I planned an educational IPE event or wrote draft documentation for a new module or programme (for the team to consider), I used my own tried and tested methods adapting them from earlier work to fit the new task. However some of the developmental work did begin at the reflection stage of the cycle (e.g. planning a research project). This reflection in itself shows that I am reusing learning and adapting materials for use in new situations over and over again to continually improve my practice.

Figure 11.1 shows my own personally developed annual cycle of management duties with regard to my programme leadership. I developed this cycle over a period of five years by continual self-study using action research methodology. Assistance and input from peers was sought on many

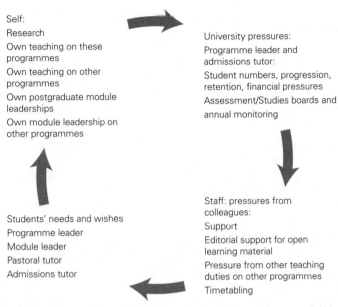

Self:
Research
Own teaching on these programmes
Own teaching on other programmes
Own postgraduate module leaderships
Own module leadership on other programmes

University pressures:
Programme leader and admissions tutor:
Student numbers, progression, retention, financial pressures
Assessment/Studies boards and annual monitoring

Students' needs and wishes
Programme leader
Module leader
Pastoral tutor
Admissions tutor

Staff: pressures from colleagues:
Support
Editorial support for open learning material
Pressure from other teaching duties on other programmes
Timetabling

Figure 11.1 Annual cycle of programme leader duties and responsibilities

occasions and suggestions gathered were carefully considered with many tried and included.

There are other methods of reflective practice widely used, however I have not found them to be better suited than the method, outlined above, for myself in my own educational practice. Critical incident methodology (Brookfield, 1990) is commonly used in clinical practice; however I have not found this approach useful to me in the educational arena because my academic work is not centred on preventing mistakes and learning from near misses in the way that healthcare must consider. My personal view is that undertaking reflection in this way is more suited to clinical practice where near misses and other incidents do unfortunately occur and suit this type of approach."

11.3 Case study 2: Ian

Professional and academic background

For the period before and during the doctorate I was Equality and Diversity Manager at a university in the UK. Based in Human Resources (HR), I was responsible for meeting the requirements of equality legislation for staff and students, and promoting an inclusive culture. I linked together students, staff and the community and represented the university at civic level in order to develop inclusive practices. By the conclusion of the doctorate I was leading on corporate social responsibility. Post doctorate, I am currently a self-employed consultant in a range of equality-related areas. I had previous personnel and HR roles in the public sector, and was a United Nations Observer at the 1994 democratic elections in South Africa. Existing qualifications included a degree and some HR qualifications including CIPD (Chartered Institute of Personnel and Development) Fellowship, and mediation and coaching qualifications.

Motivation for studying the professional doctorate

I was working in a support role in an academic environment at the university. I agree with the principles behind continuous development in terms of refreshing our learning and applying this at work and at home. I was influenced by academics I came into contact with and felt that the time was right to engage in a major academic programme. As I became increasingly involved in my doctorate, I saw that it would become a lever by which I could seek to focus on the work that interests me, and that it could be a gateway to avenues that could include specialist work, self-employment and academic involvement.

> *"Throughout my personal life and my professional working career I have been interested in principles of equality and natural justice. I am currently the Equality and Diversity Manager, based in the Human Resources (HR) Department. My role has widened from responsibilities connected with the fair treatment of staff to include working with students under an overall vision of encouraging an inclusive university community. I now engage with partner organisations and our local community in order to help deliver a positive relationship between our city and the university. My work also includes national responsibilities across a variety of themes, which have made a contribution to practice and which reflect upon the university. This holistic work has developed into a journey towards CSR (Corporate Social Responsibility), both for me and for my institution, which describes itself as a civic university.*
>
> *A Motivating Encounter: We have many experiences in our lives outside our employment in which we impact on fellow individuals positively and negatively. Before we explore the world of work, I would like to illustrate this by sharing one experience that sticks in my mind, which occurred in Manchester in 1989. I was shopping one evening at a Safeway food store just off Market Street, an area which was a favourite haunt of homeless and hungry people. Just before the store closed at 8.00 pm the price of bags of 10 doughnuts fell from £1.00 per bag to 10p per bag. I had the bright idea of purchasing 10 bags for a pound – i.e. 100 doughnuts at a penny each. Clutching my booty, I left the store looking for homeless people, only*

to discover that none were around – a slightly farcical situation of where can you find a homeless person when you want one? I decided to walk up to Piccadilly Gardens, another refuge area for homeless people and finally came across a large group. Rather naively, I approached the group and told them I had bought a hundred doughnuts, and asked if they would like any. After an embarrassed silence, one replied 'What do I want with a doughnut?' followed by 'its money I need'. At least I'd had a response so I decided to eat a doughnut and gradually the group came round with comments such as 'let's have a bit of that'. Within 20 minutes all 100 doughnuts had been passed around. I was subsequently accepted socially by this group and became for a while an unofficial mentor for Rob, the first person who replied to me, as he struggled with issues he was experiencing. His challenges were outside my area of expertise but I was able to gain a level of trust that put him in contact with a friend who worked for a homeless support agency. I learned many things from this and other experiences. I may have made some ill-judged assumptions, but for relatively little money and time a few things had happened that then led to others. They helped to make a difference that might have been very small in the scheme of things but could have been of some significance to one or two people."

The project

Title: Making a Difference – My Contribution in a Journey towards Corporate Social Responsibility in a Modern Civic University.

Abstract

"This project explores the contribution of an individual in a journey towards corporate social responsibility in a modern civic university. In an organisational context of a university that promotes a civic vision, with stakeholders who are internal and external, local and international, this report outlines a range of initiatives, from equality and diversity best practice to community engagement projects, which enhanced corporate reputation. It demonstrates how a holistic approach of encouraging an inclusive environment and a positive relationship with its communities, underpinned by principles of fairness and transparency, can generate stakeholder confidence in an organisation and pave the way towards the development of a CSR strategy and culture.

Using a methodology which combines reflection and action research, the project identifies connections between personal values and professional activities and demonstrates how both individuals and organisations can impact on partners and stakeholders. It outlines how, by working in line with shared corporate values, an individual who may not be in an executive role can influence an institution in making a difference to its communities.

The project uses action research in the development of a CSR state-ment, explores how principles were embedded into corporate strategy and practice, and benchmarks progress. In a study that captures perceptions of key stakeholders, it evaluates the impact of the CSR approach, quanti-fies stakeholder engagement and determines if the institution is seen as responsible by those who have contact with it.

In reviewing wider CSR developments and examining a contribution to CSR within an institution and to the broader community of practice, the project develops CSR principles which have wider applicability. Synthesis-ing the evidence collected and comparing existing approaches to corporate social responsibility, a new framework for CSR is proposed. The framework draws lessons for the CSR community of practice by incorporating strands of CSR activity and CSR verification across all organisational and stakehold-er levels. Informed by the experience of engagement with CSR, the report reaches conclusions that can be used by individuals and organisations that are themselves at different stages of their own CSR journeys."

Aims

The project aimed to:

- Capture a journey towards CSR in a modern civic university and my role in this.
- Evaluate the impact of CSR on stakeholders and the wider community.
- Propose a new framework for CSR in a modern civic university.

The objectives were:

- To reflect on my early experiences in order to explore my core values and to understand how individuals can make a difference.
- To critically review literature relating to CSR and the civic university.
- To undertake action research and reflect on the development of a range of activities which I propose pave the way for a CSR culture.
- To reflect on the introduction of a CSR statement and the embedding of principles into corporate strategy and practice.
- Based on the evidence in the literature and the action research and reflections above, to propose a framework for CSR within a civic university.
- To evaluate the impact of CSR at the university across its stakeholders, and wider implications for the CSR community of practice.
- To draw conclusions and lessons for practice, and propose a final framework of CSR in a civic university.

Methodological approach

I used a mixed methods research methodology, which combines research approaches in order to appropriately collect and triangulate the variety of data available. This included reflective writing, to gain understanding; a literature review, to provide context; action research and reflective practice, to set out the work and identify principles; and quantitative and qualitative research, to measure and ground the emerging theories.

I wrote in the first person throughout. I found this easier and also liberating in terms of aspects of reflection and auto-ethnography, which can make a doctorate so special.

I also deliberately numbered the supporting sections of the portfolio to directly match the relevant section of the report (i.e. Chapter 4 of the report mapped across to Section 4 of the portfolio). This made it easier for me to compile and for the reader to access, and it meant that the two documents complemented each other. The following section is taken from my report, and shows how I structured the report to reflect the methodological approach taken.

- *"Reflective Writing: To understand experiences from personal and practitioner perspectives (Chapter 1 and throughout). Winter (1989) refers to the widespread but often ignored human capacity for gaining understanding through reflecting on experience. I consider my own contributions and their impact upon me in order to share these experiences as a reflective practitioner and to help understand my role within the wider context of my involvement in CSR. I also incorporate the principles and approaches of Tenni et al. (2003), who present practical solutions to the issues raised when undertaking autobiographical research.*

- *Literature Review: To critically research; to contextualise CSR and the civic university (Chapter 3). I review literature to outline a history of CSR activities and bring this up to date in terms of current trends towards what is becoming known as corporate citizenship, which Andriof and McIntosh (2001) define as organisations giving consideration to the societies in which they operate. I review current published models and frameworks of CSR and discuss their applicability to a civic university. I examine the concept of the civic university and determine the relevance of a CSR agenda to the civic vision of the university.*

- *Action Research and Reflective Practice: To capture my contribution, assess impact and improve practice (Chapters 4, 5 and 6). Schön (1983) refers to knowing-in-action as the application of practical knowledge. He argues that if we think about what we are doing, as we are doing it, this reflecting-in-action will enable us to learn from our own practice, thereby contributing to our professional knowledge. Chapters 4, 5 and 6 are central to this report as they outline my body of work, how I reflected on my on-going practice, and learned lessons that were applied in the journey towards CSR and in the formulation of a new CSR framework. I will demonstrate how I have used action research techniques throughout the core of my chapters. McNiff and Whitehead (2002) define action research as a means of looking at practice in order to check progress, and understand either why it is satisfactory or how it needs to improve. They believe that 'the idea of self-reflection is central', as action research involves learning in, and through, action and reflection. I will show how my reflection has enabled me to identify common principles and a consistency of approach in a range of activities that were able set the scene for the introduction of a holistic CSR approach. This practice and reflection has also enabled me to recognise and refine these strands of activity into a new CSR framework. Action research is appropriate for this study as it is an approach whereby the researcher acts as a facilitator and the research relationship is one in which those involved are participants in the change process (Hart and Bond, 1995). It therefore lends itself to a process of continuous improvement derived from developing on-going relationships with stakeholders and learning from these engagements. This collaborative approach produces results that can be shared with a community of practice for wider application. Hart and Bond (1995) point out that a triangulation of research methods will deliver scientific rigour and validity; this approach is used to validate this piece of action research.*

- *Quantitative and Qualitative Research: To gauge stakeholder views on socially responsible behaviour and their perception of the university and of CSR (Chapter 7). Examination of existing staff and student survey data provides the base starting point, or 'grounded theory' (Strauss and Corbin, 1998), for measuring stakeholder opinions. These are added to by questionnaires which cover any gaps in knowledge and understanding. Qualitative contributions from key stakeholders provide insights that complement these analyses."*

Impact on the community

Having witnessed life-changing experiences such as the end of apartheid in South Africa, I was keenly aware of the impact that individuals and organisations can have on others. As an equality and diversity practitioner, I felt that progress was being made but that there was an opportunity, in the right corporate culture, for both employees and organisations to make positive contributions to the communities they come into contact with.

I therefore aimed to enhance a corporate social responsibility approach at the university and beyond. This would join up aspects of good practice already in existence, engage employees, customers and the community, and provide the environment for further contributions. I become involved in a series of pieces of work, which were broader than my initial remit but actually delivered and encouraged the principles of fairness and responsibility I was working to achieve. Initiatives included a series of water wheels in

African villages and social provisions in Columbia as a direct result of specific purchasing agreements linked to Fairtrade; a number of community events that linked the university to the city; and the introduction of some major initiatives on diversity for staff and students.

I used qualitative feedback to illustrate the impact the work had on communities and individuals. I balanced this with existing and new quantitative surveys of students and staff, which showed highest-ever ratings of the university as a responsible institution. Feedback from the city, the community and from the wider sector also helped to confirm progress in terms of stakeholder endorsement.

Since the completion of the doctorate, at the university, students and staff have embarked on a range of socially responsible projects and the university has cemented its reputation as a responsible institution. More widely, the link between the principles of equality and diversity and greater engagement with the community and with ethical practice is one that is growing in a range of organisations. I have since become a self-employed specialist in this area and am very conscious of a desire by organisations to try to do the right thing in terms of their operations, both for business and for ethical reasons.

The viva

I was examined by an Associate Dean of Faculty and relevant internal and external specialists. The mock viva was very useful for me, as my preparation and experience in that process helped when I later attended the viva. From my point of view, it was good to approach the viva as an opportunity to engage and have an informed discussion with interested colleagues rather than as a rabbit in the headlights exam. By being prepared I was able to defend my rationale if required but, and this was actually the case, was also ready to be enthusiastic about the subject and to enjoy the discussion. The examiners focused on different aspects of my work in the mock and in the actual viva. One common strand was that they found the structure of the report and portfolio easy for them to navigate and the first-person writing style appropriate to the personal content of the doctorate.

Personal experience of the doctoral journey

Anyone who embarks on a doctorate will find it a challenging, rewarding and ultimately life-changing experience. From my own viewpoint, I felt more comfortable once I became familiar with the academic principles behind the doctorate and I had begun to get something down on paper. Writing in the first person was liberating, and I found that my writing became increasingly enjoyable as I became more confident. If you are not passionate about your subject, the work can become a chore and you will need to be systematic in order to make progress. If you are passionate about your work, I would suggest trying to follow and capture that passion – it will become evident in your writing and will ultimately help you to take that direction in your future activities.

11.4 Case study 3: Max

Professional and academic background

I have worked in the marine and offshore sectors for over 40 years. Having progressed from draughtsman to vice president of a global organisation, I have been working as a consultant since 2001. Throughout my career I have been fortunate to travel extensively, experiencing the different work practices and cultures in many parts of the world. I developed an interest in management, particularly quality management, in the late 80's and successfully completed an MSc in 1996.

Motivation for studying the professional doctorate

The main reason initially was to become a doctor. Having enrolled for the study and as happened with my masters studies, I quickly realised that my education would be significantly enhanced during the study period. This did change as the course progressed and my motivation developed into one of great challenge. Several times I began to question whether I had begun something I could not finish and having faced similar scenarios during my lifetime it became another spur to push on and continue. Coming through this phase I entered a period of almost blind pursuance of the cause, often ignoring the other activities in my life.

> "The motivation for this work lies within my long standing involvement with, and interest in, quality management systems. I had been involved at a detailed level with the operation and function of quality management systems during my employment in oil and gas and latterly with a major change programme in the late 1990's. One of the many concerns I encountered from engineers and management was that quality management systems are often put in place to satisfy a client requirement and that they may offer little real value to the company or users. It is sometimes stated that systems termed 'quality systems' may actually offer little support to, and in some cases may detract from, the management function. In this report I will demonstrate how I used my experience of the oil and gas sector and my knowledge of quality management first to develop an Integrated Management System, IMS. This system was necessary to reflect a revised company structure and embodied best practice principles at that time. Building and reflecting on this initiative, I then developed and implemented the Company Management System, CMS. The CMS incorporated a core

management system which mirrored the structure and objectives of the business, whilst encompassing the principles of ISO 9001: 2000. There are eight quality management principles included within the standard which aim to improve performance and achieve success. These principles are further discussed in Chapter 3 of the report. More than this, however, the CMS embodied my own set of core principles which I propose are fundamental to good management.

In 2001 a management consultancy I had set up secured a contract for the design and management of major facilities in the oil and gas sector. The remit was quite simple. To develop and implement a management system in accordance with the requirements of ISO 9001:2000. This period of my work was used as a further development of the CMS concept. Again the development was based upon a fundamental set of core principles, as discussed in this report. The successful implementation of the system was very much a result of people engagement. Developing the system during the embryonic stage of the company facilitated the growth of an improvement-focused culture. This report provides evidence that with management support and a culture based on continuous improvement, an efficient and effective management system can be successfully developed and implemented."

The project

Title: Core Principles for a Successful Management System: A Professional Journey

A practitioner-based research programme which reflected upon my professional experience built on evidence from the academic and professional literature and centred on the development of a management information system, known as the CMS. My research revealed six principles of management systems, which I demonstrated are fundamental to the success of any organisation. The principles were further evidenced by a qualitative study of the views of senior professionals from a range of sectors.

Abstract

"This integrative doctoral report describes a research project which draws from the author's experience and knowledge of management within the oil and gas sector. Core to the research is the design and development of a company management system, the CMS. The system was designed for a new business division of an international company whose strategic vision was to gain a global presence as an engineering contractor. The research uses the formal approach of reflective practice to draw principles from the experiential work.

This reflection resulted in a series of principles which the author proposes are core to the successful development of a management system. The project entailed extensive literature research which further developed and refined the core principles. The principles were compared to the ISO standard, EFQM Excellence model and several proprietary systems. A qualitative study was undertaken to investigate the management systems in use in a selection of sectors, and to explore the applicability of the derived principles. This study established the views and opinions of senior management to systems and their attitude towards quality. The synthesis of experiential data, examination of the literature, lessons learnt from the development of the CMS and the qualitative study provided further evidence to support the six derived principles, which are: Value-based, Empowerment, Team culture, Simplicity, Continuous Improvement, and Added Value.

This work makes a contribution to both research and professional practice at several levels:

- Research into professional practice. This work demonstrates the value of undertaking a research project which is located within professional practice, and yet grounded in significant primary and secondary research.
- The six principles. The value and validity of the six principles has been demonstrated through reflective practice, exploration of the literature, a case study development of a system (the CMS) and a qualitative study. The six core principles are novel and have broader applicability than the oil and gas sector.
- The CMS. The development of the CMS has demonstrated the value to be gained by developing a management system according to sound management principles.
- Value-based vs. process-based management approaches. Finally the work demonstrates that a successful management system should be value (and culture) based, rather than process based. This piece of professional research thus makes a valuable contribution to the research of management systems both academically and specifically within the oil and gas sector."

Project aims

"The aim of this work has been to identify best practice in management systems and to propose a set of core principles which underpin a successful management system. To do this I initially completed a thorough reflection of my experience before undertaking an examination of quality and management literature. This strengthened and supported my evidence of how I developed and implemented a system which embodies best practice, the CMS. Finally I undertook qualitative research which examined senior management views on management systems."

Methodological approach

Determining how I was going to undertake this work changed several times and it was quite a while before I identified what methods I would finally employ. The key turning point was the development of a career storyboard which once analysed, identified what areas/topics I needed to research. This followed a question by a supervisor who asked: 'So what are you trying to say about your system? What makes you think it's better than others?'

I did not have any formal training although much of my professional life involved investigating and analysing work methods and practices. I did however gain significant benefit from assistance in undertaking literature research. A university librarian spent a lot of time teaching me methods and processes which I found invaluable. The data collected were diverse and in some cases voluminous. Regular discussions with my supervisors provided the direction of research.

It is important to realise that you are not alone in completing this work. Your supervisors are there to help. If you cannot convince them of the quality of your work then something must be wrong. That's why you must meet and discuss progress regularly as very often it's the simple question that starts the next phase.

Impact on the community

I aimed to influence the sectors I worked in obviously but there was an added attraction that completing this particular piece of work would establish my credibility in other sectors. My contribution has been that I have had several commissions since in varied sectors in helping people with management systems and activities. I have also been joint author of several papers which have been published and two have actually been presented at international conferences. I have been able to design, develop and implement several systems for clients without the need to convince them of the benefits. Some have gained almost immediate third party certification. The fact I have secured further commissions by international clients in this area not only in my own sector but have now moved into others is demonstration that the work is live, tangible, effective and useful. The completion of such work is now an excellent method of marketing 'Dr Max' who now can list a premier league football club, an international software company and a marketing group amongst an expanding list of clients.

The viva

I thoroughly enjoyed every second of the viva. It followed a rigorous almost torturous practice viva a couple of weeks prior during which I learnt many lessons. You never know what topics or questions will be raised; however you can prepare your method of response. That was the key for me as you will know your work inside out. Dear me you've spent three, four or even five years with it. How you can defend it becomes a skill in itself. I was a little disappointed at the end of this session as I was really enjoying the experience. The internal academic considered a matrix I had included was unclear and I offered to include another for clarity. The external academic commented the thesis was informative, comprehensive and a good piece of work. The external 'work' examiner stated he thought it was an excellent read and an accurate reflection of what existed in the oil and gas sector. He went on to say that it could have a substantial effect on how we approach work in the future. I am pleased to say he was right.

Personal experience of the doctoral journey

The first thing people must appreciate is the time and dedication necessary. The very fact that they have chosen this route suggests that they will be employed, probably in a senior position. There are no short cuts, there is no hiding place but the satisfaction of achieving such a goal is immense. Feeling the comfort and satisfaction that you have completed a major piece of work, of which original research is a fundamental property, reflects in how you can demonstrate significant enhancement of your skills and knowledge. When you reach the fourth or fifth revision of your work you seriously consider packing it up, stay with it a little longer as that's when you are nearly at the top of the hill. When you get there it's a roll down the other side, with a pot of gold at the bottom.

11.5 Case study 4: Siobhan

Professional and academic background

I am currently seconded from a local college to work full-time on two major projects and my base is an independent office where I carry out this work. The first project is being supported by a national UK group of colleges. The second project is being supported by the AoC (UK Association of Colleges).

Having completed a Certificate in Education in Further Education, full-time, I started lecturing in business and IT in 1988, after spending ten years in industry and commerce. The management roles that I have carried out over the years have included Continuing Education in the Community, New Business Development and Commercial Operations, Quality Manager, Director of a small semi-autonomous college, Work Based Learning and, more recently, Corporate Services with emphasis on efficiencies and value for money. My qualifications include a BSc(Hons) in Education and Politics, MEd in the Management of Change, MBA in Total Quality Management and (now!) a professional doctorate in Shared Services. I have been a Member of the Chartered Quality Institute since 1997.

Motivation for studying the professional doctorate

I always wanted to see how far I could go academically and wondered whether I could actually achieve a doctorate level qualification. I had over the past 15 years applied and been accepted on two doctorate programmes, but never started due to severe pregnancy sickness. By the time I started the professional doctorate, I had no intention of having any more children (or pregnancy related sickness commonly and mistakenly referred to as 'morning sickness' but in reality 24/7 sickness!!).

A Professor came along to the College I was working at and spoke to around 30 staff describing the professional doctorate and I particularly liked the idea of it being very closely related to my work. I had already done two master's degrees and an NVQ management qualification and it sounded like a blend of the two; a theoretical and practical high level qualification. Although my main aim for doing the professional doctorate didn't change, there was many a time when I progressed through the programme that I thought 'why am I doing this on top of a full-time very demanding career and a relatively young family of 4 children, not to mention my poor long suffering husband' – it did at times seem a stretch too far and certainly fine-tuned my time management skills. As with most mature students, there were family crises and bereavements, but it did help that I am a bit of an obsessive completer/finisher.

The project

Title: Shared Services in Further Education

The aim was to investigate models of shared services and to develop and evaluate a model of shared services for application in the further education sector.

Abstract

"There is very little research on the use of shared services in the further education Sector. The aims of this research are to investigate models of shared services and to develop and evaluate a model of shared services for application in the further education sector. This report investigates the case of shared services arrangements in further education using exploratory research as there appeared to be a scarcity of empirical evidence. One of the key issues that the research found was the wide and varied interpretations of what is meant by shared services. In both literature and practice, the term shared services does not have a standardised meaning and this can lead to confusion. A further major issue for principals and chief executives of colleges was the perceived lack of control when contemplating a shared services solution together with other factors such as VAT (value added tax),

competition law, information technology systems and connectivity, which the model of shared services would need to overcome.

In practice, the level of trust increased between collaborating partners in a shared service project when clear vision and strategic plans were developed during the decision-making process leading to the presentation of a business case. In addition, the research also found that the main critical success factors of a shared services solution highlights the importance of continual process improvements for achieving lower costs, high productivity and higher quality customer service.

A single case study was investigated and therefore cannot be generalised to the wider population. However, the research can be used to facilitate a better understanding of the term shared services together with the issues that are likely to be encountered when contemplating shared services in the further education sector.

The time is right for the further education sector to begin exploring shared services options as a means of being innovative, reducing costs and producing high quality services. The major barriers have been identified together with possible solutions. The key threat of independence of colleges together with concerns of control and autonomy have been explored leading to a new model of shared services that enables each partner to retain their sovereignty, while also enjoying the benefits which shared services can offer."

Project aims

The aim of this research was: To investigate models of shared services and to develop and evaluate a model of shared services for application in the further education sector.

The specific objectives of the research were:

- *To critically review the current state of the art of shared services, with particular reference to the further education Sector.*
- *To undertake a detailed case study with local further education partners to develop a shared services model to match their requirements.*
- *To analyse the case study and draw out lessons, and recommendations for, shared services, with particular reference to the further education Sector.*

Methodological approach

Exploratory case study research (Yin, 2003) was chosen as the overall approach as although much has been written about shared services (Bangemann, 2005; Bergeron, 2003; Dollery et al., 2007; Holzer et al., 2009; Janssen et al., 2007; Schulman et al., 1999; Schulz et al., 2009; Strikwerda, 2006;

Ulbrich et al., 2008; Ulrich, 1995; Whitfield, 2007; Yee et al., 2009), especially in providing cost efficiencies whilst at the same time delivering quality services (Herbert and Seal, 2009), there appears to be a scarcity of empirical evidence. Exploratory research studies are also termed as formulative studies. The main purpose of exploratory research is the discovery of ideas and insights. Inbuilt flexibility in research design is needed because the research problem tends to be broadly defined initially and then transformed into more precise meaning. This piece of exploratory research focused on the use of qualitative methodology within a single case study between further education colleges who were looking to develop a business case for shared services.

The approach I took in carrying out the research included:

- Carrying out an extensive literature review.
- Undertaking desktop research, in particular, in relation to the national Collaboration Fund projects as well as a range of other available professional and policy literature.
- A qualitative study involving in-depth, semi-structured interviews with key stakeholders (18 interviews were undertaken).
- A detailed case study of initially two further education colleges working collaboratively to develop a shared services model; this subsequently developed into seven partners working collaboratively.

I had undertaken research method training at university as an Undergraduate and also when I did my masters degrees. I had a further workshop training event organised by the university.

The fieldwork and analysis was relatively straightforward because I had been fortunate to be seconded full-time for several months to carry this work out. However, I significantly underestimated the amount of work involved in the literature review and the searches involved. It helped enormously when the professor sent me an extensive literature review report to use as an exemplar. The major difference with the professional doctorate literature review was the extensive international search and review that I had not been required to undertake with any of my previous degrees. This in-depth literature review proved to be invaluable when carrying out the analysis work.

Impact on the community

The project contributed to the limited body of research available on shared services in further education and the results clearly showed that the time is right for the further education sector to begin exploring shared services options. The raising of the profile of shared services in further education has clearly been demonstrated as a means of cost saving, increased efficiency and higher service levels, as a result of my research work. The research has been evaluated with respect to the published literature and adds to the limited body of research available on shared services in further education. The analysis, in particular the definition of most advantageous shared services that mitigates against the major barriers, can be used by other further education colleges to support their decision-making processes during this age of austerity. It has also elevated the importance of the role of procurement and some of the easy and quick wins this can bring about.

The research has fed into the development of a toolkit for the further education sector which will enable colleges to explore the possibility of setting up a shared service arrangement. The toolkit comprises modules on collaborative working, equality and diversity impact assessment, stakeholder survey, contractual and financial issues. All of these aspects have been informed by the research work which I undertook during my doctoral studies. This toolkit is of significance to the further education sector, and to anyone who is considering setting up a shared service.

Since completion of the project, I have successfully secured further funding to begin the implementation of shared services as well as investigating a federation model of delivering strategic services. The learning from the implementation phase is being captured in a guide that will be made freely available to the further education sector as an iPhone app.

"This research has highlighted the need for clarity around definitions of shared services and the emergence of a preferred model; both of which have been provided in this project. My research is the first detailed work of shared services in the further education sector. It has stimulated significant interest as demonstrated by the involvement of over one hundred colleges being involved in shared services projects, illustrating the level of understanding that the further education sector had been brought to by the dissemination of my research report.

My advice has been sought by the Association of Colleges, further education colleges and private consultants, on numerous issues relating to shared services. The project work has being lauded as 'leading the way'; the 'flagship project' by several national bodies (see Portfolio 6.1, 6.2, 6.3, 6.4, 6.7).

It is testament of the work carried out to date that the project has successfully progressed through gateway reviews and received immediate approval and funding to progress to the next stage. It is one of less than a handful of the 41 projects supported to have done this, and achieved every milestone (see Portfolio 6.5, 6.6, and 6.7).

The research has been widely disseminated in the further education sector, as well as being referred to by the private sector (see Portfolio 6.2).

Shared services have had little academic attention as revealed by the detailed literature review and this study serves as an additional primer for further research."

The viva

My examiners included an:

- Academic external examiner
- Professional external examiner
- Internal examiner
- Independent chair

Uncharacteristically, I felt very nervous, but my supervisor said that the panel could not detect it; she only knew because she could see my hands shaking under the table! I think the reason that I was so nervous was the thought of failure; all that work that had been done over a number of years and the thought of the panel not thinking it was worthy added to my anxiety. The dread I had was that I would be asked questions that I couldn't answer. In hindsight, I don't know why I inflicted this on myself. I thoroughly enjoyed the 'discussion' and felt very confident during the process because this was my work that I felt very passionate about and the time flew past! I was particularly pleased that all the examiners had said that they had enjoyed reading through my work and the discussion we had during the viva.

Personal experience of the doctoral journey

This has been a difficult journey; juxtaposing a full-time senior management career and personal family commitments; whilst at the same time trying to mesh in a demanding academic and professional doctoral research project. My knowledge and understanding of the subject, however, would not have been anywhere as near developed had I not embarked on this programme of study. I feel a real sense of achievement in being able to juggle so many demands and at the same time still managing to deliver the required outcomes to timescale.

When I embarked on the professional doctorate, I had no clear expectations other than I wanted to see if I could achieve at this level of academic and professional work. I had already undertaken several postgraduate courses. However, reflecting on my journey in undertaking this research and the deep dive into theory that I have gone through to inform my practice has really enlightened and changed the way I approach my work. I now realise that to get high quality work that I can be proud of is really (really) hard work and that it isn't enough to surface skim the theory.

I can honestly say that if my work resulted in a fail that, whilst I would naturally be disappointed, I could walk away knowing that I have personally developed in a way that I never anticipated. Consequently, I am about to embark on a further, very challenging, project on strategic shared services in further education and will begin with the hard task of deep diving into the theory of strategy and federated models knowing that this will produce the kind of outcomes that I can comfortably defend and be proud of.

Undertaking a professional doctorate is not for the faint hearted. You need to be very motivated; big doses of perseverance; dedication and commitment and the ability to be absolutely determined to see it through to the end. However, it is all worth it in the end and the personal satisfaction when you are officially awarded your doctorate will be one of the proudest days of your life.

11.6 Case study 5: Fiona

Professional and academic background

Registered General Nurse; BA in Nursing; MA in Management & Leadership.

I qualified in 1990 as a registered general nurse and enjoyed a variety of nursing, specialist nursing and nurse manager posts across acute, community and clinical networks. I took an interest in the 'errors and mistakes' that occur in healthcare as a result of my own learning experiences – not only from the error involving the patient but also because of how the 'management' managed the incident. The apparent focus on the staff over the patient, shaped my philosophical approach to nursing and management, making sure that staff understood how they contributed to the organisation and its goals as well as benefitted patients through their expertise. Now employed in a commissioning organisation, as the interim director of nursing, quality and development, I am well positioned to put patients at the centre of what the organisation does and define the desired services outcomes and experience of patients, as they would wish them to be.

Motivation for studying the professional doctorate

I had been exposed to the professional doctorate while studying in Leeds, but at that time I could not think of something that I was so passionate about to undertake a doctorate. When I joined the Primary Care Trust (PCT) I quickly realised what I was employed to deliver for the PCT was exciting and innovative, but more importantly not a 'bolt-on' to my role. It was my role, making the type of study required by a doctorate somewhat easier. The drive for this doctoral study was to develop an organisational improvement approach suited to National Health Service (NHS) commissioning and to address a gap in commissioning improvement methods. The PCT's drive for improvement was for two distinct reasons: firstly, to make improvements for patients; and secondly, to position themselves as world-class commissioners.

The project

Title: A Commissioning Improvement Framework: the development and implementation of a Lean organisational improvement approach for NHS commissioning.

Undertaken over a three year period, this piece of work used action research to show how the principles of Lean Thinking (a continuous improvement system typically associated with manufacturing) can be introduced into the day-to-day practice of NHS commissioning.

As a result of the collaborative research, a commissioning improvement framework has been developed and implemented that: positions improvement as part of the organisation's business philosophy; determines the drivers for improvement that look to add value from the viewpoint of patients, eliminate waste and increase business efficiency; standardises the process of delivering improvements, empowering staff to take forward their ideas and bring about change that benefits patients and the organisation alike.

Abstract

"This report presents the development and installation of a novel NHS Commissioning Improvement Framework (CIF) within a primary care trust context and discusses the impacts made in practice. Through a programme of action research, this study has been able to show how the principles of Lean can be introduced into the day-to-day practice of a commissioning organisation and deliver measurable benefits to both patient and the organisation through the application of the CIF.

For the past two decades, it could be argued that the improvement agenda in the NHS has been the 'silent' partner in delivering performance targets; focusing efforts on improving access to treatment. In my experience, the basic fundamental of improving patient experience has been overshadowed by the performance agenda. In recent years, there has also been a drive for improvement from a commissioning perspective. However, improvement processes are more suited to the needs of healthcare providers, thus commissioner orientated improvement methodologies are somewhat lacking.

The major contribution made by this study is a new commissioning improvement model (the CIF) which integrates the principles of continuous improvement and Lean into NHS commissioning. Structured into three main domains: Position, Process and Drivers, the new model highlights the importance of a high degree of workforce engagement and staff development. The action research process used was an intuitive part of the change process and provided a prospective view of what was required to further embed improvement into commissioning practice. Complemented by a programme of practice development and classroom education an increase in workforce improvement understanding and capability has been seen to deliver a number of measured improvements for both patient services and commissioning organisation alike.

Although there are planned changes to NHS commissioning in the future; the drive for improving patient quality, experience and commissioning efficiency will remain, regardless of who hosts the component parts of the commissioning process. There is likely to be an increase in commissioning-related organisations, with which will come a degree of fragmentation to the commissioning process. Therefore, there is an increased importance to understand the commissioning process in the emerging new world and the improvement mechanisms that will ensure increased patient value and commissioning effectiveness. Improvement frameworks, such as the CIF will have a significant role to play in 'operationalising' the new commissioning vision for the NHS."

Project aims

"The purpose of this study was to develop an organisational improvement approach in NHS commissioning using the principles of Lean."

Methodological approach

Action research was used for this study because it had the potential to challenge structures of knowledge, practice and power within a given situation. Participation of key stakeholders (such as staff members) who are normally not party to decision-making was an essential part of the research developments, and led to the project outcome being more relevant to the lives of 'ordinary' people (Bradbury and Reason, 2006). The traditional schools of quantitative (and, to some extent, qualitative) research argue against the validity of action research because of the absence of data and data analysis (Denscombe, 1998). There is a view therefore, that action research has no place in the 'research library'. Whilst data and formulation of statistical significance may not form part of the end result of an action research study, Bradbury and Reason (2006) argue that action research adds value from another perspective: it brings together action and reflection, theory and practice to conceive a practical solution. Well-implemented action research benefits from an appropriate approach that involves wide groups of people and is capable of managing complex environments.

I choose to adapt Kemmis and McTaggart's (1988) three modes of action research, with the spiral approach that is action research, as it offered an outline structure that started with the technical introduction of knowledge controlled through the 'expert'. The expert's role being to explain and predict what is needed first in practice and set the initial foundation for change and development. The second mode took the technical foundation into practice to illuminate how initial ideas operated in reality and informed future decisions, which could then be retested. The third mode, which was achieved through involving staff in practice, was emancipation, giving staff actionable knowledge and freedoms to operate.

My only tip would be to be clear at the outset about the research methodology and the stages of how that method will be described, as work-based research tends to happen all at the same time. I know I was doing multiple stages of research for different aspects of the approach in parallel. Also gather, label and organise your evidence as you go (against the research outcomes) – it is much easier and less time consuming that doing it all at the end.

Impact on the community

The focus of my work was initially directed at the leadership set of NHS commissioning organisations and professionals interested in continuous improvement per se. However, the improvement framework itself offers a broader contribution to any organisation, if the structure and principles within it are adapted to the context of the organisation. The major contribution made by this study is a new commissioning improvement model which integrates the principles of continuous improvement and Lean into NHS commissioning. The new model highlights the importance of a high degree of workforce engagement and staff development. The action research process involved was an intuitive part of the change process and provided a prospective view of what was required to further embed improvement into commissioning practice.

Structured into three components parts, the CIF provides a systematic approach and organisational platform that addresses improvement:

- Position: vision, improvement accountability and proposal, visual management system and escalation.
- Process: standardisation, process for improvement, on-the-job improvement expertise, develop capability.
- Drivers: define value from the viewpoint of the patient, build effective value-streams across the commissioning organisation, establish commissioning flow; work in response to quality, health and patient need and aspire to perfect process and provision.

This work contributes to practice because of: the new way of improvement thinking it offers commissioning organisations of the future; systematic application that develops staff and operations; and the ability to improve both patient services and organisational effectiveness. In the past, NHS improvement efforts have focused on the singular aspect of the improvement process. A major learning point of this work has been the engagement of the wider workforce in developing the CIF through practice. The additional elements of strategic position, on-going leadership support and development laid the foundations for the approach in the PCT to be sustained over the longer term. It is only because of the change in national commissioning direction that the trajectory for the PCT has altered. The study has been evaluated in two ways; one against the three modes of action research and secondly, through the impact of the approach being used in practice. Although I left the organisation once I had completed the study and returned six months later, the component parts of the commissioning improvement framework are still being used in practice.

The viva

My examiners were:

- Chief executive of a commissioning primary care trust
- Professor of nursing
- Academic from the subject area

I saw the viva as an opportunity to showcase my work and speak with people who are interested in the work I had undertaken. I had prepared well and I had 'researched' my panel members to gain some insights about their own interests. I certainly did not find it intimidating or challenging but an intellectual conversation that stretched beyond my work, which helped strengthen my final submission.

Personal experience of the doctoral journey

There were two main journeys underway in the PCT when I did my doctoral study, one of which will continue until the planned closure of the PCT, as the platform for NHS commissioning is changing. The other is mine, which ended with the PCT, due to the reduction in management costs and transition towards clinically-led commissioning. In taking this organisational development forward, not only has the organisation had to grow, so have I – examining how I interacted with the PCT and its staff. Learning more about effective organisational cultures, individual and team effectiveness and emotional intelligence has exposed me to new approaches and use of language with which to engage staff, thus lessening the impact of my perceived 'tidal wave' approach.

There have been times in my NHS career when I have been tormented by negative feedback: I was seen to be 'too challenging'; 'not living in the 'real world'; 'what planet was I on?' When I joined the NHS I did not realise the 'radical' that I was, and that it would become a central part of who I am. This PCT allowed me to use that energy and motivation to influence the behaviour and actions of others on an organisational scale for the good of the patient and the organisation itself. Consequently, I have had the opportunity to contribute to, and lead, some of the most significant organisational changes that have occurred in a single PCT – without having to renege on my philosophical outlook and values.

Being different is a personal high-risk strategy and the realities faced in practice can, in some ways, be fundamentally disempowering. Harnessed by a belief that the world can look different, my drive to improve the way services and care are organised and delivered remains my true North. Typically, individuals who have such strong convictions and values see 'a truth' that contradicts the conventions or traditional wisdoms of organisations and professional practice and yet, they are able to remain loyal to the new truth and the organisation. Such individuals are essential agents for organisations that want to learn and change.

I enrolled on the professional doctorate because I recognised that the piece of work I was about to undertake at the PCT was novel to commissioning and, in many ways, novel to the NHS. What I did not realise was the personal journey I would undergo and how it would affect the way I operate today. At the start of the doctorate process I thought I knew why I was doing what I was doing, comfortable in my skin and prepared to take on the world. However, my real journey of discovery started when I wrote the personal reflection of my life and career, identifying some of the significant events that form my own personal jigsaw. Accustomed to the practice of reflection as a nurse, I understood its value to practice, but not its value to me as a person. When I look back at the role of reflection as a clinical practitioner and as a process of understanding me, the two processes are poles apart in terms of depth and wider meaning. In reality, the reflection I undertook as a nurse offered a 'here and now' picture of what had happened, what the consequences were and what I should do next. I did not examine the personal impact, look at relationships or the impacts events had on me. It has only been through the doctorate process I have taken the time to examine the situations, events and the developments I have led in more detail, adding strength to my outlook on life.

In practice, I feel it is important for you to know who you are and what drives you, and yet, it has only been over the past three years that I have seen such clarity. As a nurse, I am not sure that my drive was about direct patient care, but about the system, or custom and practice, I operated in. Although the goal was still for patients to have a quality experience, my approach to delivering it was arguably different to others. I know when I listen to my sister as then nurse and now health visitor her clinical description of the healthcare world is very different to mine. Perhaps it is the balance of the two that can bring about an effective and quality health system. I could argue that the interest of the 'user' applies outside of healthcare. I can recall a conversation with a student peer, when I was questioning why I did not receive my student parking pass with my registration card, why was it a separate process – particularly when nearly all doctorate students will be visitors to the campus needing to pay parking fees. As I told my colleague: 'the process was not in the interest of the student, but the separate departments that managed each system'.

The professional doctorate is about an original contribution to practice. Part of the challenge in that process has been finding a way that best articulates what I have done for others to understand. Blinded by my passion at times, access to critical friends (both inside and outside of work and the university) has been vital in 'extracting' me from my world of improvement, in order to bring objectivity and meaning. Sometimes that meant having 'heated' conversations because I could see the wood despite the trees but no-one else could. Once again reflection had a role to play in relaying the message and replacing the jigsaw pieces so the picture was much clearer. The relationship of the student and tutor has been key, even though at times I wanted to 'nail them to the wall', I needed the objectivity and fresh eyes for me to look at my work through the lens of the reader.

If asked whether the doctorate process has contributed to my work, I would say yes. The combination of the two has helped – although difficult at times – maintain a degree of objectivity and take my work to another level. Without the focus on an original contribution to practice I would not have extracted the learning from past practice to enable me to formulate the CIF. My contribution would have been another organisational case study sharing numerical facts. What I presented was as valuable to my future career path as it is to other commissioning organisations. The exciting step for me will be to test the framework in other organisations or institutions.

11.7 Case study 6: David

Professional and academic background

In the early 1980s I developed an interest in computing and had a couple of summer jobs programming while I was still at school. I went to university to do an undergraduate degree in natural sciences (computing, maths and geology) in 1984. After that, five of us set up and ran a computer consultancy company, which was relatively unsuccessful and after 3 years we closed the company and went our separate ways. I then got a job as computer science researcher and worked on a joint Department of Trade and Industry/Research Council project and two European Union Framework projects. During my time at university I did register for a part time PhD (computing), but with a young family I did not manage to spend the required time on my studies and let them lapse. The projects moved with the Principal Investigator to another university, and so did I. After the projects I applied for a job as a research manager and administrator in the newly (1994) formed Research Development Office with the remit of helping academic staff to apply for research funding. Over the years my role developed and eventually (2007) I headed up research support in the university. I also again attempted a part-time PhD (computing) but once again I did not manage more than a couple of years before I realised that my job at that time was too demanding and the research overlap with my job was not sufficient.

Motivation for studying the professional doctorate

In 2008, I decided that I really should be more 'selfish' and that I would devote more time to my studies (i.e. less to work, and try to restrict myself to more or less a 40 hour week for work...). I wanted to have a doctorate for two reasons. One for my own self esteem... to show that I was 'good enough' and also (mainly I think) to be able to progress my career. For about half the director of research services jobs, a research degree was an 'essential' and for almost all the remainder a 'desirable' qualification. So it seemed that for my career progression a doctorate would be a distinct advantage. At the outset I had the option of a PhD, a DBA or a DProf. Whilst a PhD seemed like the obvious choice, with my experience of the (lack of) overlap between job and research I decided against that. A DBA might give me more credibility as a manager, but perhaps not meet the 'research degree' criterion. The DProf was then relatively new but after discussions with a professor it was clear that there would be a substantive overlap between the research and my day job, indeed it is a requirement; it is also recognised as a research degree. It also had the added advantage of being able to draw on work that I had done prior to 2008, some of which I had come to realise was in fact cutting edge, and it seemed a good way to have this work recognised in some way.

As the project progressed my main motivation stayed the same, however the cohort experience had the added benefit of re-energising me after each workshop, and there was a certain amount of healthy rivalry in term of progression. I also found the whole process of itself useful in helping (making) me take time to reflect on my work and decisions that I had taken during my career. Overall it made me realise that if I think that I have something to contribute to the 'debate' then I probably have and I should endeavour to have my work and thoughts 'published' in some way.

The project

Title: Electronic Research Administration: Reflections on Research Management and Administration (RMA) in UK universities and in particular on Electronic Research Administration (ERA) and its perceived effect on the quality and quantity of research

The project had two main strands. To reflect on and evidence my contribution to the development of research management and administration as a profession in the UK through my committee work on the national association. And, to (using evidence from and reflecting on my experience of developing Electronic Research Administration system) show whether or not the use of such systems is perceived to have a tangible impact (hopefully positive) on the actual research undertaken.

Abstract

"Research Management and Administration (RMA) is a developing profession. Many RMA staff work in Universities and other research organisations, but they can also be found in agencies that fund research; in fact anywhere where research is undertaken or managed. RMA can be defined as 'the leadership, management or support of research activities' and one area of endeavour that RMAs are involved with is Electronic Research Administration (ERA): 'IT system(s) designed specifically to support research management or administration'. The aim of my professional doctorate is two-fold: to show my contribution to the development of RMA as a profession; and to demonstrate my practical contribution to advancing ERA systems including undertaking research to address the question: 'Can ERA affect the quality and quantity of research?'.

Over the years (1997–2011) I have been involved in and led many initiatives that have helped to shape RMA. I chart my role in the development of RMA through the growth of the professional Association for Research Managers and Administrators (ARMA) and other related initiatives.

The second strand of this doctoral work reflects on the specific ERA developments that I have introduced at the university. In particular it highlights how and why the various systems were initiated, developed, enhanced and sometimes superseded. Two elements are discussed in detail and reflected upon as case studies: Costing & Pricing, which underwent a number of major changes; and Publications Information, which evolved in a more organic way. The impact of both areas is considered in terms of benefits and detriments to research endeavour.

A mixed methods study of the effects of ERA systems on the quality and quantity of research undertaken is also conducted. This report presents the results of the case studies which are complemented by the analysis of a series of national questionnaires looking at the perceptions of research managers and administrators, and academic staff regarding ERA systems.

From the evidence presented it is shown that both RMA and ERA are deemed to have a positive impact on both the quality and quantity of research undertaken. Furthermore, the evidence base for the value of research management and administration as a profession is advanced; not only for individual RMAs, but also to the research community as a whole.

Project aims

There were two main strands of work, the development of the wider profession of research management and administration (RMA) in the UK and a specific research focus of ERA systems, in particular attempting to answer the question, 'Can ERA systems improve research quality and quantity?'

Methodological approach

I used a mixed methods approach, combining information from: reflection, mainly on historical information; case studies of two elements of the systems that I had developed, informed by archival analysis, and using focus and nominal group work, then leading to a questionnaire survey. In parallel I also undertook two national questionnaire surveys informed by a workshop. I had no specific research methods training, but had used many of these techniques before, but certainly not in as robust a way. The data analysis was mainly quantitative and relied heavily on the use of Excel and SPSS; again mainly self-taught.

It is really worth spending time planning what research you will need to undertake and understanding what method(s) you will need to utilise and then making sure that you fully understand those methods. For example, if you are going to use a questionnaire then plan to do a full questionnaire, survey and analysis in order to prove the whole process to yourself; do not expect to be able to use this work in your final doctoral report – it should be a learning exercise. Above all, take advantage of any and all methodological training, even if you think that it is not what you will need. In my report I argue that by definition a (or at least my) professional doctorate will require mixed methods – you will need to know many more research methods that you will actually use.

Impact on the community

The community of practice comprises those people working (mainly) in universities that undertake research management and/or administration. From this community of practice, an association was born. I played a key role in the development of the association as a committee member from 2000–2012, seeing membership grow from around 300 to over 1,700. In particular I claim to have influenced the subset of around 200 members with a particular interest in Electronic Research Administration.

During the development of the professional association I was an advocate of RMA as a career and the use of ERA tools to provide better service. I do not think that my research findings have, to date, had much influence, but personally I hope that I have helped various people across the UK and abroad understand the issues and benefits that ERA systems can bring.

Authenticating my contribution was perhaps the hardest part (although actually perhaps the part that my examiners asked me least about, so perhaps my fears were unfounded). In general I resorted to proxies. For example demonstrating the growth in the membership of ARMA (the UK professional association) and my contributions to the committee that helped support that growth. My 'standing' was supported by my applying for and obtaining two externally funded grants in the area of ERA. Similarly this was supported by my various committee and steering group roles and presentations at conferences. Since completing, I suspect due in part to the various professional articles that I wrote during my studies, I have been asked to present for various related organisations. I have also continued contributing to the sector by serving on various steering groups.

The viva

I was examined by an internal examiner (a senior lecturer) from the computing department, an external academic (a professor) with expertise in information retrieval. My professional examiner was previously the director of the research support service in another university and is still active as a research manager and administrator.

The viva was similar but at the same time totally different from the mock viva. It seemed to focus on a (different) small subset of the work and largely ignored other areas (although perhaps this is my recollection of the event as to be honest the whole thing is a bit of a blur). The time went very quickly until I was waiting for the result of their deliberations... the longest hour of my life!

They were particularly keen to see consistency in the use of terms. I had deliberately tried to vary the words that I used to describe things (in relation to survey analysis) in order to reduce repetitiveness, however this had had the side effect of not making it clear that I was comparing 'eggs with eggs'. I was also amazed at how finicky some of the comments were (for example ensuring that the titles of tables were above rather than below). Overall it was clear that they were more than happy with my professional contribution (and suggested reducing the portfolio in that area) but less satisfied about the rigour of the description of the research – after all it is a research degree.

Personal experience of the doctoral journey

What I wish I had known then that I know now:

- It is the research that is important. Make sure that you know what research methods you are likely to want to use, and learn how to use them, and practise this. The professional work is also important.

Always keep electronic versions of everything you have done in your work life! I wish I had kept a diary of events/meetings/workshops/ etc. – however you should have started this when you started working, i.e. well before you start your professional doctorate.

● Do not be afraid to ask for help. In particular from your supervisors, but also from the library – it is well worth a visit or ten in the first few weeks, and do ask librarians for help. Keep a FULL record of everything that you have read, annotate papers (with page numbers), copy things from websites and note the date. Use reference manager software, and get to know how to use it properly; and make sure it works for you (I used EndNoteWeb®, but I think I should have switched to Mendeley® as it is much better for annotating pdfs.) Start this on day one. Also learn how to use your word processor properly, with heading styles, references and sections – and don't change versions half way through (I used Word 2007®). Think about how you might want to present your portfolio, and start collecting things sooner rather than later. (I used Excel® and OneNote® to manage my portfolio of items and my to-do lists.) I found DropBox® to be invaluable as I worked on more than one computer (and it provides and automatic backup!).

● Be prepared to throw things away (or rather not use them – although this feels like throwing them away! In the end my portfolio was I think still larger than it needed to be).

● Work out what your optimal working style is. I worked best in long tranches of time, it always seemed to take me an hour or so to get back into the 'zone'; so doing an hour here and an hour there did not help much.

11.8 Case study 7: Hamid

Professional and academic background

My previous experience included: retail banking; private business; commercial finance; and from 1989 to 2012 investment banking/internal audit/ operational risk management. I am now working in the office of the UK Regulator. In terms of qualifications I have a BSc (Hons) Financial Services/ Associate of the Chartered Institute of Bankers, an Executive MBA, and now a DProf. I am a Fellow of the Australasian Institute of Bankers (FAIB), Fellow of Securities and Investment Institute (FSI), Fellow of the Institute of Financial Services (FIFS) formerly the Chartered Institute of Bankers (ACIB), a Chartered Member of the Chartered Management Institute (CMgr) MCMI, and a Professional Member of Institute of Operational Risk (PIOR).

Motivation for studying the professional doctorate

The main motivators for undertaking the DProf were:

- Questioning the adequacy and effectiveness of the Internal Audit (IA) function to audit a complex area like Operational Risk (OR).
- Exploring IA's role during the banking crisis; and whether the IA function could have done more to limit/prevent this global financial catastrophe.
- Identifying and offering solutions to address gaps in IA coverage.
- Investigating how IA has adapted to the unprecedented changes across the industry.
- Adding to the limited published OR literature (in particular, to auditing OR).
- Understanding and applying theory to resolve complex practical issues.
- Improving my own knowledge and understanding of IA and reviewing OR control frameworks.

It became apparent in the informal preparatory discussions and literature review that IA could learn from other key stakeholders as to how IA was perceived. Many IA functions were viewed as operating in a 'bubble' with little appreciation of the interrelationships within the business world, therefore this valuable source of information was collected as part of an industry survey in order to strengthen the role of IA.

The project

Title: Measuring Operational Risk in the Context of Basel II: State of the Industry and Strengthening the Role of Internal Audit

Measuring operational risk (OR) within the financial services industry is difficult and complex. To help address this problem Basel II has set out a sliding scale of measurement across three categories of increasing risk sensitivity. [Basel II is a voluntary agreement between banking authorities.] The categories are the Basic Indicator Approach (BIA), the Standardised Approach (TSA) and the Advanced Measurement Approaches (AMA).

The main focus of this research project was to understand the role of the Internal Audit (IA) function in providing independent assurance of the Basel II approaches used to measure OR and identify areas where their role could be strengthened. Research was structured around an industry questionnaire targeting the views of two sample groups, IA and OR managers (ORm). Any emerging questionnaire feedback themes were investigated through semi-structured interviews with industry experts.

Results were presented in four published journal articles:

Article 1: Established the context in which IA operates in terms of the Basel II models being used and confirmed there is an intended transition to the AMA.

Article 2: Presented the analysis of respondent feedback using the Mann-Whitney u-test which detected a number of statistically significant differences in the mean values with responses to three specific questions between the two groups and these were explored in the semi-structured interviews. The results indicated that IA is aligned to their ORm peers with the importance of a number of pre-defined OR management building blocks, showed that IA had a 'rosier view' compared to their ORm peers and the analysis highlighted that IA had generally rated themselves higher than their ORm counterparts. The analysis identified six interrelated themes for improvement.

Article 3: Recommendations to address the six themes identified in Article 2 and strengthen the role of IA.

Article 4: Introduction of a new complementary audit approach to strengthen the classical audit approach together with a practical example illustrating how it can be implemented.

Abstract

"Measuring Operational Risk (OR) is complex and difficult. Basel II outlines a continuum of measurement approaches from the Basic Indicator Approach (BIA) to the Standardised Approach (TSA) and finally the Advanced Measurement Approaches (AMA). Regulators have prescribed approaches for BIA and TSA; but not AMA. Consequently, internal control frameworks vary greatly in quality and structure across the industry. This situation is further compounded by growing regulatory requirements because of recent banking failures. Regulators grant AMA status on the superior quality of an organisation's internal control framework. However this is not a straightforward transition from TSA to AMA (as the regulators have identified).

Internal Audit (IA) has an important role to play across all OR measurement approaches to ensure the components of the internal control framework are adequate and effective. The role of IA is supplemented by the work from OR managers (ORm); however there is potential conflict in responsibilities between these two internal assurance functions. The role of internal assurance provider is sometimes 'blurred' between ORm, the second line of defence (2LOD) and IA, the third line of defence (3LOD).

To understand the current OR internal assurance landscape and the relationship IA has with OR managers/other key stakeholders e.g. ORm, regulators, other risk disciplines, an on-line industry wide survey was carried out. Respondents from IA and ORm were asked for their views on 30 questionnaire questions (and complemented by a series of semi-structured interviews with industry experts).

Questionnaire and interview feedback provided a comprehensive base for my contribution to professional IA practice and allowed me to:

- *Clarify the status quo of Operational Risk Management (ORM) assurance within the financial services industry;*
- *Identify the main strengths and weaknesses of IA practice (and the perception of IA from key stakeholders e.g. ORm);*
- *Classify emerging themes in order to drive positive change through management awareness;*
- *Develop recommendations for improvements.*

The survey intended to identify what value IA adds to the implementation and maintenance of internal control frameworks (including AMA) and how ORm (and other stakeholders) view their contribution. Feedback from both groups will assist in identifying weaknesses across existing control frameworks and clarify 'the role of IA'.

The culmination of the research project resulted in the identification of six emerging themes and the development of an IA management model that represents part of my contribution to practice. Each of these themes together with the IA management model is explored in the journal articles linked to Chapter 6."

Project aims

"This study aims to understand the role of IA as the organisation's independent internal assurance provider of the OR framework (as perceived by the two main internal assurance provider groups i.e. IA and ORm professionals). A detailed review of the available literature and publications was carried out. The output from the literature research and industry expert informal discussions led to the following three research aims:

1. *What are the state of the art ORm practices with particular interest in the industry's view toward the Advanced Measurement Approach (AMA)?*
2. *Who provides corporate governance around the ORm frameworks?*
3. *How can IA work more effectively with the other internal assurance providers such as OR managers?"*

Methodological approach

A mixed methods approach was selected although this was a largely quantitative-led [questionnaire-based] study followed by qualitative investigation of the main survey findings. In terms of research training, this was not offered as part of the DProf curriculum in 2008; however I had previous research method training as part of the MBA degree and also used a mixed methods approach.

For the data analysis, I utilised a web-based external vendor [Survey Monkey®] to distribute, collect and sort the questionnaire feedback. However, there were three specific questions targeting an insight to IA's contribution to implementing and maintaining key parts of the OR framework. Further analysis was performed in Excel® and using the Mann Whitney 'u test' on the feedback from both groups [IA and ORm].

I learnt that planning and preparation are key. Try and set out your research question/area and plan the progressive steps to answer it [try to keep it narrow and focused]; this will give you clarity and prevent you veering off on tangents. Ideally, prepare a database in advance that you will use to store and agree on the method to analyse the feedback responses. Where possible try to keep it simple.

Impact on the community

This project was from an IA perspective with comparative input from the other main stakeholder; ORm. The output and findings from the research will influence both groups and how they approach their respective organisational assurance responsibilities as they are integral parts of the Three Lines of Defence (3LODM).

I developed the questionnaire using many different sources of information ranging from informal discussions with internal organisational experts, reading widely around the subject area, personal experiences and meeting external experts at various OR/IA seminars and forums. Similarly, I sourced experts from a diverse range of networking contacts for the semi-structured interviews, e.g. external companies, industry consultants and internal organisational experts. In terms of the output in the form of the four published journals, I estimate a personal contribution of approximately 80%. Several international reference libraries have the articles in their database.

Each of the articles was peer reviewed by representatives from the IA, ORm and industry consultant communities.

The viva

The viva was a complete unknown, so I was a little nervous; however this proved to be unfounded. My nerves dissipated quickly as the examiners made me feel at ease and were genuinely interested in the subject matter as we engaged in the discussion. I took on board their comments and challenged appropriately where I felt their view was not accurately portraying the essence of the argument. This was all exchanged in an amicable and professional manner throughout the viva leaving me feeling challenged but able to hold my ground and believing it was a shared process.

Overriding feedback was positive with a request to make the abstract more succinct and reduce the complexity around the methodology chapter to express more clearly what was done.

Personal experience of the doctoral journey

The DProf is a big (possibly life changing) commitment and needs to be given much consideration from yourself and engagement of your support network such as family members, partners and loved ones. Try and develop clarity around the topic area, a purpose statement, title and a primary research question. Remember there are milestones along the journey which will mark your progress and create self-motivation as each is reached and completed; this will keep you focused. The journey and end result in completing the DProf is a hugely rewarding experience and a challenge in equal measure. This will be a journey of self-discovery and pushing the academic boundaries giving you an opportunity to explore and write about a subject that is personal to you.

11.9 Case study 8: Liam

Professional and academic background

Undergraduate: none – left school to be an electrician (electrical qualifications), shifted to IT around 5 years after qualifying (IT professional qualifications, now out of date!). Thereafter 'university of life'! Post graduate: MSc in Quality & Safety in Healthcare (1st class).

Motivation for studying the professional doctorate

Personal achievement (needed to know I could do it if I put my mind to it) plus for my work in the Middle East meant I needed to have a doctorate or could not be employed. No change during life time of doctorate – did ensure though that I got it completed just as soon as I possibly could.

The project

Title: Developing an Integrated Framework for Healthcare Risk, Incident & Audit Management.

Abstract

"Healthcare, in contrast to any other industry, is an emotionally-charged component of world economies and societies; a deep-rooted societal system with an extremely low public tolerance for mistake or error. Healthcare does however have a history of improvements through quality, risk and patient safety initiatives. In recent years a number of prominent quality and

safety reports have highlighted the importance of developing effective, integrated and aligned quality, risk and patient safety systems which support organisational learning from failure as well as focus on the reduction of preventable patient safety incidents.

Furthermore, the healthcare literature suggests that the use of quality, risk and safety frameworks and tools are vital in meeting the requirements of 'systems-level' strategic focus – the true roots of all effective continuous healthcare quality improvement. Developing such systems and associated competencies to support effective feedback and management are crucial for healthcare organisations to foster continual improvements in quality, reliability and safety across all services.

Using a mixed methods research design, including case study research, practitioner research and action research, this project has built on existing healthcare quality and safety system design to develop a new integrated framework for the management of healthcare risk, incident and audit which can positively impact on the delivery of high quality and safe healthcare services. By design, the framework supports the systematic identification of healthcare risks and failures and the continuous development of proactive, preventive strategies. Such a framework can thus provide secure foundations for healthcare organisations to deliver high quality and safe healthcare services and ensure continuous organisational learning – surely the least that patients expect.

Keywords: healthcare, quality, improvement, safety, framework."

Aims

"To research and develop, through the discipline of a mixed methods research design, practical experience and professional peer review in Middle Eastern healthcare organisations, a practical, implementable Continuous Quality Improvement (CQI) framework for the effective integration of healthcare risk, incident and audit management systems.

The key word in this aim is 'integration'; there is evidence in the literature that implementing discrete risk, incident and audit management systems, or combinations of two out of the three, can positively impact healthcare quality and safety; however I have been unable to identify any literature demonstrating the impacts and challenges of integrating all three components and hence one of the key motivators as well as aim for this project – something apparently not done before.

In addition to my aim, the evolution of my IRIA framework has been grounded in the 'Central Law of Improvement' (Berwick, 1996: 619) which states that 'every system is perfectly designed to achieve the results it achieves' as this dictum presents an understanding that 'systems' should be at the root of all strategic approaches to making healthcare function

*better. The central law also re-contextualises healthcare organisational per-
formance from being a 'matter of effort' to a 'matter of design' – another
underpinning concept for this project."*

Methodological approach

I used a mixed methods research design, including case study research,
practitioner research and action research which evolved throughout the
lifetime of my project – I guess you could call it an 'emergent research strategy'! I had no formal research training other than modules provided on my
previous MSc programme and my doctorate programme. Mixed methods,
action and practitioner research were all completely new to me. Data analysis was carried out using PASW Statistics® version 18 (release18.0.0), Zoo-
merang® (online survey engine) and Microsoft Excel 2010®.

Do not underestimate the time required to become competent in the
use of data analysis tools as well as the understanding of data analysis itself, particularly understanding the appropriate tests which can be applied
across the reliability and validity spectrum.

Impact on the community

The community of practice that I aimed to influence was all healthcare practitioners irrespective of level or discipline. My contribution to this community was the development of a systems-level integrated framework which
could provide a secure foundation for healthcare organisations to deliver
high quality and safe healthcare services and ensure continuous organisational learning – surely the least that patients expect. I am passionate about
healthcare quality, risk and patient safety and wanted to make a difference.
The contribution was evaluated and authenticated via my portfolio of evidence – publications, seminars, conferences, consultancy, workshops, and I
have since been invited to publish in an international journal.

The viva

My viva was a relatively positive experience, shorter than I had anticipated/
prepared for (was 1 hour 10 minutes), and I was somewhat disappointed
with outcome (pass with minor amendments). What did the examiners say?
'Need to do three times more reflections in "Conclusion" chapter!'

Personal experience of the doctoral journey

Hugely positive and enriching experiencing which has without doubt made
me a better healthcare professional in my field. Key experiences included:

- Most excellent supervision.
- All staff I encountered.
- Getting to grips with the evidence-based literature and better under-
  standing my professional practice.

- Meeting fellow students and faculty on the programme
- Completely underestimating the time it would take me to complete my final report & portfolio!
- An understanding, if long suffering, family!
- Learning about the potency of reflection – I was hugely sceptical initially (border line cynical, actually), but had my eyes opened, for that My supervisor is to be applauded as without her continuing support and understanding I never would have got it.
- At times I felt had I known the time it would take & challenges I would meet, I would perhaps have not done it!

For those starting out my top tips are:

- Realistically plan.
- Realistically plan more.
- Realistically plan some more again!
- Stick to the plan, but review constantly and adapt.

Other tips:

- Confront the most brutal facts of what you need to do in your life & career to get through your doctorate (I used the 'Stockdale Paradox'; Collins, 2001).
- Do plenty of reading as grounding your work in the literature is vital.
- Pick a topic which can be a part of your daily practice (or was I just lucky?).

11.10 Summary

This chapter has presented eight detailed case studies of some of our successful professional doctorate graduates. They are from different backgrounds, completed different projects, studied for different lengths of time, and of course had different experiences along the way. So what can we learn from these? Despite the differences, there are also some common themes and important lessons that we hope will help to make the journey easier for you.

The first thing to note is that all of our graduates had quite complex career histories and had migrated away from their first disciplines to a greater or lesser extent. In their doctorates they made use of this, reflecting back on their learning journey and building their experience into their doctoral work. Their work was very practical and not simply confined to one discrete discipline as you would normally find with a more traditional PhD. They crossed professional boundaries and made a contribution that was applicable to multi-professional working environments. (We explored some of the issues related to this multi-professionalism in Chapter 3.) It was this that gave most of our candidates their motivation to do the professional doctorate. Some had previously considered doing, or even tried to do, a PhD. However, it was the opportunity to utilise their professional knowledge and to develop it further in order to make a real practical contribution that made the professional doctorate a more appealing, and ultimately successful, option for them. The words that our candidates use give us some clue as to why this might be. They talk about their real *passion* for the subject and how that drove them on. Fiona describes how she was sometimes 'blinded' by her passion for her subject; Siobhan had such belief and passion for hers that achieving the doctoral qualification almost became simply a by-product! There is an important lesson in this for anyone embarking on this journey: you should choose a research area in which you are really interested. Better still, one that you are passionate about. Siobhan tells us that this journey is 'not for the faint-hearted'. It will often be difficult, but if you are truly passionate about what you are doing you are much more likely to succeed.

Although the very practical, 'real-life' context of professional doctorate work is what gave our candidates their motivation, it brings with it some issues that they also highlight. The first of these is the construction of the portfolio. You will be aware that not all professional doctorates require the submission of a portfolio, but if yours does then you will need to plan it carefully. We go into some detail about this in Chapter 7, and the case studies reinforce that advice in a very practical way. David explains how it is important to plan your portfolio and be selective about what goes in. Your portfolio will need to reflect and provide evidence for the theme of your research, so clearly identifying that theme, and then being discriminating about the evidence you present is crucial. Tempting though it might be to fill your portfolio with everything that you have been working on for the duration of your doctorate (and perhaps for some time before that), this will not do your work justice. Your examiners will not expect to have to do the job of picking out what is relevant and what is not – you must do that job for them and present it in a way that is clear, logical and easy to follow. Ian describes how important it was for him to carefully cross-reference the report and portfolio. In complete contrast, one of our early candidates turned up for her viva with two holdalls full of additional 'evidence' to supplement her portfolio, much to the horror of the members of the examination panel! Needless to say, they refused to accept this material as part of the submission.

The need to present carefully-selected evidence in your portfolio leads us on to the next piece of advice from our cases. Our candidates quickly learned the importance of being organised and keeping records. Sometimes during our day-to-day work we can overlook the importance of some of the decisions we make and the interactions we have, so when you are undertaking your doctorate you will need to get into the habit of capturing these things – they may be important to your final submission. David and Hamid both talk specifically about the importance of organising your data as you go along.

The other common issue that emerged, which is related to the practical and multidisciplinary nature of these doctorates, was that of methodology. You will see that in all of our cases candidates initially struggled with identifying a clear methodology. Most used mixed methods, with action research featuring prominently. You will also note that almost all of the case studies talk about the importance that processes of reflection played in the development of their thinking. It is clear from these cases that some of our candidates reached a final definition of their methodology almost serendipitously. This is not unusual, and is perhaps one of the few unfortunate aspects of the practical nature of this type of doctorate. Some candidates may join the programme with the unrealistic expectation that they can write up a major project that they are undertaking at work, and that will be sufficient to achieve the doctorate. However, as we have seen throughout this book, the professional doctorate is about something much more than that. It is a true research degree that requires robust underpinning methodology and is properly informed by both the academic and professional literature, topics that we cover in depth in Chapters 4 and 5. Approaching your studies with this understanding right from the start will help to ensure that your project plan runs smoothly. You can think about the methodological approach you might use in good time, and can take advantage of appropriate training before you embark on your study, just as David and Hamid advise. You will undoubtedly be questioned in depth about your methodology at your viva, so having it well-planned will ensure that you are able to defend it confidently under examination.

This brings us to the final common theme that we wish to draw from our cases: the dreaded viva! Everyone fears the viva; it is an exam, after all. So you might have been surprised to read that our candidates, almost without exception, actually *enjoyed* the experience. Max even talks about being sad when it was over! This isn't as bizarre as it seems. The viva is probably the one chance you will ever get to talk to a group of people who have read your work in its entirety and who are interested in finding out more. It is your chance to demonstrate your expertise to a group of other experts. If you are well prepared there is no reason to fear the experience (although a little bit of controlled anxiety does not go amiss to keep you on your toes). So how do you prepare? We have devoted the whole of Chapter 10 to this subject, but our case candidates give some further practical advice that worked for them. Firstly, make sure that you have a 'mock' or practice viva – it will help you to become familiar with the process. However, do not have unrealistic expectations that this will represent the *content* of the real viva. As you can see from our cases, the questions asked in the mock will be different from those likely to be asked by the true examination panel, simply because the individuals are different and they will have their own distinct areas of interest.

The best way to prepare is simply to be fully familiar with what is in your submission. This might seem like an odd thing to say, but there can be quite a long time between when you complete and when you are examined. There is a danger that you might forget where you have put things in the report or portfolio, or indeed your thinking might have moved on to the extent that you may even now disagree with some of the things that you have included. So, make sure that you read your submission thoroughly several times shortly before your viva, and remind yourself of the rationale behind why you did the things you did (even if you have now moved on). Be prepared to explain and defend the work. Some people like to prepare a list of questions that they anticipate from the examiners, but you will see from our cases that this is rarely helpful (see, for example, Max's comments). There are a few general areas of questioning that are easy to predict – for example, you will undoubtedly be questioned on your contribution to knowledge and your methodology – but other than that, the questioning will be determined by the particular areas of interest of your particular examiners. You can be cheered by Max's reflection on his viva:

> *"You never know what topics or questions will be raised; however you can prepare your method of response. That was the key for me as you will know your work inside out. Dear me you've spent three, four or even five years with it."*

Like Max, *you* will be the person who really knows your work in detail. You are the expert, and you can relish the opportunity to demonstrate your expertise to a group of interested peers.

No doubt as you read our case studies there will be some that interest you more than others, dependent perhaps upon the professional area or project description. However, the common themes that we feel that every reader can learn from are:

- Be passionate about your research area. Passion will keep you motivated through difficult times, and will make your arguments more convincing (but don't become 'blinded' by your passion to the extent that you don't see other ways of doing things).
- Be meticulous and systematic with the collection of evidence to support your work. Do not throw away anything that might eventually be included, but be prepared to discard material when you come to collate your final submission. Prepare your submission clearly and logically, so that examiners can easily see the evidence for the work you have done.
- Plan your methodological approach, and undertake appropriate training in methods with which you are unfamiliar.
- Good preparation means you need not fear the viva. It can be enjoyable!

12 Summary and the Future

On completion of this chapter you will:

▶ have checked out the major points which relate to your doctorate, and ensured that you cover all necessary stages
▶ have considered how your doctorate has impacted upon you as an individual, and how you might continue your learning journey in the future

12.1 Introduction

This chapter briefly draws together all of the main points raised throughout the text, and summarises them as a checklist. It also gives some final reflections on the authors' experiences of working with professional doctorate candidates. Finally, we encourage you, as a student, to reflect on your own doctoral experiences, and to continue to work at doctoral level and to explore your practice after graduation. The chapter also addresses the question of what happens next, and encourages you to view your professional doctorate study as one part of a lifelong journey.

12.2 Summary of main points

In the checklist on the following pages we have grouped together the main points from each area of your professional doctorate. You might find this useful for reference as you progress through your doctorate.

CHECKLIST OF MAIN POINTS: 1	Have you covered these?
Personal Motivation	
• Do you really want to do it?	
• Do you have the opportunity to impact upon practice?	
• Does your project relate to your work activities?	
Motivation for the project	
• Does your project have a clear aim and purpose?	
• Is it something which you are passionate about?	
• Is it clear who will benefit from your work?	
Literature Review	
• Have you completed a critical review of the state of the profession and of relevant academic literature?	
• Have you included the relevant policy documents/professional papers/articles?	
• Have you covered up-to-date academic papers which relate to your topic?	
Methodology	
• Have you decided which methodological approach to use?	
• Have you decided which method(s) to use?	
• Does your methodology help you to explore your professional issues?	

CHECKLIST OF MAIN POINTS: 2	Have you covered these?
Reflection	
● Are you keeping a reflective diary?	
● Are there things you have done which evidence your contribution to practice?	
● Can you evidence why you took certain decisions?	
Community of practice	
● What is your community of practice?	
● Who do you benchmark yourself against?	
● Who do you need to influence?	
Dissemination	
● How will you disseminate your work to your colleagues and others within your community of practice?	
● What dissemination vehicles exit?	
● Have you produced a detailed dissemination plan?	
Potential for contribution	
● Will your work make a clear contribution to practice?	
● Have you collected evidence of your impact?	
● Have you evaluated your work?	

CHECKLIST OF MAIN POINTS: 3	Have you covered these?
References	
● Are all your references in a standard style (e.g. Harvard format)?	
● Have you got sufficient up to date (recent) references?	
● Are all references cited within the body of the text?	
Project Plan	
● Have you included timescales through to completion?	
● Is your plan realistic?	
● Have you included review points, and the possibility for changes?	
Doctoral Report/Thesis	
● Have you started to draft chapters of your final report/thesis?	
● Have you agreed the contents list with your supervisor?	
● Is your abstract clear and concise?	
Portfolio (if applicable)	
● Does your portfolio of evidence cover the early stage of your project?	
● Have you agreed the structure with your supervisor?	
● How will your report relate to your portfolio?	

CHECKLIST OF MAIN POINTS: 4	Have you covered these?
Ethical issues	
● Have you considered the ethical issues?	
● Have you obtained informed consent?	
● Have you applied for ethical approval through the appropriate university committee (or agreed with your supervisor that this is not required)?	
Supervisors	
● Have you been meeting regularly with your supervisors?	
● Do you send them written work in advance of the meeting?	
● Are you open and honest with them about your progress?	
Professional Contacts/Mentors	
● Who do you respect in your community of practice?	
● Who understands best practice?	
● Who understands the national picture?	
Viva (Oral examination)	
● Have you prepared sufficiently by working through possible questions?	
● Have you had a mock/practice examination?	
● Have you checked the date and time?!	

12.3 Authors' reflections

The authors have had the privilege of working with groups of professional doctorate students for a number of years. Each student has their own personal motivation for studying on the doctoral programme, and every project is different. What is common is the enthusiasm and passion that the students have for their professional practice, and the professional doctorate programme, gives them the tools to develop their practice in a formal, rigorous, critical and evaluative manner.

Although students come to the programme with many different motivations and aspirations, our experience is that they all find the doctoral journey one of fulfilment, challenge and personal transformation, in a way that they never imagined. We believe passionately in the professional doctorate as a vehicle which enables professional people to develop their practice to doctoral level, in a way that just wouldn't be achieved by a traditional PhD.

The professional doctorate offers many advantages to the PhD model. In particular a professional doctorate gives you the opportunity to:

- Work with a cohort of other students.
- Benefit from taught elements, which help to focus the project and hone the skills of reflection and research methodology.
- Base your doctoral project on your work activities.
- Work within your community of practice to demonstrate impact.
- Add academic theory and the rigour of established research methods to your practice.
- Gain support from tutors, supervisors, other students and professional mentors.

12.4 What happens next?

When you graduate you will, of course, have a feeling of great achievement. You have worked very hard, you deserve your doctorate and you should feel very proud of yourself. However, this should not be the end of your journey. Studying for a doctorate is a journey of personal transformation, and part of the product of the doctoral process is YOU!

Every one of our graduates has observed a transformation in themselves. They feel more reflective, more able to take decisions based on evidence and more confident in their own professional practice. And each and every student has continued to research and develop their practice after completion of their doctorate. They have also all wished to keep in touch with supervisors, tutors and fellow students, and all come back and give seminars on their own doctoral journey.

In the words of two of our candidates:

"In conclusion, studying a professional doctorate has introduced me to the power and practical application of reflective practice and as an autobiographical researcher I can see how my projects have benefitted from this additional perspective. I feel, having almost come to the end of my doctoral journey, that it is only now that I feel clarity about the process and the knowledge that I have gained."

"I can honestly say that if my work resulted in a fail that, whilst I would naturally be disappointed, I could walk away knowing that I have personally developed in a way that I never anticipated. Consequently, I am about to embark on a further, very challenging, project and will begin with the hard task of deep diving into the theory knowing that this will produce the kind of outcomes that I can comfortably defend and be proud of."

We would encourage you to continue to use the skills which you have developed within your professional doctorate in your professional life. For example, you should consider continuing to publish your work along with your supervisors after you graduate. It is likely that you have produced a lot of material during the course of your doctorate, and some of this could probably be quite easily converted into papers for academic or professional journals. It might be possible to publish your work as a book chapter or, in some cases, as a book.

You will have made many contacts, and expanded your sphere of influence during your studies. You can use the links which you have made to further develop your career in the future.

You will have learned a lot about doing research, collecting data and using evidence to back up your decisions and the arguments that you present to others.

Several of our candidates have used their professional doctorate to further develop their career. We thought that you might be interested in learning what graduating with a professional doctorate has meant to each of the graduates featured in Chapter 11.

Claire, the pharmacy lecturer who explored different models of interprofessional education in her teaching, has left the higher education sector and returned to pharmacy practice as a consultant. She continues to undertake research with colleagues from a local university, and has just published a paper in a high-quality refereed journal.

Ian, the equality and diversity professional who developed a model for corporate social responsibility (CSR), is now undertaking consultancy work in the area of diversity and CSR. He is considering writing a book on the topic of CSR, based on his doctoral studies.

Max, the local businessman who followed a doctoral project in the area of quality and management information systems, is using his doctoral qualification and experiences to do consultancy around the world, and is also developing a new career as an expert witness. He feels strongly that the core management principles which he developed during his doctoral studies will be of use to others, and is considering writing a popular book based on them.

Siobhan, the senior member of staff from a local college who undertook a project in the area of shared services, continues to work on her shared service project and is now recognised as a national expert on how to develop a shared service. She regularly speaks at national conferences and other events on the subject of shared services.

Fiona, the healthcare professional who developed a commissioning framework, took a year's break from work after her doctoral studies. She has returned to work for the health service, putting into practice the framework that she developed for her professional doctorate.

David, the senior university administrator who explored the area of research administration systems, has moved to a more senior position and continues to publish and develop new systems. He has a role in a national research evaluation exercise.

Hamid, the financial risk auditor, has moved into a senior position within financial regulation, and is often asked to speak on his research.

Liam, the health information systems specialist, has been offered a promotion, and is now implementing the model which he developed during his professional doctorate project.

We hope the above stories demonstrate that research shouldn't stop with your doctorate. In many ways your journey has only just begun. We hope that you have enjoyed this book and that it has helped you on your doctoral journey. We have enjoyed the experience of writing it, and of working with doctoral students. We certainly intend to continue to develop our own practice, and hope that you will use your doctoral studies to do the same.

References

Anderson, S.C., Jones, C.O.H. and Huttly, S.R.A. (2010) 'Reflections, refinements and revisions: thirteen years' experience of a professional doctorate in public health', *Work Based Learning e-Journal*, 1(1).

Andriof, J. and McIntosh, M. (eds) (2001) *Perspectives on Corporate Citizenship*, Greenleaf, Sheffield.

Argyris, C. (2002) 'Double-loop learning, teaching, and research', *Academy of Management Learning & Education*, 1(2), pp. 206–18

Armsby, P. and Fillery-Travis, A. (2009) 'Developing the coach: using work-based learning and doctorate programmes to facilitate coaches learning', UALL Work-Based Learning Network Annual Conference: The Impact of Work Based learning for the Learner, University of the West of England, 13–14 July.

Arter, J.A. and Spandel, V. (1992) 'Using portfolios of student work in instruction and assessment', *Educational Measurement: Issues and Practice*, 11.

Ashford, R., Carson, A.M., Lloyd-Jones, N.J. and McCabe, S. (2012) 'Working on the boundary between professions and the academy: the future of professional doctorates', 3rd International Conference on Professional Doctorates, 2–3 April 2012, Florence, Italy, Middlesex University and UK Council for Graduate Education.

Baas, M., De Dreu, C.K.W., and Nijstad, B A. (2011) 'When prevention promotes creativity: the role of mood, regulatory focus, and regulatory closure, *Journal of Personality and Social Psychology*, 100(5), pp. 794–809.

Bangemann, T. (2005) *Shared Services in Finance and Accounting*, Aldershot: Gower.

Bargh, J.A. and Chartrand, T.L. (1999) 'The unbearable automaticity of being', *American Psychologist*, 54, pp. 462–79.

Barnes, T. (2011) *The Engineering Doctorate: Professional Doctorates in the UK*, UK Council for Graduate Education.

Barnes, T. and Stanley, D. (2012) 'The EngD – Perspectives on 20 years' experience at Warwick and Manchester', 3rd International Conference on Professional Doctorates, 2–3 April 2012, Florence, Italy, Middlesex University and UK Council for Graduate Education.

Baumard, P. (1999) *Tacit Knowledge in Organisations*, London: Sage.

BBC (2012) 'Jenny Clack – how creatures from the sea conquered the land', *Beautiful Minds: Series 2*, first shown 5 April.

Benner, P. (1984) 'From novice to expert: excellence and power in clinical nursing practice', *American Journal of Nursing*, 84(12), p. 1479.

Bergeron, B. (2003) *Essentials of Shared Services*, Hoboken, NJ: John Wiley & Sons Inc.

Berwick, D. M. (1996) 'A primer on leading the improvement of systems', *British Medical Journal*, 312(7031).

Blaikie, N. (2007) *Approaches to Social Enquiry: Advancing Knowledge*, Cambridge: Polity Press.

Blair, S.E.E. (2011) 'Containing anxiety and supporting resilience in students undertaking a professional doctorate, 2nd International Conference on Professional Doctorates, 20–21 April 2011, Edinburgh, Middlesex University and UK Council for Graduate Education.

Blanchard, K., Hearsey, P. and Johnson, D.E. (1986) *Management of Organizational Behaviour*, New Jersey: Prentice Hall.

Bolton, G. (2010) *Reflective Practice: Writing and Professional Development*, London: Sage.

Boud, D. and Tennent, M. (2006) 'Putting doctoral education to work: challenges to academic practice', *Higher Education Research and Development*, 25(3), pp. 293–306.

Bourdieu, P. and Wacquant, L. (1992) *An Invitation to Reflexive Sociology*, Chicago: University of Chicago Press.

Bourner, T. and Bowden, R. (2001) 'Professional doctorates in England', *Studies in Higher Education*, 26(1), pp. 65–83.

Bradbury, H. and Reason, P. (2006) 'Conclusion: broadening the bandwidth of validity: issues and choice-points for improving the quality of action research', *Handbook of Action Research*, pp. 343–51

Bronckart, J.P. (1991) 'Imagination' in R. Doron and F. Parot (eds), *Dictionaire de Psychologie*, Paris: Presses Universitaires de France.

Brookfield, S.D. (1990) 'Using critical incidents to explore learners' assumptions' in J. Mezirow (ed.) *Fostering Critical Reflection in Adulthood: A Guide to Transformative and Emancipatory Learning*, San Francisco: Jossey-Bass.

Brown, K. and Cooke, C. (2010) *Professional Doctorate Awards in the UK*, UK Council for Graduate Education.

Bryman, A. (2008) *Social Research Methods*, 3rd edn, Oxford: Oxford University Press.

Capobianco, B.M. and Feldman, A. (2010) 'Repositioning teacher action research in science teacher education', *Journal of Science Teacher Education*, 21(8), pp. 909–15.

Carr, S., Lhussier, M. and Chandler, C. (2010) 'The supervision of professional doctorates: experiences of the process and ways forward', *Nurse Education Today*, 30(4), pp. 279–84.

Carr, W. (1986) 'Theories of education and practice', *Journal of Philosophy of Education*, 20(20), pp. 177–86.

Christianson, B. and Adams, S.R. (2011) 'Arty-facts: the role of performance in the "conventional" PhD', 2nd International Conference on Professional Doctorates, April, Edinburgh, Middlesex University and UK Council for Graduate Education.

Chynoweth, P. (2012) 'The harvesting of professional knowledge: methodological perspectives on the legitimization of tacit and Mode 2 knowledge in the professional doctoral thesis', 3rd International Conference on Professional Doctorates, 2–3 April 2012, Florence, Italy, Middlesex University and UK Council for Graduate Education.

Clarke, G., Fell, A.F. and Fillery-Travis, A. (2012) 'Design and delivery of research supervisor training for professional doctorates', 3rd International Conference on Professional Doctorates, 2–3 April 2012, Florence, Italy, Middlesex University and UK Council for Graduate Education.

Collin, R. (2011) 'Dress rehearsal: a Bourdieusian analysis of body work in career portfolio programs', *British Journal of Sociology of Education*, 32(5), pp. 785–804.

Collins, J. (2001) *Good to Great: Why Some Companies Make the Leap ... and Others Don't*, New York: HarperBusiness

Commonwealth Association (2010) *Overview of Case Study Models and Methodology*, Commonwealth Association for Public Administration and Management, available at ww.capam.org/_documents/reportoncasestudymethodologies.pdf.

Cormack, D.F.S. and Benton, D.C. (1996) 'The research process' in D.F.S. Cormack (ed.) *The Research Process in Nursing*, 3rd edn, Oxford: Blackwell Science.

Costley, C. and Lester, S. (2012) 'Work-based doctorates: professional extension at the highest levels', *Studies in Higher Education*, 37(3), pp. 257–69.

Council of Australian Deans and Directors of Graduate Studies (2007) *Guidelines on Professional Doctorates*, Adelaide: Council of Australian Deans and Directors of Graduate Studies.

Council of Graduate Schools (CGS) (2008) *Task Force Report on the Professional Doctorate*, Washington, DC: CGS.

Creswell, J.W. (2007) *Qualitative Inquiry and Research Design: Choosing among Five Traditions*, 2nd edn, Thousand Oaks, CA: Sage.

Critten, P., Squire, P. and Leppenwell, G. (2010) 'The university in the workplace: extending the boundaries of academic jurisdiction', UALL Work Based Learning Network Conference, Teesside University, 13–14 July.

de Waal, C. (2005) *On Pragmatism*, Belmont: Wadsworth.

Delamont, S., Atkinson P. and Parry, O. (2000) *The Doctoral Experience: Success and Failure in Graduate School*, London: Falmer Press.

Denscombe, M. (1998) *The Good Research Guide*, Buckingham: Open University Press.

Denzin, N. and Lincoln, Y. (2000) *Book of Qualitative Research*, Thousand Oaks, CA: Sage.

Dobrow, S.R. and Higgins, M.C. (2005) 'Developmental networks and professional identity: a longitudinal study', *Career Development International*, 10(6/7), pp. 567–83.

Dollery, B. and Akimov, A. (2007) 'Critical review of the empirical evidence on shared services in local government', Centre for Local Government, University of New England, NSW, Working Paper Series 06.

Doncaster, K. and Thorne, L. (2000) 'Reflection and planning: essential elements of professional doctorates', *Reflective Practice*, 1(3), pp. 391–9.

du Plock, S. (2012) 'In assessing professional doctorates should what is deemed useful also be morally and ethically "good"?', 3rd International Conference on Professional Doctorates, 2–3 April 2012, Florence, Italy, Middlesex University and UK Council for Graduate Education.

Duffy, F.D. and Holmboe, E.S. (2006) 'Self-assessment in lifelong learning and improving performance in practice: Physician Know Thyself', *Journal of the American Medical Association*, 296(9), pp. 1137–9.

Duncan, M. (2004) 'Autoethnography: Critical appreciation of an emerging art', *International Journal of Qualitative Methods*, 3(4), Article 3. Retrieved 19 July 2012 from http://www.ualberta.ca/~iiqm/backissues/3_4/html/duncan.html.

Dyche, L. and Epstein, R.M. (2011) 'Curiosity and medical education', *Medical Education*, 45, pp. 663–8.

Eisenman, S., (2008) *Building Design Portfolios: Innovative Concepts for Presenting your Work*, Beverly, MA: Rockport Publishing Co.

Ellis, C. (2004) *The Ethnographic I: A Methodological Novel about Autoethnography*, Walnut Creek, CA: Alta Mira Press.

European University Association (2005) *Bologna Seminar on Doctoral Programmes for the European Knowledge Society*, Brussels: European University Association, http://www.eua.be/eua/jsp/en/upload/Salzburg_Conclusions.1108990538850.pdf.

Evans, C. and Stevenson, K. (2011) 'The experience of international nursing students studying for a PhD in the UK: a qualitative study', *BMC Nursing*, 10 (11).

Evans, T. (1998) 'Issues in supervising professional doctorates: an Australian view', Staff and Educational Development Association: Good Practice in Post Graduate Supervision, SEDA.

Fell, A., Flint, K. and Haines, I. (2011) *Professional doctorates in the UK*, UK Council for Graduate Education.

Feyerabend, P. (1975) *Against Method: Outline of an Anarchistic Theory of Knowledge*, London: New Left Books.

Fillery-Travis, A. and Robinson, L. (2011) 'The DProf advisor/candidate relationship – a coaching model?', 2nd International Conference on Professional Doctorates, 20–21 April, Edinburgh, Middlesex University and UK Council for Graduate Education.

Fulton, J., Smith, P., Sanders, G. and Kuit, J. (2012) 'The role of the professional doctorate in developing professional practice', *Journal of Nursing Management*, 20, pp. 130–9.

Gibbons, M., Limoges, C., Nowotny, H., Schwartzman, S., Scott, P. and Trow, M. (1994) *The New Production of Knowledge: The Dynamics of Science and Research in Contemporary Societies*, London: Sage.

Gibbs, P. and Armsby, P. (2011) 'Recognition is deserved, qualifications are merited. Where does that leave fairness in accreditation?', *European Journal of Education*, 46(2).

Golde, C.M. and Dore, T.M. (2001) 'At cross purposes: what the experiences of doctoral students reveal about doctoral education', A report for the Pew Charitable Trusts, Philadelphia http://www.phd-survey.org/report.htm Accessed 18 July 2012.

Green, H. and Powell, S.D. (2007) *The Doctorate Worldwide*, Buckingham: Open University Press.

Hammersley, M. and Atkinson, P. (1995) *Ethnography: Principles in Practice*, 2nd edn, London: Routledge.

Hargrove, K. (2009) 'From the classroom: 'In My Classroom' – reflections on our year in school', *Gifted Child Today Magazine*, 32(3), p. 64.

Hart, E. and Bond, M. (1995) *Action Research for Health and Social Care: A Guide to Practice*, Buckingham: Open University Press.

Heikkinen, H.L.T., Huttunen, R. and Syrjälä, L. (2007) 'Action research as narrative: five principles for validation', *Educational Action Research*, 15(1), pp. 5–19.

Herbert, I. and Seal, W. (2009) 'The role of shared services', *Management Services*, 51(1), pp. 43–7.

Hessels, L. and van Lente, H. (2008) 'Re-thinking new knowledge production: a literature review and a research agenda', *Research Policy*, 37, pp. 740–60.

Higgins, M.C. (2001) 'Changing careers: The effect of social context', *Journal of Organizational Behaviour*, 22(6), pp. 595–618.

Holzer, M., Fry, J, Charbonneau, E., Shick, R., Burnash, E., Ceesay, A., Kwak, S., Lin, W., Nayer, G. and Schatteman, A. (2009) *Literature Review and Analysis Related to Costs and Benefits of Service Delivery Consolidation among Municipalities*, Local Unit Alignment, Reorganization and Consolidation Commission, Rutgers University.

Hyland, K. (2001) 'Humble servant of the discipline? Self-mention in research articles', *English for Specific Purposes*, 20 (3), pp. 207–26.

Ibarra, H. (1999) 'Provisional selves: experimenting with image and identity in professional adaptation', *Administrative Science Quarterly*, 44(4), pp. 764–91.

Jameson, J. (2012) 'The mouse that roared, phonetically speaking: doctoral student development in the professional doctorate in education', 3rd International Conference on Professional Doctorates, 2–3 April 2012, Florence, Italy, Middlesex University and UK Council for Graduate Education.

Janssen, J., Joha, A. and Weerakkody, V. (2007) 'Exploring relationships of shared service arrangements in local government', *Transforming Government: People, Process and Policy*, 1(3), pp. 271–84.

Johnson, S. (2001) *Who Moved My Cheese?*, London: Vermilion.

Joyner, R. W. (2003) 'The selection of external examiners for research degrees', *Quality Assurance in Education*, 11(2), pp. 123–7.

Kemmis, S. and McTaggart, R. (1988) *The Action Research Planner*, 3rd edn, Geelong, Australia: Deakin University Press.

Kincheloe, J.L. and Berry, K.S. (2004) *Rigour and Complexity in Educational Research: Conceptualizing the Bricolage*, Maidenhead: Open University Press.

Kirkham, J., Cole, C. and Clark, M. (2012) 'Action inquiry and research: the DBA learning experience', 3rd International Conference on Professional Doctorates, 2–3 April 2012, Florence, Italy, Middlesex University and UK Council for Graduate Education.

Klenowski, V. (2002) *Developing Portfolios for Learning and Assessment: Processes and Principles*, London: Routledge.

Kolb, D.A. (1984) *Experiential Learning*, London: Prentice Hall.

Kreber, C. and Cranton, P.A. (2000) 'Exploring the scholarship of teaching', *Journal of Higher Education*, 71 (4), pp. 476–95.

Kuhn, T.S. ([1962], 1996) *The Structure of Scientific Revolutions*, 3rd edn, Chicago, IL: University of Chicago Press.

Kuit, J.A., Reay G. and Freeman R.D. (2001) 'Experiences of reflective practice', *Active Learning in Higher Education*, 2(2), pp. 128–42.

Langer, E.J. (1989) 'Minding matters: the consequences of mindlessness-mindfulness', *Advances in Experimental Psychology*, 22, pp. 137–73.

Langer, E.J. (1997) *The Power of Mindful Learning*, Cambridge, MA: Perseus Books.

Langer, E.J. (2005) *On Becoming an Artist: Reinventing Yourself Through Mindful Creativity*, New York: Ballantine.

Lave, J. and Wenger, E. (2009) *Situated Learning: Legitimate Peripheral Participation*, Cambridge: Cambridge University Press.

Laverty, S.M. (2003) 'Hermeneutic phenomenology and phenomenology: a comparison of historical and methodological considerations', *International Journal of Qualitative Methods*, 2(3), pp. 21–35.

Lee, A. and Boud, D. (2003) 'Writing groups, change and academic identity: research development as local practice', *Studies in Higher Education*, 28 (2), pp. 187–200.

Lee, A. and Boud, D. (2008) 'Framing doctoral education as practice' in D. Boud and A. Lee (eds) *Changing Practices of Doctoral Education*, London: Routledge.

Lee, N.-J. (2009) *Achieving your Professional Doctorate: A Book*, Maidenhead, Open University Press.

Leshem, S. and Trafford, V.N. (2002) 'Starting at the end to undertake doctoral research: predictable questions as stepping stones', *Higher Education Review*, 35(1), pp. 31–49.

Leshem, S. and Trafford, V.N. (2007) 'Overlooking the conceptual framework', *Innovations in Education and Teaching International*, 44(1), pp. 93–105.

Lester, S. (2004) 'Conceptualising the practitioner doctorate', *Studies in Higher Education*, 29(6), pp. 757–70.

Levinthal, D. and Rerup, C. (2006) 'Crossing an apparent chasm: bridging mindful and less-mindful perspectives on organizational learning', *Organization Science*, 17(4), pp. 502–13.

Maguire, K. (2012) 'Transdiciplinarity and professional doctorates: facilitating metanoia between candidates and advisers', 3rd International Conference on Professional Doctorates, 2–3 April 2012, Florence, Italy, Middlesex University and UK Council for Graduate Education.

Malfroy, J. (2005) 'Doctoral supervision, workplace research, and changing pedagogic practices', *Higher Education Research and Development*, 24(2), pp. 165–78.

Martin, P. J. (2006) *Professional Doctorate Portfolios: Helping to Select and Present Best Practice*, London: Higher Education Academy.

Mathews, D. (2001) *Looking for a Fight*, London: Headline.

Maxwell, J. (1996) *Qualitative Research Design: An Interpretive Approach*, Thousand Oaks, CA: Sage.

Maxwell, T.W. (2003) 'From first to second generation professional doctorate', *Studies in Higher Education*, 28(3), pp. 279–91.

Maxwell, T.W. (2011) 'Australian professional doctorates: mapping, distinctiveness, stress and prospects', *Work Based Learning e-Journal*, 2(1).

Maxwell, T.W. and Kupczyk-Romanczuk, G. (2009) 'The professional doctorate: defining the portfolio as a legitimate alternative to the dissertation', *Innovations in Education and Training International*, 46(2), pp. 135–45.

Maxwell, T.W. and Shanahan, P.J. (1997) 'Towards a reconceptualisation of the doctorate: issues arising from comparative data relating to the EdD degree in Australia', *Studies in Higher Education*, 22(2), pp. 133–49.

Mayer, J.H.L. and Land, R. (2005) 'Threshold concepts and troublesome knowledge: epistemological considerations and a conceptual framework for teaching and learning', *Higher Education*, 49 (3), pp. 373–88.

McIntosh, P. (2010) *Action Research and Reflective Practice: Creative and Visual Methods to Facilitate Reflection and Learning*, London: Routledge.

McNett, J.M., Wallace, R.M. and Athanassiou, N. (2004) 'Tacit knowledge in the classroom: a strategy for learning', 29th Improving University Teaching Conference, Bern, Switzerland.

McNiff, J., and Whitehead, J. (2002) *Action Research: Principles and Practice*, London: Routledge Falmer.

Moon, J.A. (2004) *A Book of Reflective and Experiential Learning: Theory and Practice*, London: Routledge Falmer.

Muir, P. (2007) 'Action research in the scholarship of L & T', *Ed. magazine*, 2(3), http://emedia.rmit.edu.au/edjournal/Action+research+in+the+scholarship.

Muncey, T. (2010) *Creating Autoethnographies*, London: Sage.

Murray, R. (2006) *The Book of Academic Writing*, Buckingham: Open University Press.

Murray, R. (2011) *How to Write a Thesis*, Buckingham: Open University Press.

Nonaka, I. (1994) 'A dynamic theory of organizational knowledge creation', *Organization Science*, 5(1), pp. 14–37.

Nonaka, I. (2007) 'The knowledge creating company', *Harvard Business Review*, Jul–Aug.

O'Mullane, M. (2005) 'Demonstrating significance of contributions to professional knowledge and practice in Australian professional doctorate programs: impacts in the workplace and professions' in T.W. Maxwell, C. Hickey and T. Evans (eds) *Working Doctorates: The Impact of Professional Doctorates in the Workplace and Professions*, Geelong, Vic: Deakin University.

Oja, S.N. and Pine, G.J. (1989) 'Collaborative action research: teachers' stages of development and school contexts', *Peabody Journal of Education*, 64(2), pp. 96–115.

Olesen, H.S. (2001) 'Professional identity as learning processes in life histories', *Journal of Workplace Learning*, 13(7/8), pp. 290–7.

Olesen, V.L. and Whittaker, E.W. (1968) *The Silent Dialogue: A Study in the Social Psychology of Professional Socialization*, San Francisco: Jossey-Bass.

Parahoo, K. (1997) *Nursing Research: Principles, Process and Issues*, Basingstoke: Macmillan.

Paul, R. and Elder, L. (2006) *The Art of Socratic Questioning*, Dillon Beach, CA: Foundation for Critical Thinking.

Paulson, F.L., Paulson, P.R. and Meyer, C.A. (1991) 'What makes a portfolio a portfolio?', *Educational Leadership*, 48(5), pp. 60–3.

Petty, N.J., Cross, V. and Stew, G. (2012) 'Professional doctorate level study: the experience of health professional practitioners in their first year', *Work Based Learning e-Journal*, 2(2), pp. 1–28.

Plowright, D. (2011) *Using Mixed Methods Frameworks for an Integrated Methodology*, Thousand Oaks, CA: Sage.

Plowright, D. (2012) 'To what extent do postgraduate students understand the principles of mixed methods in educational research?', 3rd International Conference on Professional Doctorates, 2–3 April 2012, Florence, Italy, Middlesex University and UK Council for Graduate Education.

Powell, S. and Long, E. (2005) 'Professional doctorate awards in the UK', UK Council for Graduate Education.

QAA (Quality Assurance Agency) (2012) *UK Quality Code for Higher Education. Part B: Assuring and enhancing academic quality*, Chapter B11: Research Degrees, pp. 19-20, http://www.qaa.ac.uk/Publications/InformationAndGuidance/Documents/Quality-Code-Chapter-B11.pdf.

Raney, K. (2012) 'Integrating theory and practice in a fine art doctorate', 3rd International Conference on Professional Doctorates, 2–3 April 2012, Florence, Italy, Middlesex University and UK Council for Graduate Education.

Rinne, K. and Sivenius, P. (2007) 'Rigorous science – artistic freedom. The challenge of thesis supervision in an art university', *South African Journal of Higher Education*, 21(8), pp. 1091–102.

Rozuel, C. (2012) 'Moral imagination and active imagination: searching in the depths of the psyche', *Journal of Management Development*, 31(5), pp. 488–501.

Sanders, G. (2010) 'Towards a model of multi-organisational work-based learning: developmental networks as a mechanism for tacit knowledge transfer and exploration of professional identity', *Learning and Teaching in Higher Education*, 4(1), pp. 51–68.

Sanders, G. and Kuit, J.A. (2011) 'Professional researcher or researching professional: developing the professional identity of professional doctorate candidates', 2nd International Conference on Professional Doctorates, 20–21 April Edinburgh, Middlesex University and UK Council for Graduate Education.

Sanders, G., Kuit, J., Smith, P., Fulton, J. and Curtis, H. (2011) 'Identity, reflection and developmental networks as processes in professional doctorate development', *Work Based Learning e-Journal*, 2(1), pp. 113–34.

Savin-Baden, M. (2008) *Learning Spaces: Creating Opportunities for Knowledge Creation in Academic Life*, Maidenhead: McGraw-Hill.

Schatzki, T., Knorr Cetina, K. and von Savigny, E. (eds) (2000) *The Practice Turn in Contemporary Theory*, London: Routledge.

Schein, E.H. and Schein, E. (1978) *Career Dynamics: Matching Individual and Organizational Needs*, vol. 24, Reading, MA: Addison-Wesley.

Schön, D. (1983) *The Reflective Practitioner: How Professionals Think in Action*, New York: Basic Books.

Schulman, D., Dunleavy, J., Harmer, M. and Lusk, J. (1999) *Shared Services: Adding Value to the Business Units*, New York: PriceWaterhouseCoopers and James S. Lusk.

Schulz, V., Hochstein, A., Uebernickel, F., and Brenner, W. (2009) 'Definition and classification of IT Shared Service Center', Proceedings of the Fifteenth Americas Conference on Information Systems, San Francisco: California.

Smith P., Curtis, H., Sanders, G., Kuit, J. and Fulton, J. (2011) 'Student perceptions of the professional doctorate', *Journal of Work-based Learning*, 2(1).

Stake, R.E., (1995) *The Art of Case Study Research*, Thousand Oaks, CA: Sage.

Starkey, K. and Maban, P. (2001) 'Bridging the relevance gap: aligning stakeholders in the future of management research', *British Journal of Management*, 12, pp. 3–26.

Stewart, D.W. (2010) 'Important if true: graduate education will drive America's future', *Change*, 42(1), pp. 36–44.

Strauss, A. and Corbin, J. (1998) *Basics of Qualitative Research: Techniques and Procedures for Developing Grounded Theory*, Thousand Oaks, CA: Sage.

Street, I. (1986) 'Mathematics, teachers, and an action research course' in D. Hustler, T. Cassidy and T. Cuff (eds) *Action Research in Classroom and Schools*, London: Allen & Unwin.

Strikwerda, J. (2006) *The Shared Service Centre: Change, Governance and Strategy*, Business School, University of Amsterdam.

Taylor, A. (2007) 'Learning to become researching professionals: the case of doctorate education', *International Journal of Teaching and Learning in Higher Education*, 19(2), pp. 154–66.

Tenni, C., Smyth, A. and Boucher, C. (2003) 'The researcher as autobiographer: analysing data written about oneself', *The Qualitative Report*, 8(1).

Tsoukas, H. (2005) *Complex Knowledge: Studies in Organisational Epistemology*, Oxford: Oxford University Press.

Ulbrich, F., Bergstrom, R. and Ianni, A. (2008) 'Transforming general performance objectives into specific measurements for shared service centres' in P.B. Srinivasan (ed.) *Shared Services Management: A Global Perspective*, Hyderabad: Icfai University Press, pp. 37–57.

Ulrich, D. (1995) *Shared Services: From Vogue to Value*, University of Michigan.

Verger, J. (1999) 'Doctor, doctoratus', *Lexikon des Mittelalters*, 3, Stuttgart: J.B. Metzler.

Vince, R. and Reynolds, M. (2009) 'Reflection, reflective practice and organizing reflection' in S.J. Armstrong and C.V. Fukami, *The Sage Handbook of Management Learning, Education and Development*, London: Sage.

Vitae (2012a) *Managing and Supporting your Researcher*, http://www.vitae.ac.uk/policy-practice/14884/Managing-and-supporting-your-researcher.html.

Vitae (2012b) *Realising the Potential of Researchers. Using Professional Development Planning (PDP),in Researcher Degree Programmes*, http://www.vitae.ac.uk/policy-practice/14881/Using-Personal-Development-Planning-PDP-in-Research-Degree-Programmes.html.

Wacquant, L. (2012) 'Symbolic power and urban inequality: taking Bourdieu to town', Workshop: York European Centre for Cultural Exploration (YECCE) and the Centre for Urban Research (CURB), 31 May–1 June, University of York.

Wagner, R.K. (1987) 'Tacit knowledge in everyday intelligent behaviour', *Journal of Personality and Social Psychology*, 52(6), pp. 1236–47.

Walker, R. (1998) 'Writing down and writing up in the professional doctorate journals and folios' in T.W. Maxwell and P.J. Shanahan (eds) *Professional Doctorates: Innovations in Teaching and Research*, Faculty of Education, Health and Professional Studies, University of New England.

Webb, C., Endacott, R., Gray, M., Jasper, M., Miller, C. and Scholes, J. (2002) 'Models of portfolios', *Medical Education*, 36, pp. 897–8.

Weick, K.E. and Sutcliffe, K.M. (2006) 'Mindfulness and the quality of organizational attention', *Organization Science*, 17(4), pp. 514–24.

Wenger, E. (1998) *Communities of Practice, Learning, Meaning and Identity*, Cambridge: Cambridge University Press.

Wenger, E. (2010). 'Communities of practice and social learning systems: the career of a concept' in C. Blackmore (ed.) *Social Learning Systems and Communities of Practice*, London: Springer, pp. 179–98.

Whitfield, D. (2007) *Shared Services in Britain*, A Report for the Australian Institute for Social Research and the Public Service Association.

Winter, R. (1989) *Learning From Experience. Principles and Practice in Action Research*, Lewes: Falmer Press.

Woolgar, S. and Ashmore, M. (ed.) (1988) *Knowledge and Reflexivity*, Thousand Oaks, CA: Sage.

Yee, J., Chian, F. and Chan, T. (2009) 'A preliminary decision model for shared services: insights from an Australian university context', 20th Australasian Conference on Information Systems, Melbourne.

Yin, R.K. (1984) *Case Study Research: Design and Methods*, Newbury Park, CA: Sage.

Yin, R.K. (2003) *Applications of Case Study Research*, 2nd edn, Applied Social Research Methods Series, 34, Sage Publications, Inc.

Zubizarreta J (2009) *The Learning Portfolio: Reflective Practice for Improving Student Learning*, San Francisco: John Wiley & Sons.

Appendix: Sample Coursework Assessments

These coursework assessments are included to give you an example of some assessments from the taught element of a professional doctorate programme.

Professional Doctorate: Reflective Practice

Assessment schedule

Assessment overview

This module is assessed by a portfolio based on two tasks. The individual parts of the assignment are not weighted and each part must be passed in order to gain a pass grade for the module. The tasks will explore professional learning and identity from two perspectives: that of the profession as a community of practice, and that of the individual learner. You will be asked to reflect critically on these two perspectives in order to construct an appropriate framework for your learning during completion of your doctoral programme. We start in Task 1 with your reflections on your current profession.

Module learning outcomes

Students will be able to demonstrate the following knowledge:

- K1. Narrative and autobiographical writing as vehicles for documenting and reflecting upon a participant's professional norms, values and behaviours.
- K2. The place of value systems in professional practice and how these shape the participant's professional identity.
- K3. A conceptual understanding of current research that enables the participant to evaluate critically their personal and professional identity in the context of the relevant literature.

and the following skills and abilities:

- S1. Establish both an ideological and practical foundation for self-transformation.
- S2. Reflect and critically review personal norms, values and behaviours in the context of professional norms, values and behaviours.
- S3. Reflect on complex issues in professional practice and demonstrate self-direction in tackling and solving problems.

Task 1   Identification of core professional norms, values and behaviours through critical incident analysis and reflection

We have looked at what reflection means in terms of organisational learning and self-development, compared some examples of reflective writing, and learned about the application of critical incident technique as a tool for self-reflection. You were asked to start keeping a critical incident diary which will be used to support the work that you will produce for the assignments. (Note that we will not ask to see the diary itself.)

Now we want you to select a critical incident from your current profession to explore the professional norms, values and behaviours that underpin professional practice in your field. (Note that in this piece of work we want you to focus on your profession as a community of practice – the opportunity to reflect on your own place within that profession will come in Task 2.)

You must produce a piece of reflective writing that:

- Describes a critical incident that you see as significant in the demonstration of the way professional norms, values and behaviours are exercised in your field.
- Explores your assumptions about this incident critically, drawing on relevant literature. (You should consider what your assumptions were before the incident, what they were immediately after it happened, and what they are now.)
- Reflects on how critical analysis of the selected incident has altered or shaped your knowledge and understanding of professional practice with respect to norms, values and behaviours in your field.

Your work must draw extensively on relevant literature to provide a theoretical perspective on the reflective approach adopted. Your report should be between 2,000 and 3,000 words in length.

We also will be looking for:

- Appropriate selection of critical incident. You should select a critical incident which you feel was important in shaping your professional practice.
- Clear articulation of the assumptions that you select for analysis.
- Clear evidence of critical reflection.
- Well structured academic writing.

Assessment of learning outcomes for Task 1 (this task assesses learning outcomes K1, K2, S2, and S3)

NB: In the following tables, the column headed 'Achievement' will contain an indication of your level of achievement for each learning outcome and comments on your performance in each section. The attainment of general criteria is also reported on a scale from 'Needs improvement' to 'Good'.

Your work will be assessed according to the following learning outcomes and criteria:

Learning outcomes	Achievement Not achieved ⇨ Fully
Narrative and autobiographical writing as vehicles for documenting and reflecting upon a participant's professional norms, values and behaviours	
The place of value systems in professional practice and how these shape the participant's professional identity	
Reflect and critically review personal norms, values and behaviours in the context of professional norms, values and behaviours	
Reflect on complex issues in professional practice and demonstrate self-direction in tackling and solving problems	
General criteria	Needs improvement ⇨ Good
Academic writing style	
Structure and presentation	
Evidence of use of literature	
Evidence of critical reflection	

Task 2 Professional autobiography and critical review of personal norms, values and behaviours underpinning your professional identity

We have asked you to explore your own values, motives and beliefs and how these relate to your professional behaviours. Now we would like you to produce a piece of reflective writing that elaborates on this theme, drawing on your own professional experiences.

Write a 'Table of Contents' that outlines the chapters of your working life autobiography. Then select the chapter that most interests you to concentrate upon. This should include your narration of an experience in your work history (from a single interaction to a day or an overview of a longer time period). Then explain how you feel your own values, beliefs and motives have affected your professional behaviour during this experience, and how they subsequently affected your professional journey.

Then you should revisit the writing you did for Task 1 and explore how the norms of your profession interact with your own professional identity. How much have they influenced you? Are there any mismatches between who you feel you are as a professional and who the profession expects you to be?

Your writing should conclude with a concise definition of what you feel your profession to be, the explanation of which should be clear from your report. Your report should be between 3,000 and 5,000 words in length. Your work must draw extensively on relevant literature to provide a theoretical perspective on the reflective approach adopted and should be presented as a well structured piece of academic writing.

Assessment of learning outcomes for Task 2 (this task assesses learning outcomes K1, K2, K3, S1, S2 and S3)

Your work will be assessed according to the following learning outcomes and criteria:

Learning outcomes	Achievement Not achieved ⇨ Fully
Narrative and autobiographical writing as vehicles for documenting and reflecting upon a participant's professional norms, values and behaviours	
The place of value systems in professional practice and how these shape the participant's professional identity	
A conceptual understanding of current research that enables the participant to evaluate critically their personal and professional identity in the context of the relevant literature	
Establish both an ideological and a practical foundation for self-transformation	
Reflect and critically review personal norms, values and behaviours in the context of professional norms, values and behaviours	
Reflect on complex issues in professional practice and demonstrate self direction in tackling and solving problems	

General criteria	Needs improvement ⇨ Good
Academic writing style	
Structure and Presentation	
Evidence of use of relevant literature	
Evidence of critical reflection	

Professional Doctorate: Research Methodologies

Assessment schedule

Assessment overview

For the assessment for this module you are required to write an evaluation of the methods of enquiry within your community of practice. The purpose of this piece of work is for you to explore and evaluate the methods which are available to you for use in your project, and provide a foundation upon which you can develop a detailed project proposal within the next module.

Module learning outcomes

Students will be able to demonstrate the following knowledge:

- K1. A range of research methodologies relevant to the workplace.
- K2. The broader ethical issues which relate to research investigations.
- K3. The methods of enquiry relevant to the individual's community of practice.

and the following skills and abilities:

- S1. Critically evaluate a variety of research approaches and methodologies relevant to the individual's area of practice.
- S2. Critically analyse the issues involved in research design.
- S3. Critically evaluate the role of research in addressing workplace issues.

Assessment structure

Your assignment should be in two parts:

Part 1 should cover, and evaluate, the range of research methodologies, and methods which are relevant to your area of practice. You should also discuss the broader ethical issues which relate to research investigations in your area of practice.

Part 2 should evaluate the ways in which your project might be developed. In particular, you should critically analyse the issues that may be involved in your research design and evaluate the potential role of research in addressing your workplace issues.

Your work should be evidenced by reference to the literature, including references to papers which demonstrate the use of specific methodologies within your own community of practice. The assignment should be between 3,000 and 5,000 words long, and Parts 1 and 2 should be approximately equal in length.

Assessment of learning outcomes (this piece of work assesses all learning outcomes)

Your work will be assessed according to the following learning outcomes and criteria:

Learning outcomes	Achievement Not achieved ⇒ Fully
A range of research methodologies relevant to the workplace	
The broader ethical issues which relate to research investigations	
The methods of enquiry relevant to the individual's community of practice	
Critically evaluate a variety of research approaches and methodologies relevant to the individual's area of practice	
Critically analyse the issues involved in research design	
Critically evaluate the role of research in addressing workplace issues	

General criteria	Needs improvement ⇨ Good
Academic writing style	
Structure and presentation	
Evidence of use of relevant literature	
Reflection of the relationship between theory and practice	
Structure and clarity of argument	
Level of critical analysis	

Professional Doctorate: Contextualisation and Planning

Assessment schedule

Assessment overview

For the assessment for this module you are required to write a comprehensive and detailed report which presents your project proposal. The module is assessed by a report and a presentation, during which you will be present your proposal to a small assessment panel.

Module learning outcomes

Students will be able to demonstrate the following knowledge:

- K1. The primary literature in their particular area of interest.
- K2. The state of practice within their profession.

and the following skills and abilities:

- S1. Design a detailed programme of work which will apply theory and practice to create solutions or innovation within their workplace.
- S2. Reflect upon their work and recognise its limitations and the contribution which they as individuals are making to the profession.
- S3. Self-direct, manage and deal with complex issues.
- S4. Communicate with other professionals to exchange knowledge and good practice.

Assessment structure

This component is assessed by a report and a presentation.

The report

You are required to write a report which makes a very detailed proposal for your doctoral project. The report will be assessed by a review panel. The report (between 5,000 and 7,500 words) should cover the following areas:

- Title of the work.
- Abstract. A brief summary of the content of your report.
- Issue(s) to be addressed/aim of the work.
- Motivation (why do the work?).
- Review of the state of the profession and of relevant academic literature. This should be a critical review of the literature and how it will inform your project.
- Methodology. Detail your overall methodological framework and the method(s) which you will use in your project.
- Reflective log of relevant work already undertaken, including deliverables which could form the basis of a portfolio of work.
- Community of practice. Which community of practice will benefit from your work?
- Dissemination plans.
- Potential for contribution to the profession.
- Conclusion.
- References.

APPENDICES to the Report
- Project plan, including deliverables which will form the basis of your portfolio of work.
- Draft contents list of doctoral report.
- Draft contents list of portfolio.
- Discussion of ethical issues/ethical approval.
- Discussion of any health and safety issues/risk assessment(s).
- Notes of meetings with supervisors.
- Details of professional contacts/mentors.

Presentation

You will also be required to prepare a 20-minute Powerpoint® presentation of your work and present this to, and discuss it with, a panel which will comprise your supervisors and other independent members.

Assessment of learning outcomes

Your work will be assessed according to the following learning outcomes and criteria:

REPORT (the report assesses all learning outcomes)	
Learning outcomes	**Achievement** Not achieved ⇨ Fully
The primary literature in their particular area of interest; demonstrate a clear grasp of the state of the art in the profession and relevant academic theory	
The state of practice within their profession; present a clear statement of how the proposed work will impact upon professional practice, and make a contribution to knowledge	
Design a detailed programme of work which will apply theory and practice to create solutions or innovation within their workplace; clearly state the direction and focus of the work; present a clear methodology which will deliver the desired outcomes, is feasible in the timescale and is grounded in academic theory	
Reflect upon their work and recognise its limitations and the contribution which they as individuals are making to the profession; present a critical and balanced reflection on any work already undertaken	
Self-direct, manage and deal with complex issues; present a clear plan with definite milestones and deliverables	
Communicate with other professionals to exchange knowledge and good practice	

General criteria	Needs improvement ⇨ Good	
Academic writing style; clear and correct use of English; well evidenced and grounded in the literature; clearly reaching postgraduate level, and approaching doctoral level; evidence of critical analysis and review		
Structure and presentation; report accessible to a variety of audiences		
Evidence of use of relevant literature; a complete set of up-to-date references in standard format		
Consideration of ethical issues		
Interaction with supervisors; records of meetings signed by student and supervisors		

PRESENTATION (the presentation assesses learning outcomes K1, K2 and S4)

Learning outcomes	Achievement Not achieved ⇨ Fully	
The primary literature in their particular area of interest; demonstrate a clear grasp of the state of the art in the profession and relevant academic theory		
The state of practice within their profession; demonstrate a clear understanding of the relevant professional issues and how the proposed work will impact upon professional practice, and make a contribution to knowledge		
Communicate with other professionals to exchange knowledge and good practice; well presented; good visuals; well timed; good interaction and response to questions		

Index

246